THE COMPLETE

SNOW CAMPER'S GUIDE

THE COMPLETE

SNOW CAMPER'S GUIDE

by Raymond Bridge

CHARLES SCRIBNER'S SONS   NEW YORK

7 9 11 13 15 17 19 M/P 20 18 16 14 12 10 8

Printed in the United States of America
Library of Congress Catalog Card Number 72–37223
SBN 684–12769–5 (cloth)
SBN 684–13130–7 (paper, SL)

This book is dedicated to Maddie and Diane, Walt Sticker,
Bob and Gloria Smith, Bob and Sheryl Philpott,
Bill Engs, Clare and Bill Bucher,
Erwin Goldsmith, Dick Koch,
and all my other companions in wild places.

Contents

THE COMPLETE

SNOW CAMPER'S GUIDE

Introduction

Custom dictates that an author owes the reader some justification before asking him to delve into a book—a reasonable requirement in an age when trees and leisure are scarcer than words on wood pulp. So, why this book?

One morning a couple of years ago, I drifted slowly into wakefulness from a warmth made blissful by the contrasting cold of the air on my face. I pulled on my clothes inside my sleeping bag and crawled out of the small mountain tent, moving carefully to avoid knocking frost from the walls onto my sleeping companion.

Outside was a world so fantastically bright and new and sparkling with white light that my first reaction of exultation was replaced by a wonder that I should be allowed to be there at all. The clarity of colors—orange tent, green trees, blue sky—stood out against the snow, and above it all stood the peaks of the Sierra Nevada—the Snowy Range—renamed the Range of Light by John Muir.

The day before, we had skied to this spot in "whiteout" conditions—snow blowing so hard we could see nothing. We struggled with the tent in the wind, finally pitching it well enough to last the night, and tumbled into our sleeping bags inside. The roar of our cooking stove competed with that of the wind, and the meal completed a kind of existential sense of well-being that seems only to come with hard physical effort.

Now, the next morning, the fruits of the storm sparkled on the branches of lodgepole pines—the miracle of the Spartan, pristine, incredibly beautiful world of winter—a world born clean and new with every snowstorm.

This is a book about some of the pedestrian aspects of exploring that world—a how-to-do-it book for the beginning cold-weather wilderness traveler. It deals with the techniques of exploring the white wilderness on foot and of living there while traveling.

WHY WINTER?

The most important reason for going hiking, camping, snowshoeing, and skiing in the winter is that it is a beautiful time of year. There is a unique loveliness in the hills and woods when snow is on the ground. The obvious difficulties which often scare off the fair-season camper become happy challenges to the devotee. Advantages not immediately apparent are learned when one travels much in the cold seasons. Many areas that receive heavy snows are much easier to visit in winter than summer—impenetrable brush is covered over with a highway of snow. Watery regions are often passable on foot only when temperatures remain below freezing.

I have a more selfish reason for visiting the woods in winter, though. Many of my favorite wilderness areas are no longer wilderness except in winter.

The great interest shown by all sorts of Americans in the outdoors and the wilderness has had the laudable effect of giving many people a taste for the magnificence of those wild places that have escaped "progress" in some degree. Unfortunately, this growing enthusiasm has also made it increasingly difficult to find those things for which many of us go to the woods in the first place—solitude or the companionship of chosen friends in an atmosphere of beauty and simplicity. For good reasons and bad, the pressure on wilderness and semi-wilderness areas has increased tremendously in the last few years. It has increased fastest in those areas that are accessible on weekends and during short annual vacations. Such short periods are all the time most of us have available for a wilderness experience.

For those who have discovered the fact that the wilderness can only really be experienced on its own terms there are still some ways out. Luckily, most of the highly mechanized Americans who are creating the pressure on readily accessible wilderness areas are gone after Labor Day. They depart when the first snows begin to fall and cover the beer cans with beauty.

The areas of the country that are covered by snow in the winter still offer the challenge of discovery to those willing to make some effort to learn the skills necessary to travel the winter wilds on foot. Until just a very few years ago, vast areas that are crowded in summer were rarely visited in winter at all. A hundred yards from the nearest plowed road or ski trail one entered a world where one could travel for weeks, never meeting a soul. In some areas this has changed quite a bit with the advent of the snow machine (about which I will have more to say in the last chapter), but it is still possible to experience far more of the beauty of this country on short winter trips than on much longer summer jaunts.

I have tried to present all the information that would be needed by a person with some experience in mild-weather camping who would like to broaden his horizons by traveling on snow. It is not necessary to climb a 14,000-foot peak twenty miles from the road-head to have a fine wilderness experience. Though this is a worth-while endeavor, which I recommend to you when you are ready for it, a short hike and an overnight camp can be quite satisfying and valuable.

Modern lightweight wilderness camping, whatever the season, is very different from the camping done by the men who wrote many of the classics on the outdoors. Modern equipment has completely changed the techniques and possibilities of lightweight back-coun-try travel, but so have modern problems, pressures, and conscious-ness. Modern equipment makes it possible for a small woman in only reasonably good physical condition to comfortably carry an outfit that will enable her to live in luxury. An outfit with the same capacity a few years ago would have worn down one of the legendary supermen of the past. At the same time, in the areas that most of us visit it is criminal in fact, if not in law, to use a lot of the old north-woods techniques of camping. The environment simply cannot stand it. The days are gone when trees could be cut without thought for every whimsical temporary need. Most of the books on wilderness living that are now available are written about the kind of camping that may still be appropriate in the great wilderness areas of the north woods but is completely out of place in the California Sierra, the tableland of Katahdin, or even in many of the now heavily used camping areas of the north

Why winter? 3

woods. This type of camping is based on very low population density, and that is something you have to travel a long way to find these days.

The good modern wilderness traveler still tries to travel self-sufficiently, without depending on stores, restaurants, or hotels for reasonable comfort under expected conditions or for survival in unexpected emergencies. However, he also realizes that his wilderness is fragile, and if he expects to continue enjoying it, he cannot "live off the land."

This book is a description of the techniques necessary for this sort of travel in winter, and it attempts to help fill the need for books on modern methods and equipment.

GETTING STARTED

An obvious division in the subject of winter travel is between travel techniques proper—hiking, snowshoeing, or skiing—and the methods of cold-weather camping. This is a good division for the beginner to follow, since the two can be learned separately. You can begin by camping near your home or car, or you can start by taking short ski tours or snowshoe hikes. The separation reduces the number of difficulties and expenses that have to be dealt with at one time.

The choice of the best way to start may be dictated by your inclinations and the finances, location, and equipment you already possess. If you live in snow country outside urban areas, you may be able to start snowshoeing or ski touring near your home, even on weekdays. Equipment costs are low, and you can extend your activities to overnight trips when you feel ready. Even basic camping techniques can be learned in your back yard.

On the other hand, if you have to drive one or two hundred miles to snow country, you may want to learn snow camping first. Then you will have a base of operations for touring without paying for accommodations. Summer backpacking and car-camping equipment is sometimes adaptable to winter use with the addition of some warm clothes. The dictators of fashion in civilian and military life have fortunately made it possible to get good cold-weather clothing cheaply.

However you start, winter travel is not very expensive, once you buy the equipment. Most good lightweight equipment will give years or decades of hard service. The initial investment is not high, but it's certainly not low for those who live on budgets like mine. Fortunately, not everything has to be bought at once. A judicious use of rental equipment, plundering of surplus stores and storage chests, careful comparison shopping in catalogues, and taking advantage of sales and second-hand equipment can greatly reduce costs and spread them out. Making some of your own equipment, either from scratch or from kits, will cut expenses even more. Once it is acquired, it costs almost nothing to keep your outfit in repair.

The beginner is faced with a choice of several ways to travel over the snow. If it isn't deep, he will simply walk, but even then he must be prepared for more snow if he goes far. When the snow drifts deep, it is time to get out the webs or skis.

If you have never skied, don't try Alpine ski-touring equipment until you have learned some basic downhill skiing. This is no problem for the person who plans to do his touring on flat ground and rolling hills. In this terrain the beginner can learn either ski touring or snowshoeing easily. Take your pick after reading the chapters on each.

Novices who haven't skied and want to be able to handle mountain terrain without any intermediate fuss should get a pair of snowshoes. You can learn to walk on them in an hour, though you may not win any races until your second weekend.

Confirmed skiers will pick the slats on any terrain. The type of equipment will depend on the country in which you'll be skiing.

The main thing is to get out in the snow. You don't need fancy equipment to start—there's a lot of it discussed in this book, but there's also advice on cutting corners. Get a five-dollar pair of Army bearpaw snowshoes, dig out grandpa's heavy wool trousers, and take a walk in the woods. You'll soon be a confirmed enthusiast.

A few words are in order about the intended limitations of this book. I have made no attempt to discuss the kind of camping and travel used in deep wilderness areas on true expeditions. This book describes the methods used in the sort of camping where the traveler carries everything he needs on his back. The increasing weight of food limits this experience to about two weeks, though caches or airdrops can be used to extend it indefinitely. Weather conditions are assumed to be those prevailing in the "temperate" regions, which can be quite severe in winter, especially in the mountains. This book does not talk about winter conditions on Mount McKinley or at the South Pole. The weekend camper probably won't be going to either on his first few trips.

Mountains are the natural provinces of the winter traveler in those parts of the country where they are available. In midwinter he walks the snows at all altitudes, but as spring arrives he follows the beloved white stuff up into the hills and peaks. The mountains, along with their many other virtues, are the poor man's Arctic expedition. For every thousand feet of altitude gained, the climber sees a climatic change equivalent to a latitude 300 miles north. In a weekend trip to the Sierra Nevada or the Cascades, the West Coast dweller gets his Alaskan expedition—well, almost. The New England mountaineer will experience Arctic conditions on the summit plateaus of Mount Washington or Katahdin. Winter lasts longer in the high country, so that the white wilderness may still be found there when the lowlands are in the heat of early summer.

There is no discussion of mountaineering techniques on difficult terrain in this book. I have drawn my line at the point where a rope is necessary for safety. There is some description of the use of the ice ax and crampons on moderate slopes, but covering the techniques necessary on difficult terrain would either expand this book to twice its size or mislead the reader with a superficial treatment of a serious subject.

Finally, a note on the way the book is arranged. A great deal of emphasis has been placed on the discussion of equipment. This has been done for two reasons. The first is that one of the problems confronted immediately by the beginner is the choice of his outfit, so that he needs more help with this than some other things. My main motive is that the discussion of choosing equipment necessarily includes details about its use and the conditions that dictate a certain design. This method places an unfortunate emphasis on means rather than ends, however, as talk about equipment and technique must. The book may place undue stress on gadgets, but the reader can easily redress the balance by getting out into the woods, where man and his works take on their proper perspective.

I

Heading Out in Winter

Traveling the wilderness in the cold seasons doesn't require any kind of supernatural physiology or masochistic desire to undergo terrible ordeals. Still, the beauty of nature at this time of year is of a much starker kind than when the flowers are in bloom, and it is well for the would-be lover to be prepared for a cold rebuff. Nature is not forgiving of foolish mistakes in the winter. The traveler must know what he is about.

The cardinal rule of winter camping and travel is not to exceed your limitations. Your knowledge and skill will increase rapidly with experience, and as they do your trips will become more ambitious. The trick is not to attempt a trip until your skill and knowledge are adequate to it. All this is not meant to discourage the adventurous. Push yourself, but don't push your luck.

Winter travel and camping are fun, and they should be. It's pleasant to have a balance between larks and trips with more bite and challenge, but if you consistently exceed your limitations, you'll find winter travel a series of grim survival struggles.

HOW TO KEEP YOUR BODY RUNNING

The big difference in winter camping is, of course, that it's cold outside. The human body will only function when it is kept at the right temperature. If the temperature of the body's central core, where the vital organs are, varies a few degrees in either direction, essential functions start to deteriorate rapidly. The body has its own mechanisms for regulating its temperature, and it is important for the winter sojourner to understand them.

When the core of the body becomes too hot, circulation to the surface of the skin is increased, perspiration is excreted to produce cooling by evaporation, and there is a general inclination to avoid exercise which will produce more heat. Most people are aware of these reactions, but they don't always realize what happens in the cold. When the body's core temperature drops, a reverse process occurs: the blood vessels near the surface of the skin contract, the blood supply to all the extremities except the head is greatly reduced, and if the core temperature continues to drop, violent involuntary exercise of the muscles occurs in the form of shivering. The snow camper has to help his body prevent excessive heat loss, since the naked human body can't handle low temperatures by itself.

Heat loss. There are several ways that your body can lose heat. "Lose" is the key word here, since heat is a form of energy, and cold is simply the absence of heat. If you sit down on the snow in a thin pair of pants, the cold snow absorbs energy from your nether regions; this is heat loss by conduction. The cold wind blows air molecules against your face which absorb more heat; this is heat loss by convection. If you have sweated a lot climbing up a hill, the wind will also dry some of the sweat, producing heat loss from evaporation. Finally, if you are sitting under the black night sky you are losing some more heat by radiation directly to the sky.

Your body tries to reduce all these forms of heat loss by allowing the skin temperature to drop, reducing the difference between it and the temperature of the air. Heat energy is only transferred when there is a temperature difference, and the smaller the temperature difference, the less the heat loss will be from any of these effects. Your body is trying to reduce the temperature difference between the skin and the surrounding air. The way to keep your body warm is to put an insulating layer around the body. The principle is simple: the outside of the insulating layer remains at about the temperature of the air or ground outside, so that little heat is transferred. The inside of the insulating layer is the same temperature as your skin. The layer is effective if heat passes only very slowly from the warm side of the insulating layer (you) to the other side.

The insulating layer provided by your clothing or sleeping bag is what prevents the heat from your body from escaping too rapidly into the world around you. At the same time, your body continues to produce heat, using the food you eat as fuel. Some heat is always being produced by the body at a basal metabolic rate, even when you are sleeping. Digestion of food produces additional heat, and metabolism of some foods produces more heat than others. Heat is also produced as a side product when the muscles are exercising. The intelligent winter camper can use all of these principles to help his body keep warm. Eating fats before bed, for example, will produce extra heat throughout the night. A working knowledge of such tricks is what separates the experienced traveler from the beginner.

A few of the first rules for winter travel follow pretty obviously from what has already been said. Heat is produced from food, so that if you want to keep warm, keep eating. Trail snacks kept in the pocket are munched on the trail throughout the day, making the period between breakfast and supper a sort of continuous lunch. Since exercise produces heat, you can keep fairly warm without much insulation while you are going up a hill, but when you stop for a rest at the top, you had better put on some clothes right away, or you will get a chill.

WIND CHILL

Before going into more detail on protecting the body from the cold, it's important to talk a little more about what we mean by "cold." Everyone knows that low temperatures will rob your body of heat much faster than higher temperatures, but few people realize how important the wind is in chilling your body. Wind has just as important an effect as temperature. Thirty degrees below zero may not feel too cold if you are protected from air movement, but when a strong wind comes up it can freeze exposed flesh in short order. Wind is dangerous in cold weather. Respect it and treat it with caution.

The effects of wind chill are generally measured by stating the calm-air temperature that would produce the same effect as a particular wind and temperature. A glance at the chart will show how

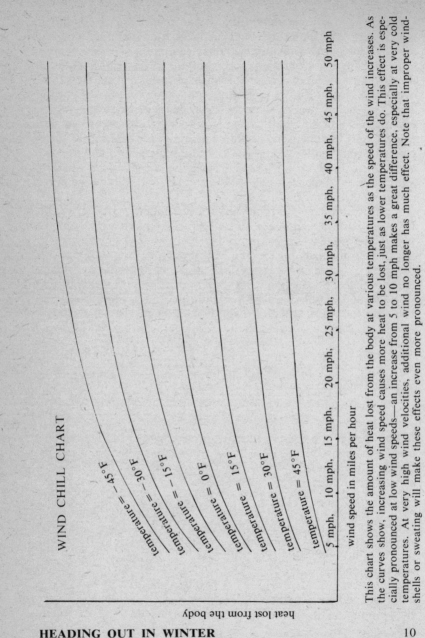

WIND CHILL CHART

heat lost from the body

temperature = −45°F
temperature = −30°F
temperature = −15°F
temperature = 0°F
temperature = 15°F
temperature = 30°F
temperature = 45°F

5 mph, 10 mph, 15 mph, 20 mph, 25 mph, 30 mph, 35 mph, 40 mph, 45 mph, 50 mph

wind speed in miles per hour

This chart shows the amount of heat lost from the body at various temperatures as the speed of the wind increases. As the curves show, increasing wind speed causes more heat to be lost, just as lower temperatures do. This effect is especially pronounced at low wind speeds—an increase from 5 to 10 mph makes a great difference, especially at very cold temperatures. At very high wind velocities, additional wind no longer has much effect. Note that improper windshells or sweating will make these effects even more pronounced.

HEADING OUT IN WINTER

this works. Very small amounts of air movement have considerable chilling effect because they carry away the thin layer of warmed air that builds up near the body. Increasing wind velocity has the effect of lowering temperatures up to about forty miles per hour. Wind velocities higher than this produce little additional cooling effect.

The chilling produced by both wind and water will be mentioned in more detail later. Besides its direct cooling effect, wind robs certain types of insulation of their effectiveness, and this is also the danger presented by wetness. A temperature of thirty-five degrees above zero with a cold, wind-driven rain is more to be feared than a windless thirty-five below.

INSULATION

The function of the insulating layer has already been mentioned. It serves to prevent heat from escaping from the body to the cold environment. The insulator itself is almost always the same: air. Air that is held in numerous small compartments and prevented from moving around in little breezes is the most practical insulator because it weighs almost nothing and is readily available anywhere on earth. The trick is to hold it still so that convection currents cannot start moving about, carrying body heat with them. Wool sweaters, down sleeping bags, Dacron jackets, foam pads, fur coats, and Orlon blankets all serve primarily to trap a layer of air cells next to your body. The actual insulation is provided by the air, and for this reason the amount of insulation provided by the layer depends only on its thickness, not on its weight, color, space-age design, or much of anything else.

Other forms of protection—against wind and water—are also necessary in winter, but without an insulating layer they are of no use. The main principle of cold-weather clothing has already been mentioned: thickness counts. A very tight-woven, heavy sweater is not a better insulator than a light, fuzzy one of the same thickness. The tight one may be more durable or wind-resistant, but when it is worn under a wind-proof shell garment, the extra weight is wasted.

A second principle of insulation for cold-weather dress is the use of layers of clothing. Two medium-weight fuzzy sweaters are generally better than one heavy fuzzy sweater weighing the same amount. A layer of still air is trapped between the two sweaters and provides extra insulation. Even more important, the two sweaters are more versatile. You can't put on one half of a heavy sweater. This flexibility is very important, for reasons which will be discussed in detail a bit later.

Insulating materials are many, and their advantages overlap in such a confusing hodgepodge that many week-long blizzards in high-mountain bivouacs have been whiled away with arguments over the virtues of various combinations. Some blessings and evils are undisputed, however, and these are the ones the beginner must learn. They are part of the basic knowledge of winter travel, and should be acquired early. You can take more time in developing an interesting set of prejudices.

The best insulator is northern goose down. The amount of down required to provide a given insulating layer weighs less and takes up less space when compressed and packed than any other insulator. Down is the underlining of the breasts of waterfowl, and it is distinct from feathers, which have quills. True down consists of tiny central pods, each with a myriad of filaments extending out. Down has numerous disadvantages, but its insulating qualities are unequaled for the traveler who must carry a lot of light, compact insulation.

Down is expensive; it has characteristics that make it expensive to work with; it cannot be woven into fabric but must be enclosed by other material, and it becomes useless when wet. It is best used in equipment where so much insulation is required that other insulators would be impractically heavy or bulky. Sleeping bags are the best example. Another use is in big down parkas for extremely cold weather. The advantages and disadvantages of down will be discussed in more detail in the chapters on clothing and sleeping gear.

Dacron batting has similar characteristics to down, but it is not nearly as good an insulator. Dacron providing the same amount of insulation as a certain amount of down will weigh more, will not compress so much, will not breathe as well, and will not recover as well from compression. It will, however, cost less and be cheaper to work with. Dacron is usually used for cold-weather equipment by those who do not have the requirements of light-weight travelers, but it may sometimes serve as a substitute for down. Some clothing insulated with Dacron or other material may be preferable if there is a danger of getting clothes wet.

Wool is the winter traveler's greatest friend because of a unique virtue: besides being a fairly good insulator, wool retains a fair amount of its warmth even when it becomes wet. For this reason, most basic clothing for winter mountaineering is made of wool. Some bulked Orlon fabrics are almost as good as wool in this respect, and they are stronger.

Cotton is undesirable for winter wear. It is not an exceptionally good insulator, and when it becomes wet it is heavy, clammy, provides no insulation, and is hard to dry. Its main use is in outer shells, where it is often combined with nylon. Good cottons make the most water-resistant breathing fabrics.

Nylon is very useful for its great strength, mainly to enclose down or Dacron and for shell garments, tents, packs, and the like.

THE SHELL GAME

An extension of the principle of dressing in layers brings us to the outer shell of clothing. This layer is not generally used for insulation but consists of light, tough garments designed to be windtight and water-resistant, preserving the insulation value of the inside layers. If the weather is such that rain or sleet may be encountered, it is also necessary to have a truly waterproof shell system, usually very light, to shed the rain. The outer clothing may be used over any necessary amount of insulation, and its value is incalculable. It will not eliminate the wind-chill factor, which simply makes low temperatures more effective at chilling, but it will insure that the insulating layers can do their work. Wind can blow through a fuzzy sweater as if it were not there. A wind shell reduces this problem.

KEEPING WATER OUT

Wet, cold weather, besides being miserable, is dangerous. Dry snow creates no real problems for the winter traveler, but wet snow, sleet, or rain can soak all your clothing and make it practically useless. A cold wind can then make short work of the strongest man unless shelter or dry clothing is found quickly. When weather like this is at all possible, the winter traveler must carry water*proof* equipment, and if he is caught without it, he should find shelter before he gets wet.

Waterproof rain gear cannot be substituted for the normal outer wear because if it is fitted tightly enough to keep out the wind, it will trap the body's own moisture inside. This will not soak insulation quite as fast as a cold rain, but in the long run it can be just as deadly. This is also the objection to waterproof tents: if they are waterproof and tight enough to withstand winter storms the occupants will soon drench their gear, even when there is no visible perspiration. The quantity is likely to be larger during the day. All clothing must "breathe," that is, the water vapor must be able to pass out, and there is still no fabric that breathes well and that also will shed a lot of water without leaking.

GETTING WATER OUT

Wet clothing and sleeping gear is the winter traveler's biggest problem. As long as you keep your gear dry, you can sit out almost any storm. Get it wet, and you have an emergency situation. The obvious dangers of precipitation have been discussed, but the novice should keep reminding himself of the less obvious danger of perspiration. One of the reasons for the layer system is that the spaces between layers help water vapor to escape through the clothing. This will be discussed at greater length in the next chapter, but no clothing can disperse very much perspiration. When traveling in cold weather, it is essential to avoid sweating. Novices always tend to peel off a layer of clothing a bit too late, after they have already worked up a sweat. The rule is to remove a layer of clothing *before* you really get warm and start perspiring. At the same time, various means are employed to help the body get rid of unfelt perspiration through adequate ventilation, a subject that will be continued in the next chapter.

GETTING WATER IN

The importance of food intake and insulation have been discussed, but one other winter problem should be mentioned here. With snow all around, obtaining water would seem to present little problem in winter, and in one way it does not. The winter traveler never runs into the problem of water being completely unavailable, but, oddly enough, dehydration is often a problem because liquid water is often unavailable. It is a good idea to eat moderate amounts of snow throughout the day, perhaps combined with small snacks. Whenever liquid water is available, the traveler should "tank up," drinking as much as he comfortably can, and filling canteens or water bottles. Observation of these rules can save fuel and time in the evening, for if thirst is not quenched during the day, the body's liquid supply will have to be taken care of then.

One reason for avoiding mild dehydration follows from its consequences in emergency situations. Dehydration aggravates the syndromes of shock and hypothermia (exposure). The body will be better able to deal with serious situations if it is kept adequately supplied with food and water throughout the day.

HAZARDS AND EMERGENCIES

It is difficult to write about the dangers of winter conditions in a way that conveys the proper perspective to the reader. One sounds either like a Pollyanna or a Cassandra. The winter wilderness is no place for the careless or foolhardy; there are quite a few dangers, and a party is required to avoid them or meet them with its own resources, without any helpful bystanders to get them out of trouble once they get into it. Winter hazards really hold no terrors for those with reasonably level heads who are willing to learn from their adventures. The rules to keep out of trouble are fairly simple, and when they don't suffice, one can still usually get out of difficulty without too great a sacrifice. One of the great lessons of the wilderness is that you can manage very nicely by yourself when you know you have to. I have had several skiing injuries on commercial slopes, but not one in the hundreds of miles of wilderness skiing I have done, despite the fact that the latter was usually done under more difficult conditions.

The main dangers of wilderness travel in winter are: avalanches, storms, becoming lost, and personal injury or medical emergency. All will be covered in some detail in later chapters, and all have certain unique aspects in connection with cold weather. Avalanches will be the most unfamiliar to the experienced backpacker newly arrived to the cold seasons. They are treacherous even for the expert, and it takes years to become an expert in this field. Anyone going into mountain country in the winter must learn to exercise the utmost care concerning steep snow. Chapter XI offers an introduction to the problem of avalanches.

EQUIPMENT

The obvious dodge for the author talking about equipment is to tell the beginner to take everything he needs but not one ounce more. Good advice, except that even the expert never really knows what he may need. Most of us arrive at the solution of taking only what we *know* we'll need, plus a light combination of *essential* emergency equipment. Appendix D may be used as a check list.

The novice is faced with a greater equipment problem than the expert; he must not only decide what to take but also what to buy. The best rule is to buy only what you need for the next trip. If you're learning your way by taking day trips, don't buy a mountain tent until you plan on using it. This will spread out your costs and enable you to make intelligent choices of equipment based on more experience. Both costs and experience may be spread out even farther by judicious use of the rental services of any backpacking or mountaineering stores in your area.

The reader will find most equipment discussed in the chapter concerned with its use. Advice about technique is often handled easily by discussing the merits of various sorts of equipment, and I have used this plan frequently. There is a risk in this method of placing too much importance on the equipment itself, which is, or ought to be, of secondary importance. This book is about equipment and technique, but what is important is the traveler's experience of the wilderness itself. It's always fun to talk about equipment, but this can become a fetish. I hope I have not obscured the real meaning of the white wilderness in this book, but the problem will be easily solved if the reader gets out and experiences it. No piece of equipment is so essential it cannot be done without or replaced with a substitute.

II

Cold-Weather Clothing

The art of dressing for cold weather is fairly simple when the principles discussed in the preceeding chapter are followed. Your clothing must provide enough insulation to keep you warm in the temperatures you will encounter, with wind chill taken into account. It must breathe well enough to pass the water vapor produced by your body into the outside air. It must be readily adjustable for varying temperatures and exercise. It must be roomy; binding clothes cut circulation and compress insulation. You must have shell clothing that is windproof and capable of shedding any precipitation you might encounter.

If cost is no object, you can simply buy your outfit from a good outfitter and be done with it, but for most people clothing is the best part of the outfit on which to save money. You probably have a lot of clothing that will do very well in your closet or in a trunk, and if you don't, someone else does. Military surplus is also an excellent source for some items. Other clothing is easy to make, since baggy fit is desirable rather than detrimental.

Underwear. True net underwear, originated by Nordic fisherman using fish nets, is excellent for a couple of reasons. When worn

What the well-dressed snowshoer will wear. Down parka, mittens, and wool-lined poplin pants are shown. The tight woven outside layer of the pants helps turn wind and snow.

COLD-WEATHER CLOTHING   18

under another layer it forms cells of trapped air which give significant insulation. Its greatest advantage is that it provides a layer of air next to the body in which small amounts of perspiration can vaporize, rather than immediately being soaked into the clothing. Net underwear is formed of a rather coarse mesh. It is not the same as the "waffleweave" types, which provide the insulation but not the drying effect of net. Net underwear is best made of one of the synthetics or wool, though it is more readily available in cotton.

Net underwear can either be worn directly under regular clothing or inside another layer of underwear, depending on the temperatures to be encountered. Additional underwear should be pure wool or should contain as much wool as you can wear comfortably. Cotton underwear soaks up perspiration and becomes damp and cold. Wool underwear can often be worn comfortably over net, but if you can't take wool at all, you may have to use one of the double-layer types of underwear with wool on the outside only.

Shirts and sweaters. These should be all wool, or nearly so. A garment that may be worn on the outside should have a hard finish that will wear better and shed some wind and snow, but more insulation will come from fuzzy weaves. Windbreaking qualities are best left to the shell clothing. Several layers are better than one. They aid in temperature control, provide extra insulation by trapping insulating layers of air between layers of clothing, and help the body to dispose of water vapor. Shirts and sweaters should be long. Short ones will pull up in active use, exposing the kidneys and fraying the temper.

Excellent shirts and sweaters can often be pulled out of mothballs for use on a snowy day. Fashion can be ignored by males, since the snow-bunny population in the back country is very low. Women are also best advised to save their stretch pants and other tight garments for the ski runs equipped with bars or warming huts at the bottom. Excellent wool shirts and sweaters can often be bought at surplus outlets for a fraction of what it costs to make them. Incidentally, virgin wool is warmer than reprocessed wool. Orlon is also a satisfactory material for shirts and sweaters.

Pants. Pants should be made of a hard-finish wool or Orlon. The hard finish wears better and doesn't collect snow. Orlon whipcord is excellent, since it is warm and very strong. Wool fabrics are not quite so resistant to tearing and abrasion as the synthetics, but this

Cold-weather clothing 19

Good standard cold-weather wear. Net underwear, wool shirt and sweater, hard-weave surplus wool pants with knit cuffs and foam-padded seat and knees.

may not be important. It depends on how much punishment you expect them to take. Various types of military-surplus wool pants are nearly ideal for winter wear and need only to be modified at the cuff. One type of Air Force pants can be obtained for four dollars a pair; they are of heavy wool with knit cuffs and foam insulation at the seat and knees. The old type of ski pants that were made before stretch pants became popular are also excellent. Stretch pants should be avoided for wilderness travel.

Cuffs on pants can be normal, knit, drawstring-tightened, or ski-pants type with a heel strap. If the type you choose does not form a snow-tight closure with your boots, you will have to wear gaiters in deep, loose snow.

Whatever the cuff style, the pants should be loose enough so that you can take large steps without having them bind or pull your cuffs out. Long pants or knickers are equally good, but knickers will require gaiters and knicker socks to be worn with them. Knicker socks are more expensive than short ones, but they wear out just as fast. Knickers have the advantage of binding the leg less than long pants.

COLD-WEATHER CLOTHING   20

Shell clothing. Though insulation may sometimes be included effectively in the outer shell, it is usually best kept separate; the layer principle continues to apply. The most indispensible piece of this type of clothing is the parka or anorak. This should be a roomy, windproof covering for the upper body, from the thighs to the head. It should have a hood with a drawstring that can be tightened so that most of the face is covered and a drawstring at the waist. It can be made either in a pullover pattern, with a ventilation opening at the neck, or like a jacket, opening all the way down the front. The former is simpler, lighter, and proof against zipper failure, while the latter allows much better temperature control, especially when you are wearing a pack.

The material for the parka should be determined by the weather in which you plan to wear it. Coated, waterproof material should never be used for this item of clothing; it will become a portable steam bath. The material used must breathe. Reevair, a coated nylon fabric, does not breathe enough for a general-use parka, and its pores tend to clog up as it is used, becoming more watertight with age. Pure nylon fabric is light and abrasion-resistant, and it can be made into a good windbreaking layer that breathes, but its use should be restricted to use in very cold weather when no wa-

Shell clothing for cold, windy weather. Nylon surplus wind pants and a parka of nylon-cotton cloth.

ter-repellency is needed. Wind-tight parkas that will shed some water—always a necessity except in very cold temperatures—are best made from cotton or nylon-cotton combinations. Nylon fabrics do not accept water repellents well and cannot be made to tighten in the rain as cotton and combination fabrics can. The most water-resistant cloth is made from pure, long-fiber cottons. Cotton-nylon combinations sacrifice a little water-repellency for more abrasion resistance. Either makes an excellent anorak material.

Wind pants are needed in extreme conditions as an outer layer for the lower part of the body. The same types of material are used as for the parka, though an abrasion-resistant material is desirable. Waterproof rain pants may be substituted in emergencies.

Shell clothing must include a waterproof shell if wet, cold conditions may be encountered. The rain poncho is a rectangle of waterproof fabric with a hood for the head almost in the middle and snaps to close the sides. Some are big enough for a pack to be worn underneath. Ponchos are excellent for walking, except when the wind is bad, because they provide plenty of ventilation and reduce the problem of condensation. The poncho is also versatile and has many utility uses. In high winds it becomes a curse, and it is not ever convenient for doing chores. It is very poor for climbing on steep terrain. Rain parkas solve all these problems, but with them condensation becomes a problem. A compromise is the canoeist's rain shirt or the climber's *cagoule,* which are long, very baggy, waterproof anoraks. They provide good wind protection, and since they have arms, they are more convenient for chores and climbing. Ventilation through the wide bottom is better than a parka but not as good as a poncho. Choice among the three designs will depend on the country in which you intend to use it and your judgement. None even approaches the ideal. For the mountains, where high winds coupled with freezing rain are common, I recommend the cagoule or the parka. The cagoule is also an excellent piece of bivouac gear, since the legs can be drawn up inside and the arms pulled inside.

Rain protection for the legs will depend on your choice of an upper garment. A rain parka requires rain pants. With the cagoule or the poncho you can also use rain chaps, which are simply leg coverings with no seat or front. The tops attach to your belt. Plans for a cagoule and rain chaps may be found in Appendix A.

Material for rain gear may be some sort of coated nylon, which is light, durable, and expensive. Alternatively, you may get a plas-

Two types of waterproof wet-weather gear. On the right a commercially made rainsuit. On the left a home-manufactured cagoule.

Cold-weather clothing

The cagoule is good bivouac equipment. Arms and legs can be pulled inside.

COLD-WEATHER CLOTHING   24

tic rain set for emergency use. These are light, not very durable, but inexpensive. If you expect to encounter a lot of cold, wet weather, try to get nylon gear. If you are only preparing for a freak warm spell in midwinter, a light plastic emergency set is fine.

All closures (waist, cuffs, neck) on raingear should be adjustable with drawstrings, snaps or some similar arrangement. Fixed elastic prevents control of air circulation. Seams in nylon should be as infrequent as possible, should be French fell seams (see the illustration in the chapter on making your own equipment), and should be sealed after sewing. Raingear should be bought as large as you can wear it; this allows room for both warm clothing and ventilation. Ponchos should have an extra length at the back, which can be snapped up when not in use, to accommodate your pack. A pack can't really be worn over a poncho.

Hats and face masks. Hats are not optional in cold conditions. Because the brain is an essential organ, the body does not shut down the blood supply to the head when the cold temperature drops, as it does to the other extremities. The unprotected head can easily pump over half of the body's heat production into the great outdoors. The old-timer who said, "If your feet are cold, put on your hat," knew what he was talking about. This is a good place to indulge your individuality, but any hat you choose should include ear protection. One of the best choices is the balaclava helmet, which rolls up into a stocking cap in moderate weather, and rolls down to protect the face and neck in very cold weather. An opening is provided for the eyes. This opening is also large enough for ski goggles, a feature not found on most face masks. The material should be wool or Orlon. Additional ear protection can be provided for any hat with an ear band or ear muffs. The hood of the parka or anorak covers the hat. An extra balaclava is worth its weight and cost on a winter trip.

For very severe conditions some sort of face protection is necessary, and if a balaclava is not worn, a face mask should be carried. Wool and Orlon are the usual materials and work well in combination with the parka hood. Deerskin masks are excellent.

A hat that turns into a face mask, and heavy wool shirt.

COLD-WEATHER CLOTHING 26

DOWN CLOTHING

Despite all space-age developments, down is still the ultimate insulating material when it gets really cold. Down clothing is not necessary for most winter travel, though it is pleasant and convenient to have a few down items. Down clothing becomes necessary when the effective temperature drops so low that the amount of normal layer insulation needed would be unmanageably heavy, constricting, and bulky. .

The biggest disadvantage to down clothing, besides its expense, is the fact that it becomes useless when wet. Down clothing should be avoided in wet, cold conditions when temperatures are around freezing. Wool is better under such circumstances. Wetness is rarely a danger in the very cold weather that necessitates the use of down, providing the body is adequately ventilated.

If you do decide to buy down gear, consider what you plan to use it for. Really cold conditions may dictate the purchase of a "big downie"—the expedition down parka. If you're buying your down gear as a luxurious supplement to other clothing, though, you may get more use out of a lighter and less expensive garment —a down sweater, jacket, vest, or lightweight down parka. The expedition parka is heavier and bulkier, and you won't be able to wear it while exercising in moderately cold temperatures. The other down gear can be used in your normal layer system.

Mountaineers often use the big downie because they expect very cold conditions, but also as a bivouac equipment, for belaying in cold weather, or because they are going to very high altitudes, where body resistance to cold is less. One of these uses may persuade you to buy one. The use of the down parka for bivouacs is discussed in Appendix A.

Down garments for the upper body range from the big downies to the down vest. Most of the weight and the expense goes into the construction of the walls that hold the down, rather than the down itself. The easiest way to make them is to quilt the outer and inner shells into large squares or tubes, with the down in between. This method makes excellent vests and light to medium jackets. The sewn-through seams have no insulation along them, though, so where very warm gear is needed this method of construction won't do. Overlapping quilting or tubing, or sewing baffles between layers eliminates the cold seams. This is an expensive feature, but it is important where it's needed. Don't let anyone sell you an expensive down parka with sewn-through seams. The illustrations in Appendix A will give you an idea of down construction.

When you are buying down gear, don't forget, *thickness is warmth*. Nicely tailored ski parkas with slim lines are fine in their place, but they aren't worth the money for insulation purposes. A couple of sweaters and a shell parka will keep you warmer than many of them for less money and with more protection.

All down parkas should have attached or attachable hoods, and these are a good idea with down jackets. If you need the insulation of down on your body, you need it even more on your head. The discussions of closures below apply to down garments as well as others, but with an expensive down garment, you should make sure there is no cold seam along the front. A down tube or overlapping front should cover the opening. Uncoated nylon fabric is generally best for down equipment.

For most people, a down sweater, vest, or jacket is a better purchase than a full down parka. Any of these pack a lot of extra warmth into a corner of your pack. When worn over a sweater, shirt, and underwear, and underneath a shell garment they can make an active man comfortable under pretty extreme conditions. I've toured in the high mountains of the West in severe winter conditions many times with no down gear at all, without ever feeling the need for it. As soon as you buy it, of course, the laws of human nature make it essential. When you stop for the night, down gear does become important, and it is recommended for sleeping bags. Down pants are only necessary in exceptionally severe conditions.

Many mountaineers make a big down parka double for a sleeping bag, when combined with a half-bag for the feet. This method is excellent, and it is discussed in Appendix A, but it is not really very suitable for beginners in winter conditions.

Zippers and other closures. The closures on your outer clothing are important. Failure can be dangerous, and the design of closures is also one good indication of the over-all quality of a garment. Parkas, shell and down, should have two front closing systems if they open like a jacket. The double closure serves to seal out drafts and also is insurance against jammed zippers and ripped buttons or snaps. Zippers should work perfectly; a zipper that sticks in the store is not something you want to struggle with in icy conditions. Larger zippers, especially nylon ones, are less likely to jam. Light snaps are undesirable but acceptable for a wind seal; they are unacceptable as a main closure. Heavy snaps are excellent for an alternate closure and on a down parka with a wide overlap may be used for both closures. They are not very good for main closures on shell parkas or for pants flies, since they aren't windtight. The same considerations apply to buttons as to snaps. Velcro tape that uses two mating surfaces that stick together makes an excellent closure for pockets or wind seals, but it will not substitute for a long zipper.

Well-made zippers are quite reliable; they can jam, but buttons and snaps can rip off. Double closures on important seams and a few safety pins carried on a belt loop will take care of emergencies.

Mittens and gloves. Mittens are much warmer than gloves because the fingers warm each other, and they are are to be preferred for wilderness conditions. A good and inexpensive choice is a pair of unlined leather or fabric and leather outer mitts, with wool liners. Extra liners can be carried to replace wet ones. The outer mitts should have gauntlets long enough to overlap with the parka

Two good types of surplus mittens. Wool liners are used.

Down clothing 29

High gaiter and an anklet.

sleeves, and it should be possible to make a tight seal. In very cold weather a pair of silk or nylon inner gloves can be worn inside the mitts. These provide a bit of extra warmth, but their main use is to prevent the skin from freezing to metal objects if the mittens are removed for handling a camera, fixing a ski binding, etc. Down gloves and mittens are available for those who can afford them or who are wintering on Mount McKinley. Whether or not you choose the shell-lined method, at least one change of mittens (or liners) should be carried.

Gaiters and anklets. A snowproof closure between the pant legs and the boots is essential in winter. If you are wearing long pants, little zippered anklets or *stop-touts* are available. They have zippered sides about six inches high and elastic at top and bottom to keep the snow out. A cord goes under the boot to keep them down, and the zipper allows them to be put on without removing the boot. They are best made of waterproof fabric.

Long gaiters, now usually made of light nylon fabric, serve the same function but reach to the knee. These cover the socks of knicker-wearers and give extra protection in deep, wet snow for those who have long trousers. They are made with zippered sides

COLD-WEATHER CLOTHING 30

or in a tube large enough to fit over the boots and tightened with a shoelace type of arrangement. Some special types of footwear like mukluks make the use of gaiters and anklets unnecessary.

Socks. At least one pair of heavy wool or Orlon pile socks is standard wear for active foot travel, especially in winter. The springiness, wicking action, and wet warmth of these materials are more important for the feet than any other part of the body. Whether or not you choose to wear light inner socks is a matter of personal preference and of your choice of heavy socks. Cotton is completely out of place as a sock material, except in small amounts (ten percent or less). Nylon reinforcement increases wear. My own preference is for heavy wool Norwegian ragg outer socks and light Orlon liners. Many prefer the pile-lined "thermal" or "wicking" socks; many are good, but check the cotton content.

The number of outer socks to be worn depends on conditions and your means of travel. Boots and other footwear will be discussed in chapters on particular methods of travel; a mukluk may be excellent for cold-weather snowshoeing, but it just won't do for mountain ski touring. Desirable sock combinations depend on other footwear.

One important thing to remember with any type of footwear is that putting on an extra pair of socks will not make your feet warmer if they cramp circulation. Tight boot-sock combinations are one of the major causes of frostbitten toes.

A reasonable number of extra socks should be carried on every winter trip. Wet, dirty socks are bad insulators and blister raisers. Socks should be changed at least every day, and dry socks should be worn to bed at night if you are chilly.

DRESSING FOR THE COLD

Cold temperatures do not usually require nearly so many clothes as people think they will. Most novices do not become cold because they don't have enough clothing, but because it is the wrong type or is not used properly. All clothing should be roomy rather than tight; socks should be neither too tight nor loose enough to form blister-raising wrinkles.

Dressing for the cold   31

The most common mistake of all is to wear too many clothes during active exercise. I have traveled quite a few miles in winter during fairly cold weather with only a net undershirt on above the waist, and even when the wind comes up, I rarely need to add more than a shirt and shell anorak. Stopping is a different matter: a lunch stop calls for immediate donning of extra clothes.

A lot of thick clothing is needed by the ice fisherman, the sentry, and the belayer in ice climbing, all of whom have to stand still in the cold for long periods. The active wilderness traveler needs far less, and he must keep aware of how much he needs. The novice generally takes off that extra sweater about ten minutes after his shirt becomes damp with perspiration. This is a dangerous mistake, because he won't have the warmth when he needs it.

It *is* necessary to have adequate clothing available on wilderness trips, however. A lot of downhill pleasure skiers injured on the slopes are getting pretty cold when the ski patrol reaches them ten minutes later. The wilderness traveler has to be equipped for the emergency situation himself, even if it never happens to him. Some of his protection will be carried in his sleeping gear, but clothing needs to be sufficient for fatigue and storm conditions. The most likely person to get caught is the snowshoer, ski tourer, or climber out for a day trip. If you are going off patrolled or well-used trails, carry emergency clothing. Carry it, but don't wear it while you are sweating up that hill!

III

Sleeping Warm

If you intend to enjoy a trip, instead of just enduring it, you should pay particular attention to the equipment necessary for a good night's sleep. Food and sleep can ease the memory of a lot of daytime discomforts, but a bad night or an empty stomach will sour the finest day. Obviously you can't get a good night's sleep if you're cold, and since we're talking about cold-weather conditions, our concern is mainly with ways to keep warm at night.

Carrying your gear on your back pretty well precludes the possibility of carrying a stove and fuel for heating. This means that unless you are traveling in an area where there is plentiful supply of wood, your gear will have to be capable of maintaining your body warmth without any outside help. The use of outside sources of heat will be dealt with later in the book, but it should be noted that the modern winter traveler is placed more and more in the position of having to provide his own heat even in wooded areas due to conservation problems. You may well decide to cook over an open fire, but an all-night fire to keep you warm is quite a different matter; a very much larger quantity of wood is required.

Modern equipment has greatly lessened the problem of keeping warm at night. Even a very competent woodsman has to spend a lot of time putting up a lean-to, making a bough bed, and collecting enough wood for an all-night fire. You can set up a mountaineering tent and be inside it in your sleeping bag in ten or fifteen minutes. Then you lie back and relax while the gas stove heats supper and takes the chill out of the tent. Good sleeping gear can also make an improvised shelter a warm and cozy place to sleep. The gear consists basically of a sleeping bag or a substitute for it and something to insulate you from the ground.

A sleeping bag is the most expensive and the most essential piece of equipment the winter traveler has to buy. As soon as you graduate from day trips to overnight trips on weekends, you'll have to buy or rent a sleeping bag, and for real winter conditions it should be a good one.

Some of the principles of insulation have been discussed already, but the compromises that are necessary in choosing and making clothing are not such a problem in constructing a sleeping bag. When you are asleep your body produces heat at the basal metabolic rate unless you are cold and shivering. This means that you need a lot more insulation than you do when you are climbing a hill, but it also means that you won't have to vary the amount of insulation with your rate of exercise. Also, the bag won't have to take the kind of punishment that an outer garment will.

The standard cold-weather sleeping bag for the lightweight traveler is a down-filled bag with a nylon shell. Some of the reasons

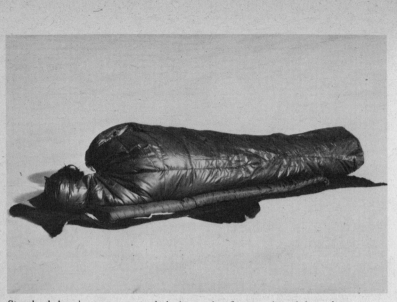

Standard sleeping gear: ground cloth-poncho, foam pad, and down bag.

for this have already been discussed, but they'll be summarized here. Down provides more insulation per unit weight than any other material; it will compress to a smaller packed size, and it can be compressed again and again, returning each time to essentially the same volume. Finally, down-insulated bags breathe well. Most of the disadvantages of down are not very important in sleeping gear, though the reader will probably disagree when he goes to buy his own bag. Down *is* expensive!

The great compressibility of down can be thought of as a disadvantage as well as an advantage, because it is this characteristic that makes a bed underneath the body an absolute necessity, especially in winter. The down layer is compressed to negligible thickness at the points of the body which are bearing weight. The sleeping bag has to be supplemented with an insulating layer that keeps those points from resting on the ground. In principle this layer could be included in the sleeping bag, but in practice, when down bags are being used, a separate layer has been found to work best.

Methods of providing this additional layer will be covered after a further discussion of the sleeping bag itself.

SLEEPING WARM   34

HOW MUCH SLEEPING BAG DO YOU NEED?

The purpose of a sleeping bag is to keep you warm by preventing your body heat from being lost at a greater rate than you are producing it. If the bag fails to do this for any length of time, your body will first begin to shut down blood circulation to your skin and extremities, the most apparent result of which will be cold feet. You will probably begin to sleep badly, and eventually you will wake up shivering as your body becomes alert to the need for increased heat production.

Clearly then, an adequate sleeping bag for you is one that will prevent this uncomfortable train of events from occurring where you will be using the bag. In this chapter the factors that make a bag warm will be discussed in a way that will give you a basis for comparing bags. The evaluation of your own needs is something you will have to make on the basis of your own experience with your body, your estimation of the conditions you will encounter, and consideration of the other equipment you plan on using.

The biggest variable in this equation is your own body. Different people are in better or worse physical condition, have different metabolic rates, different amounts of body fat to insulate them, and different circulatory characteristics that may help or hinder their staying warm. Some people "sleep cold," while others tend to "sleep warm." For example, my wife and I can sleep in identical sleeping bags, on identical pads, in the same tent; I am likely to be warm as toast sleeping nude inside my bag, while she is just barely keeping warm wearing a big down parka inside her bag. Clearly, she needs a heavier bag than I do under the same conditions.

The conditions you will meet are complicated, but fairly obvious. You need to consider the lowest temperature at which the bag will normally be used. Inside a tent, or out? Well-protected from breezes? With or without a sleeping-bag cover? Sheltered from the sky? With how much additional allowance needed for fatigue, dampness, and the like?

One other condition that might not be so obvious is the altitude at which you plan to use the bag. Altitude affects both temperature and weather, of course, in ways that are discussed more fully in the section on weather. In addition, however, it affects the body functions directly, especially in an individual who has come recently from lower altitudes. Decreased oxygen pressure and some other more complicated effects have the general result of depressing all the body functions, so that your capacity to produce heat is liable to be decreased the higher you go. For this reason you can expect to need a warmer bag for zero temperatures at high altitudes than for the same temperatures at sea level. To make things even more complicated, the altitude may make you sleep badly to begin with, so that cold feet are more likely to keep you awake than they would be at sea level.

Finally, in evaluating your needs for a sleeping bag, you'll have to consider the other equipment you plan to take. It is hard to overstress the need to make every piece of equipment serve as many purposes as possible on any lightweight trip, and this is much more true in winter than in more temperate seasons. Your dry clothing will serve to extend the range of your sleeping bag, and it should be taken into account when you decide how warm a bag to purchase.

It isn't necessary to wear every stitch of clothing you have with you every night. What you should try to do is to adjust the combination of clothing and bag so that it is adequate to handle the worst conditions you can reasonably expect to meet. Then on warmer nights you won't need it all, but on cold nights you will be adequately protected without carrying unnecessary weight or spending more on your outfit than necessary.

In particular, if you decide to get down clothing, this can be used to extend the range of a sleeping bag, and this is the way many of us make our summer bags serve double duty in the winter. One minor caution that you should observe in your planning is to allow for the possibility of some of your clothing being wet and therefore of no use in helping you keep warm at night.

A BUYER'S GUIDE TO SLEEPING BAGS

The materials and construction are of equal importance in the construction of a good sleeping bag, and they also share equally in the high cost of this piece of equipment. (The cost is only high as an initial investment; a good sleeping bag gives wear and service that is truly phenomenal with almost negligible maintenance costs.

In fact, it's hard to advise others on the merits of different bags because you can't wear out enough bags in one lifetime to get a very wide selection, except by borrowing from your friends.) This section assumes the use of down as an insulating material; other insulators will be discussed briefly later in the chapter.

Down. The quality of the down itself is an important factor in the warmth of a bag. Down is a natural material and does not have the uniformity of some man-made materials. It is important to distinguish down from feathers. The latter have quills, but down consists of a mass of filaments extending out from a tiny pod. Down always has small feathers mixed with it, but a down-and-feather mixture, labeled as such, is greatly inferior in insulating quality to true down.

The best down is plucked from geese raised in a cold climate, and it is not surprising that it is expensive. Its quality is measured by the volume of air that a given weight of down will immobilize. Unfortunately, the manufacturers of quality bags do not all use the same grading system in describing the down used in various bags, so that grades (prime, A, AA, etc.) are useful mainly in comparing the bags of one manufacturer. Color—gray or white—is not important in down quality.

There is one happy consequence to the fact that construction and materials are equally expensive in making down clothing. Manufacturers who skimp on one invariably skimp on the other, too. This means that you can generally judge the quality of the down, which you can't see, by the other features of a bag, which you can. A good outfitter will not spend an extra twenty dollars on some fine points of construction and then try to save five by using inferior down.

Fabric. The standard material for sleeping bags these days is nylon, and the reasons for this are so good that there are practically no excuses for deviating from the rule. The use of other materials is generally the first sign of an inferior bag. I know of only one manufacturer of quality bags who still uses cotton fabric, and even his lightweight bags use nylon. The reasons are simple: for a particular fabric weight, nylon is stronger and will take more wear than any other type of cloth; it is not subject to mildew or rot; it can be woven tightly so that it is downproof. The major disadvantage of nylon cloth is that it cannot be treated very effectively with water repellants, but this is of little importance in sleeping bags.

The disadvantage of initial expense is offset by the durability of nylon. A cotton cover, even a quite heavy one, will wear out long before the down it is enclosing.

The lightness of high-strength nylon fabric gives greater freedom to the sleeping-bag designer, because a heavyweight fabric will tend to reduce the expansion of the down by its very weight. Even so, a well-designed sleeping bag uses different weights of fabric throughout the bag. The heaviest weight fabric is used on the outer shell, while the inside of the bag is made of a durable lightweight material, tightly woven enough to prevent escape of the down. An even lighter fabric is used between the two layers for down baffles, and it is also the proper material for a removable liner.

Shape. The shape of a bag for lightweight winter use should be roughly the same as the shape of the human body—a so-called "mummy" bag. The big rectangular bags tend to be prohibitively heavy even in summer, and in winter weights, they are even heavier. They are also very expensive when they are made of down. The reason is twofold: not only is the bag itself larger, using more materials, but it is also much less efficient so that a thicker bag is needed.

Within the mummy classification, however, there is a lot of room for choice, because bags are now made which range all the way from a modified rectangular bag tapered at each end to reduce weight and surface area to extremely lightweight bags that fit very closely. The standard bags offered by most mountaineering supply stores fall somewhere in between these extremes, and this compromise is a good one for most people. The bags fit closely enough to be really warm and efficient, while still having enough room inside to allow a little movement and to allow any down clothing you may wear to fluff up. The narrower bags—the superlight, slimline, etc.—are excellent for those who want to pare off every possible ounce, but they are usually designed for a temperature range not extending more than ten or twenty degrees below zero, and this factor should be considered, especially since down clothing inside them is less effective than in other bags. The larger bags, sometimes called modified-mummy, are usually designed for moderate temperatures, and are best left there, but they might be considered by people who really feel cramped in the standard bags.

A well-designed bag should taper rapidly at the top, to the hood, should be fairly broad through the midsection, from shoulders to hips, and should then taper down to the foot. There should be a bottom large enough so that when you are lying in the bag with your feet sticking up, they do not press against the bag. Otherwise, there will be a cold spot.

Construction. The internal construction of sleeping bags is complicated, and the better the bag the more complicated it becomes. The object behind it all is, of course, to get the most insulation for the least weight. As with clothing, the insulation a sleeping bag provides will be proportional to the thickness of the layer of dead-air spaces it holds around your sleeping body. You can get a rough idea of the insulating power of any bag from its *loft.* The loft of a bag is its thickness lying flat—approximately double the thickness of the layer that will cover you. The loft gives one basis of comparision between the bags of different manufacturrers, but catalogue claims should be considered as only a rough indication, since different makers measure the loft in different ways.

One important feature in the design of a cold-weather bag is a *differential cut.* Any bag will actually consist of two bags, one inside the other, with the insulation in between. If the two bags are the same size, then whenever you stretch inside the bag you will push the inner bag against the outer one, and the down in between will compress. You will then have a cold spot at each pressure point. With a differential cut the inner bag is cut smaller than the outer one, so that when you press against it the outer bag will still be held away from the inner one by the down insulating layer.

It is considerably more difficult to make a bag with a differential cut than to simply cut the inner and the outer shells to the same pattern, and even some of the best outdoor suppliers manufacture economy down bags without this feature. Such bags are not well-suited for cold-weather use; under winter conditions when you scrunch up from the cold, you will soon find that your back is freezing because you have pressed the inner shell against the outer one. Sleepers who don't move around much may not need the differential cut, but I feel that a properly designed differential cut greatly improves the bag.

Between the two shells of your bag is the down, but down is made up of a great many filament clusters, which will shift around if left to themselves. If they were not held in place, it would be necessary to put so much down in the bag that no empty spots could form. This would be inefficient, heavy, and very expensive. In order to get efficient use from each little cluster of down, it is necessary to separate the volume between the two shells into many small compartments, each containing just enough down to expand it completely. One easy way to form these compartments is to quilt the bag. Just sew the inner shell to the outer one in squares or tubes. This method is very poor for cold-weather bags, however, because each of the seams is a "cold seam." That is, it has no insulation along it, so that it allows heat to escape. This method is usually used only with inferior types of insulating material, such as down-feather mixtures, and it is good only for making warm-weather bags.

The method used in high-quality sleeping bags is to sew very thin baffles between the two shells of the sleeping bag. These walls allow the two shells to be pushed apart by the down, but at the same time keep the down from shifting around inside the bag. Some of the methods of baffling are shown in Appendix A, but in general they can be summarized in this way: the smaller the compartments are, the more efficiently a certain amount of down can be used for insulation. In other words, the number of pounds of down and the quality of the down are not the only things that determine how warm a bag will be. Unfortunately, sewing small compartments in between two layers of fabric and then filling them with down is an expensive proposition, and this is why good sleeping bags cost so much money. It is the design and construction of these compartments that make one bag of the same weight from the same manufacturer cost twice as much as another and give it a comfort range forty degrees lower.

Closures. Most lightweight sleeping bags have an opening that is closed by a zipper running at least halfway down one side or the top of the bag, as well as being open at the head of the bag. The zipper should be a large size with opening tabs both inside and outside the bag. It should operate perfectly, and a sticking or jamming zipper these days is the sign of an inferior bag. Don't buy it. Most of the better-quality bags now use nylon zippers, but there is nothing wrong with a good metal one. Inside the bag there should be sewn along the opening a down-filled tube that covers the zipper from the inside when it is closed. This tube prevents a cold breeze from blowing through the zipper at night and dusting your spine with powder snow. Other closures besides zippers are possible, but they are not currently being used by the manufacturers of good down bags.

Other considerations are of less importance than good zipper operation and down tube. A side zipper has some advantage over the top one. When the weather warms up a bit and you want ventilation, or when you open the zipper for freedom of movement, the side zipper allows some air circulation without having the bag fall completely off your chest, as happens with the top zipper. A full-length zipper has some advantages in drying the bag on sunny days, a matter worth consideration of the small extra weight and expense. Finally, many manufacturers now make all their bags that have full-length zippers in such a way that they will zip together as long as the zippers are on opposite sides.

Most hood designs are adequate. When you buy a bag, test the operation and make sure the hood can be opened all the way and closed to any desired degree down to an opening large enough for the tip of the nose. The simpler the whole operation, the better. When the call of nature gets strong enough to make you brave the midnight cold, fussing with fifteen different tangled and unidentifiable strings is annoying—to say the least!

The old miniature awnings at the head of the bag, which are often depicted as shedding torrential rains from the head of the peacefully sleeping camper, are rarely found on lightweight bags. They are useless, and their presence on bags you are being shown should send you packing to another store.

Occasionally, you may find ultra-light bags with no side openings; entry is through the top. Most manufacturers don't make these bags because of their major disadvantage: they lack flexibility in temperature range. If you need a really ultra-light bag for one temperature range and can afford it, you can either make a bag of this type or have one custom-made. Usually, they are not worth the weight saved.

Liners and covers. These are extra features available from many manufacturers. For those who feel the advantages are important, but who cannot afford the cost, they are excellent do-it-yourself projects, requiring less experience than do many other pieces of equipment, but not holding up your trip schedule if you don't finish them in time.

Most liners are designed simply to keep the bag clean. They are worthwhile for this purpose, since a liner will cut the number of cleanings or washings necessary to a quarter of what they would be. Bags usually get dirty inside first. Liners are a matter of personal preference, with four main types in common use for lightweight bags. My own strong preference is for extremely lightweight nylon ripstop. These liners weigh practically nothing, and they can be washed and dried during a short break on a sunny day. The biggest advantage to my mind, though, is that they are slippery nylon, which prevents the material from binding—an important feature for comfort in a form-fitting bag. Others dislike the silky feel of nylon and prefer flannel liners. These weigh a bit more than the nylon, and they can't be dried as easily, but they contribute some insulation. An inexpensive answer is liners made from normal bedsheets, often cut from the better parts of worn sheets at home. The final alternative is a nylon fleece, which offers a more luxurious and expensive version of the advantages and disadvantages of the flannel type. All told, liners should be considered for their value in keeping bags clean and their catering to the tastes of their owners; the insulation value they offer is always less than what would be gained by having a heavier down bag.

Another type of liner is really a second sleeping bag made to go inside the first one and extend its temperature range. Two bags of this type make an excellent and versatile combination, though the combination is not quite so efficient as a single bag of the same weight. The inner bag is usually made with sewn-through seams, since cold seams are not a problem.

Sleeping-bag covers are a bit different matter from liners. They also offer some protection for your expensive bag, but this is less useful than that offered by liners. The main advantage offered by a sleeping-bag cover is that it can be used to extend the temperature range of a bag. They should be seriously considered by those who possess bags that are not quite heavy enough for extremely cold weather. Their use as bivouac equipment will be discussed later in the book.

The covers are quite useful for those (like myself) who like to sleep without a tent on quiet nights. They reduce condensation on the bag, make it warmer, and if they have waterproof bottoms, they double as groundcloths. Some covers incorporate insulating pads under the hips, shoulders, and feet. This seems a good idea, but it never quite works out, since the insulation usually ends up on the side of the bag somewhere while your posterior sits in the snow. The best type of cover, in my opinion, is made of very light material, waterproof on the bottom and breathing on top. It is shaped just like a big flat paper bag, and has room for equipment beside the sleeping bag. It is made by several outfitters, and there are plans in the do-it-yourself section.

Double bags or zip-togethers? For couples who plan to do their snow camping together or for friends of the same sex who go on trips together and consider warmth more important than nighttime privacy, heat is greatly conserved with togetherness in some kind of a double bag. Two can sleep warmer than one. There are also some financial advantages. Several manufacturers sell a double bag, which is simply a wide mummy bag with special arrangements for two heads at one end. These are much less expensive than two bags, but they are for truly inseparable couples—or for those well enough off to afford several sets of bags. You cannot take half the bag with you on a trip when your spouse is away for the weekend. Also, you will find yourself at a disadvantage if you should spend a night at a ski shelter provided only with narrow single bunks. In efficiency, financially and thermally, however, double bags have great advantages.

The alternative arrangement is a set of zip-together bags. Several manufacturers are now making all their bags with the same length zipper, separating at the bottom, so that any two of their bags will zip together, providing one has a left and one a right zipper. This arrangement offers great flexibility in meeting individual needs. For example, my wife and I do a lot of camping together in pretty cold weather, but I also go off by myself occasionally on insane Spartan jaunts. I sleep much warmer than she does. We are still trying to wear out an old set of zip-together bags, but if I were buying a set now, I would get one very warm bag and one moderate-weight one. On trips together, I would sleep in the lighter bag, while my wife had the luxury of the super-warm model. On solo trips I could take whichever bag best suited my needs. Many other adjustments are possible.

One other advantage to the true double bag should be mentioned. Since it is designed for two people rather than being comprised of two bags designed for one, it has some better-thought-out features. The most important is that the arrangement at the head of the bag is usually well-suited for individual temperature

A buyer's guide to sleeping bags

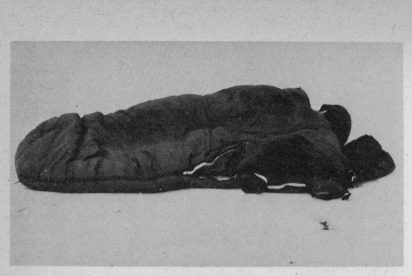

A double bag with outside zippers. Two hoods and provision for closure at the center are essential.

control, though you should check this. The other is that the zippers are on the sides of the bag and can still be used for ventilation and individual exit. On zip-together bags, the zippers are sacrificed to the joining operation.

Choosing your bag. The use of rentals has been mentioned earlier in this book, and sleeping bags are especially profitable to rent. Borrowing from a friend is a cheaper equivalent, of course, if this alternative is available. If you know from previous experience what kind of bag you need and you have the money to buy it, don't go through the expense and inconvenience of renting. By the same token, if you have a medium-weight bag and enough clothing to extend its range for winter use, don't rent a heavier bag you can do without. But if you don't own a bag that can be made adequate for cold-weather use and you either aren't sure what type of bag to buy or don't have the money to put out at one time, rent your sleeping bag the first few trips. If you get a different bag each time, you can build up more experience with different makes of bags than some old-timers have built up in years. Sleeping bags last so long, most active mountaineers don't use more than two or three before retiring. Obviously, this alternative is only open to those who are lucky enough to have a mountaineering-backpacking shop nearby.

Let us say that you have only very limited knowledge of snow camping and can't try out equipment by renting or borrowing. (Obviously, if you can get such experience you will be ahead of the game; you will rapidly develop your own prejudices and can ignore some of mine.)

The first step in buying a major piece of equipment like a sleeping bag is to get all the catalogues you can. Even if you end up buying your bag at a store, you will have a better idea of what is available after reading the offerings of other manufacturers. There aren't too many manufactures of lightweight outdoor equipment in this country, and you can write most of them for literature in an evening. A fairly complete list is found in Appendix C. Many of the catalogues available from these houses contain very valuable advice and information. With a bit of work and consideration of the features discussed in this chapter, you should be able to compare the bags offered and get some idea of the comparative prices of different manufacturers. There are some pretty big differences, though price is a good guide to relative quality in any one maker's line.

One minor caution is to read all the information about each bag. Most reputable manufacturers of lightweight bags readily admit that temperature ranges are only suggestive: they tell you that one bag made by Joe Smith is warmer than another but not that it is warmer than one by Frank Jones. The same thing applies to loft measurements, down ratings, etc.

Finally, if you do go to a store, take a good look at the catalogue before you get into a discussion with the sales clerk. Almost all good stores selling this type of equipment put a lot of care into their catalogue statements. Their customers demand honesty and frankness, but they cannot be expected to screen their clerks quite as carefully. Some are very good indeed. (I mean this; that salesman you're talking to may very well be one of the best living mountain climbers in the world.) Unfortunately, some are not. They may have strong opinions but weak experience, or they may simply have developed a cynical attitude toward customers. Do your homework beforehand and then listen to the salesman; he may be very helpful, but he will be more so if you know what you want.

A buyer's guide to sleeping bags   45

Insulators other than down. Some people are allergic to feathers and down, and they will have to use other types of insulation. The best substitute is a mummy bag using Dacron batting as insulation. Two or three of the outfitters listed in Appendix C carry such bags. They may also be the answer for the poverty-stricken winter camper who sleeps warm and does not expect extremely severe conditions.

What's underneath it all? Obviously, if you sleep directly on the snow, you're going to get cold, no matter how well-protected you are from chilly breezes above. Yet sleeping on the snow is almost what you're doing without some sort of ground insulation; the thickness of a compressed sleeping bag and a tent floor doesn't present too much of a barrier to the cold. In any season, ground insulation of some sort is important, because sleeping right on the ground is a very inefficient way to use a sleeping bag. In winter, when heat loss to a snowy ground is much greater, a proper ground bed becomes a matter of survival.

Two major types of ground bed are generally used—air mattresses and foam pads. Air mattresses will be discussed first, mostly to dispose of them, and the use of bough beds will be covered in another chapter. Air mattresses have one major advantage: they can be folded to a very compact size when deflated, whereas foam pads are somewhat more bulky, even though they usually weigh a bit less. The only mattresses worth considering are the lightweight coated nylon fabric type. Standard rubberized fabric is very heavy, and plastic is too fragile, though it is quite light. All this is relevant mostly in moderate seasons, though, for the air mattresses are cold compared with foam pads, and many consider them less comfortable, anyway.

The reason that air mattresses are cold is a simple one; even though they are thick, they have only one unbroken layer of air which is not compartmentalized to prevent convection currents. This means that all the thermal energy transmitted from your posterior to the air in the mattress is rapidly dissipated to the snow below by air currents inside the mattress. For this reason I recommend foam pads to cold-weather travelers, but for those of you who are incurable air-mattress buffs, there is one easy conversion that will make your beloved air mattress the equal in insulating power to any pad.

The modification is simple: a small slit is made in each tube of the mattress and a few ounces of down are inserted. Only a little is needed—just enough to break the convection currents that normally make the mattress colder than a pad. One of the slits should be made near the valve and a piece of gauze or mesh glued over the valve opening on the inside to prevent the down from escaping. After all this is completed, patch all your holes and you will have a priceless possession—a warm air mattress. Complete credit for this idea goes to that great outdoorsman, Calvin Rutstrum, for I have seen it mentioned nowhere except in one of his books, and no manufacturer I know of has made such an air mattress commercially.

For those of you who are not already committed to the air mattress, there is a more readily obtainable and less expensive alternative to a down filled mattress—the foam pad. The necessity of choosing is still with you, however, for there are two major types. The first type is the sort of foam used in furniture—an open-cell foam like sponge rubber. The lightweight camping version is made of a plastic foam, usually polyurethane. These pads are very comfortable, usually a little lighter than an air mattress, and for winter use they should be one and a half or two inches thick. Because they are permeable, they are best covered with some sort of nylon cloth to keep them from getting wet, and also to protect them from being torn when riding on the outside of the pack. This type of foam pad coupled with a good sleeping bag provides the winter outdoorsman with luxury undreamed of by the hardy woodsman of old.

The second type of foam pad is a more recent innovation, and is generally the best alternative for the winter traveler. This is the closed-cell foam pad, often called Ensolite or Thermobar after the most frequently used brands. Closed-cell foam is just that; it is a foam in which each air cell is completely closed off from all the others. Hence, there are no convection currents, and a very thin sheet will give as much insulation as a much thicker open-cell pad. I know of no published test figures, but in my own experience, three-eighths of an inch of closed cell foam is about the equivalent of two inches of polyurethane foam and is much warmer than any commercially available air mattress. Closed-cell foam doesn't provide the padding that open-cell does, but this is not too important to the winter traveler, since snow generally presents a fairly smooth sleeping surface. Closed-cell foam is lighter for equivalent insulation; it is more compact, even though it can't be compressed

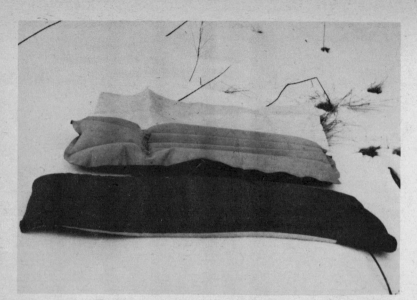

Three types of ground insulation. In the foreground is an open-cell foam pad with a cover, the most expensive, comfortable, and bulky type. In the center is an air mattress, which is too cold for most winter use. Top is closed cell foam, as warm as the lower pad and much cheaper, but not so comfortable.

much, and it is cheaper because there is no need for a cover; the closed cells can't absorb moisture. Closed-cell foam can be bought in various degrees of hardness—type M is best—and various thicknesses—a quarter inch is good for emergency and moderate-weather use, three-eights or a half inch are best for sleeping on snow.

No matter which type of ground insulation you choose, get the "shortie" or hip-length type. This takes care of the major weight-bearing points of the body, from shoulders to hips. The legs and feet can be insulated quite easily with a bit of spare clothing, pack, climbing rope, food bags, and other contents of the pack.

Keeping warm and sleeping warm. Even with the proper equipment there is a lot of know-how separating the shivering novice from the toasty veteran. The important thing is to remember that it *is* know-how. The old verse and current cliché goes, "A little knowledge is a dangerous thing," and the novice, knowing that physiological differences *do* cause some people to sleep and wake

SLEEPING WARM 48

warmer than others, is likely to attribute the expert's comfortable state to "warm-bloodedness," when it is actually due to techniques that have been cultivated for so long that the fellow doesn't remember what he is doing himself. Some of the tricks for keeping warm have been covered in the preceeding chapters, and some will be discussed with other camping techniques, but there are a few that deserve special consideration here.

The first technique for sleeping warm is *keeping* warm. During the day you will usually keep warm from sheer physical effort, combined sometimes with the welcome rays of the sun. You will notice at every rest stop, though, that the air is cold, and when you stop you feel it. This is much more true on stopping toward the end of the day, for the sun is usually going down, and your tired body joins dropping temperatures and damp clothes to produce a situation where very sudden chilling often results.

The proper way to meet this situation is simple. Make your camp and then get into your sleeping bag before you start to feel cold. If you're still warm, the sun is in the sky, the woods invite exploring, and camp is made, by all means answer the call. However, watch your body, and always try to bed down before you get cold. If you use a stove, the standard pattern in winter is to cook supper in your sleeping bag. At any rate, your camp should be completely ready before you start exploring. The days are much shorter in winter, and the cold really seeps into your bones in a hurry when the sun goes down and you stop moving. Even if you don't get into your sleeping bag, change to dry socks and mittens, and loosen boot laces. Put on extra clothes if you are sitting around.

Keep your body warmth in mind as you are pitching camp. Follow the techniques for choosing a warm campsite, which are discussed later in the book. Then arrange your bed so that you are well-protected underneath. If you are cold in your bag, then it is only common sense to use all the insulation you have available. There shouldn't be any extra dry sweaters in your pack.

Even if you aren't using a double sleeping bag, there shouldn't be any gear or much space separating bags. Placing bags next to one another conserves a lot of warmth. Fluff the bags up well.

For all-night warmth, you need food; the digestion of food releases energy in the form of heat. There is one slight qualification here: if you are really cold when you first get into your bag, start off with hot drinks and perhaps something sweet. Though you need lots of food to keep you warm, eating a lot of heavy things forces the body to divert blood to the stomach, when you need it temporarily for thawing out.

To warm up when you get in your bag, snug everything tightly, and then try contracting your muscles hard, a few at a time. This serves the same function as shivering: the muscular activity produces warmth. The contractions are good because you avoid moving around and creating air currents to carry away the heat you are producing.

If anyone is *really* cold, don't neglect the possibility that he may be suffering from hypothermia, popularly known as exposure. This subject is discussed in another chapter, and the symptoms should be memorized by cold-weather campers. It is important for each person to take responsibility for his companions, since a person suffering from too much heat loss often becomes irrational and may not realize he is seriously sick. A person suffering from hypothermia cannot always generate enough heat to get warm inside a sleeping bag; someone else must get in with him.

One piece of clothing is often neglected at night, though it can cut more heat loss than almost any other. If you're cold, *wear a hat*. High blood circulation is maintained in the surface skin of the head, even when the body is cold, and this can result in tremendous losses of heat. This is particularly true at night, when cooking and other chores are still being done from the sleeping bag, so that the hood isn't covering the head. *If your feet are cold, put on your hat*.

Drying out clothes. If you want to start a good argument in a group of experienced winter campers, just inject this subject into the conversation, and then sit back and watch the fun. The question is whether to wear your damp clothes to bed at night in order to dry them out with your body heat.

Those who favor this technique argue that "During the earlier and warmer part of the night much of the moisture from damp clothes can be evaporated and will pass right through the sleeping bag in the form of water vapor. This way you wake up with dry clothes, rather than a frozen heap at the foot of the tent, and you have a particular advantage if the sun doesn't come out."

"Nuts!" says the opponent, the sleep-in-dry-clothes man. "You probably won't succeed in drying your clothes very much, but you will have a bad night's sleep. What is more dangerous, if you do this regularly on a long trip, your sleeping bag will pick up more and more moisture, eventually becoming useless and losing significant insulation even the first night."

Obviously, there is some truth in each of these arguments, and your practice should be governed by personal trial coupled with a few basic principles. The first is fairly obvious: if you use body heat to evaporate water from your clothes, that heat is not available for keeping your body warm. Clearly, you should never try to dry out wet clothes in your bag unless you are quite warm and can afford the heat loss. Also, it is clear that the amount of drying you can expect to do is limited, and it should be confined to damp woolens, which aren't too uncomfortable. It is absurd to lose a night's sleep trying to dry out clothes. If you can't sleep, you're making a mistake.

The major problem, however, is the problem of wetting the bag. It works like this: the air inside your bag is warm, and some of the water in your clothes evaporates in this air, mixing with insensible perspiration from your body. Since this air doesn't circulate very much, the humidity inside the bag gets quite high. Gradually the water vapor circulates through the air cells trapped in the down insulation of your sleeping bag, and those air cells are colder near the outside of the bag. The colder air cannot hold as much water, and if too much water vapor is being produced, the water may condense into dew in the down. This may not be serious if the weather is not too cold, since the water may evaporate again later. If the weather *is* very cold, the air cells in the outer part of the bag are often well below freezing, so that when the water vapor condenses, it freezes, forming ice crystals in the down. In very cold weather these keep forming, and the bag finally becomes completely useless. On long trips, this can be a problem even if clothing is not dried in the bag, since insensible perspiration can cause the same difficulty. The problem arises much more quickly if clothes are dried in the bag.

The condensation is also serious in damp weather around the freezing point. Under these circumstances the moisture does not freeze in the down, but it condenses into liquid and does not evaporate because the air is already too wet. As with the dry-cold problem, the only real solution is to either dry things in the sun or before a fire.

The reader has probably guessed that the author tends to side with the sleep-in-dry-clothes advocates. The main reason is that

A buyer's guide to sleeping bags   51

clothing is generally a lot easier to dry than a sleeping bag. A damp sleeping bag on a cold weather-trip is a very serious matter. So are damp clothes, but except for down clothing, nothing you wear is nearly so hard to dry as your bag. Finally, as I suggested at the beginning of the chapter, a little misery in the day is soothed a lot by a good night's sleep. A wet bag will at best make the whole trip an ordeal.

Caring for your sleeping gear. Aside from the obvious matter of repairing rips and broken hardware, the two main things you can do for your sleeping gear, at home and in the field, are to keep it dry and clean. Dirt and moisture both rob down of its insulating value. When the opportunity arises on a trip, open the bag and air it out, preferably in the sun. When you get it home, hang it out in the sun or in a warm spot in the house until you are sure it is thoroughly dry. Then store it in a dry place.

Unless you spill the stew on your bag or perspire much in it, you won't need to clean it too often. Most dirt will rub off on the liner if you have one, and this can be cleaned separately. Too much perspiring in a bag will get salt in the down, and this in turn will absorb moisture when the bag is in use. A bag can be cleaned by a reputable dry cleaner, but you should be sure he uses no detergents, since these remove necessary oils from the down. Don't use a coin dry cleaner, because these will not dry the bag adequately. It is very important that all the solvent be evaporated before the bag is used, since it is quite toxic and many deaths have resulted from the use of dry-cleaned bags that still contained solvent. If you take the bag to the dry cleaners, smell it when you get it back, and either leave it with the cleaner if it still has the characteristic dry cleaning odor, or take it home and air it until the smell is gone. You should air it for a day or two, anyway.

I prefer to wash the bag myself. Use warm water and mild soap, squeeze most of the water out of the bag, and then dry it. The easiest way is in a drier set on low heat, which still takes a while. If it is necessary to dry the bag in the house or the sun, you will have to fluff it occasionally as it dries to keep the down from balling.

After the washing is done, fluff the bag up; it will be restored to its original loft. A good bag will take years of hard use. Pads and air mattresses require washing only when good taste demands it.

IV

Camping on Snow

The fascination of winter is hard to grasp fully until you have
tried camping on the snow. On day-long tours with skis or
snowshoes you can experience the beauty of brilliant white slopes
meeting blue sky in a line somehow sharper than any seen in summer. Still, it is only during longer stays that you can feel the full
intensity of the background silence, sometimes bright and clear,
sometimes muffled and close.

The challenges of winter are also felt more strongly when one
lives for a time on the snow, in addition to walking on it. Challenges are often worth meeting for their own sake, but there are
other more important reasons for snow camping. Especially when
you begin snow camping, before the techniques become second
nature and begin to make you feel at home, you may feel very
strongly how tenuous your existence is in this world of cold and
light. The beginner has one great advantage over the expert in this
situation, because this consciousness of not belonging in the cold,
stark, and beautiful world around you can lead to a realization of
the independent value of that world—a value that can only be
experienced in its own terms.

To meet the winter on its own terms you have to get away from
the knowledge that a warm cabin is waiting. To me this is what
snow camping is all about. It's also a great challenge in its more
extreme forms. Finally, it can be a lot of fun.

GETTING STARTED

It's best to get your first couple of experiences camping on snow that's not too far from your base. If you live in a woodsy area, try walking into the woods behind your house for the first try. Otherwise, get just far enough from the road for peace and quiet. A little experience in easy conditions can prevent your first real trip from turning into a survival ordeal. There's a lot to learn about snow camping, and you might just as well learn it pleasantly.

Incidentally, this go-slow approach is particularly important for men taking their wives, families, or girl friends snow camping. The best way to get them to go again is to avoid any unpleasant experiences the first time around. (Women who may be reading this know their own minds well enough so that they don't need any advice of this kind from me.)

For your first trip pick a weekend that seems to offer reasonable prospects for decent weather. Winter weather is unsettled enough so that you'll have your chance to experience a blizzard soon enough; try to avoid it the first time out.

If you have bought or rented new equipment, make sure to inspect it and try it out at home or at some other warm location. A cold, snowy evening is no time to find out how to operate a self-priming gasoline stove from the Swedish directions, or to find out that the last guy who rented that tent left the zipper on top of Horrible Ridge. Incidentally, later on you'll find that this applies to the first trip of every season, anyway. By then you will have forgotten that broken fortzwaffler that you were going to fix during the summer—and never did.

This is a good place to mention again a couple of principles in getting equipment. The old rule of thumb is to never buy anything you don't need for the next trip. This way you don't get a lot of stuff that you don't need and you are likely to make more intelligent selections of the things that you do need. Naturally, you'll have to modify this rule a bit if you're buying equipment by mail order from a place that takes six weeks to reply.

If there is a store near you specializing in mountaineering and backpacking equipment, they probably have a rental service. Renting is obviously a good way to spread the cost of basic equipment over a reasonable period. It is also a good way to try out various types of gear before putting out the large sums needed to purchase them.

SHELTERS TO CARRY WITH YOU

For winter camping you will almost always need a shelter, whether it is one you carry with you or one you construct in the field. It needs to do a good deal more than is required of the type of shelter used in most summer camping, and for this reason many of the types of tents and shelters that are used in summer camping are inadvisable for camping on snow. An example is the plastic tube tent, which is an ideal shelter in many areas during the summer. At best it is emergency equipment in the winter; you should not plan on camping in it. At worst it can be a death trap.

Shelters that are made on the spot will be discussed later in the chapter, but it might be useful to point out that they will usually come later in your camping experience, too. You won't be able to plan on using improvised shelters until you have had quite a bit of experience, and this means you'll have to carry a tent at least while you're learning.

Except in the mountains, most tents for use in the warmer seasons on the trail function mainly to shed the rain. In crowded campgrounds the matter of privacy becomes important, but for go-light campers, this does not usually need to be considered. Open-front tents have had great and well-deserved popularity, because they cover a lot of area without weighing or costing too much, and because they don't give one the feeling of claustrophobia that many closed, lightweight tents do.

Especially with the widespread use of down sleeping bags, these tents aren't used primarily to keep warm. Many backpackers, myself included, prefer to sleep without a tent when the weather permits. This can sometimes be managed even in winter, but as a rule the tent in winter has to help keep you warm, to protect you from snow and from cold winds. Usually, this means either a closed tent or an all-night fire. The traditional north-woods arrangement of a lean-to (tent or boughs) and all-night fire is fine if you're camping where plenty of wood is available. However, if even part of your trip will be in an area that is not heavily forested or where the use of wood must be restricted, a closed tent is definitely advisable. In the mountains where high winds may be expected they are essential.

The closed tent may or may not have a sewn-in floor, but for winter camping a floor is essential, whether or not it is sewn to the tent. If it is not, the tent should have a sod cloth all the way around the edge, which can be used to form a weather-tight seal by burying it in snow. The advantages to a sewn-in floor are a ready-made weather seal, easier pitching, and easier striking. If you are buying or renting a tent for winter use, you should definitely get one with a sewn-in floor, which is waterproof and preferably extends up the sides six inches or so. If you already have a tent for summer use, you may be able to get along with it providing it isn't made of coated nylon fabric. The disadvantage to the sod cloth or buried side for a frequently moved camp is that it freezes in the snow and has to be chopped out. Tent sides treated in this way don't last very long.

A few words about car-camping tents will be in order later in the chapter, but we are generally considering tents light enough to be packed on your back. The reasons for choosing closed-cell tents have already been mentioned, but if you will be traveling entirely in wooded areas and plan to make do with an open-front tent, remember to choose one with a roof that is pitched steeply enough to shed snow. The comments later in the chapter on the use of improvised lean-tos will apply also to open-front tents.

A Logan-type, or modified pyramid, tent.

CAMPING ON SNOW

A two-man mountain tent in a mild storm. This one is tapered toward the rear.

Before choosing a tent, you will have to decide how many people it is going to accommodate. A four-man tent is usually about the largest practical one for cold-weather lightweight travel. The four-man is roomier for each person than the two-man tent, and it weighs and costs less per man, but it costs more per tent, and it is heavy for regular use by two people. Party size is considered in a later chapter, but your own circumstances will be the main determinant. The main type of four-man tent for this use is some variation of the Logan tent—a pyramid tent with a central pole, guyed out on the sides for stability and extra room. These have the great virtue of making it possible for someone to stand up in the center, a virtue impossible to fully appreciate until you have waited out a blizzard in a two-man mountain tent. There are several variations of the standard Logan design, including somewhat larger and smaller versions. They are all fine tents, which can be used year-round for backpacking, canoe camping, and car camping. Any of them are good for their size. If you are doubtful, try to rent one for a weekend and try it out. If you get it by mail, try it in your backyard, protecting it from the ground with a plastic sheet. Any of the outfitters listed in the appendix will refund your money if you are not satisfied and return the tent in good condition.

Shelters to carry with you 57

The standard cold-weather tent for two people is the two-man mountain tent. This design is basically pup-tent-shaped, though there have been so many improvements that this is a different tent. This tent is efficient—which is to say rather cramped. Size and weight vary somewhat. The ends may both be full height, in which case there should be entrances at each end. This extra room is not functional at night, but it is handy when you are sitting up to dress or cook, and the two entrances are very convenient. Weight may be saved by building the end near the feet lower, losing one entrance. Excess weight is eliminated not only in fabric but in poles and guys.

Poles at the entrance to a mountain tent should be arranged as a set of two outside poles meeting at the top. The single pole in the center takes up too much space, and poles inside make the tent harder to pitch. The sides of mountain tents are held out by various arrangements of guys and wands (very light rods arranged to curve outward). Each added feature should be considered with a jaundiced eye, not only as a convenience but as a weight in the pack and a complication waiting to go wrong in the first blizzard.

Materials. The basic fabric in a winter tent should *never* be waterproof. Such a fabric will condense all the moisture produced by your body, your breathing, and your cooking. This moisture will then rain back down on your sleeping bag and freeze, forming another waterproof layer which will then trap body moisture in the bag itself. The floor should be waterproof, of course. For the rest of the tent there are two alternatives, each with its own advantages.

Cotton and nylon-cotton mixtures may be made into fairly light, water-resistant materials that will shed a reasonable amount of rain. These tents are cheaper than all-nylon types. They do not need flies for most weather, and they do not condense as much moisture or build up as much frost as the all-nylon tents. The pure cotton tents are better in all these respects than the cotton-nylon, but are not so strong.

All-nylon tents will not withstand any significant amount of rain by themselves, so a completely waterproof fly, a second tent roof, is pitched a few inches above the tent itself. This makes the tent completely waterproof, and rain will not wick through when the roof is touched. The fly helps to insulate the tent when it is used, keeping it somewhat warmer, though not as much as is often claimed. In very cold weather, when there is no danger of rain, the fly can be left home, reducing the weight of the tent. The all-nylon tents cost quite a bit more, and condensation is more of a problem even when the fly is used. When the fly is carried, the nylon tent usually weighs about the same as the cotton or cotton-nylon versions.

Frost liners and inner tents are made of light material and are hung from ties inside the tent to form a layer of air an inch or two thick between the liner and the inner wall. The inner tents are made of heavier material, and are intended to form an insulating layer. The frost liners are very light and serve mainly to reduce the problem of frost formed from moisture condensing on the cold tent walls. Unless you have extra money to spend, these features are probably not worthwhile for the reader of this book. They are useful mainly for expeditions of considerable duration.

Entrances. The two main entrance designs are the zipper front, which has several versions, and the tunnel entrance. Zipper entrances are usually more convenient for all-weather use, while tunnel entrances are best where high winds may be encountered, as in winter use above timberline. Mountain tents with two full-size ends should have both types of entrances: that's the main advantage to the design. Otherwise, take your pick. Some Logan-type tents can also be bought with two entrances.

Zippers on entrances should, of course, work faultlessly. A zipper in the floor through which snow for cooking can be scooped is handy. Other features can be left to the reader's judgement. Most really successful innovations by one manufacturer are immediately appropriated by all the others, anyway.

CAMPSITES

If you are using fires for cooking or for heat, your main consideration in picking a campsite will be the availability of wood. By the same token, if you are camping using improvised shelters, you will have to look mainly for a suitable shelter site. For tent campers using a stove for cooking, the main consideration in choosing a site should be the availability of liquid water, which will save fuel and time.

Wherever the campsite is located, the camper must be certain that no dangers are present. This is mainly a problem in the mountains, where the possibility of avalanches exists, a matter which is discussed at some length elsewhere in the book. With tents, some care should be exercised in the woods to be sure that large quantities of snow and dead branches will not fall onto the tent from nearby trees. Some special dangers applicable to improvised shelters are discussed later in the chapter.

With real luck, the winter camper may be able to find a campsite that is not only safe and supplied with plentiful amounts of firewood and water, but is warm as well. If there are strong winds, of course, it's well to seek protection from them. With real storms, though, beware of the lee side of a ridge. A large drift often builds up at this point, and moving a tent out from under a snow-drift in the middle of the night is not conducive to restful sleep.

In the absence of prevailing winds, remember that cold air sinks. On a calm night the bottom of a bowl may be twenty degrees colder than a knoll fifty feet higher. Also, if the bowl is a large one, the gullies leading into it are usually the paths for rivers of cold air flowing down at night. Pitch your tent a little out of the gully from which you're getting your water.

Radiational cooling accounts for the fact that clear nights tend to be the coldest. Under a clear sky your tent will get colder than it will if it is sheltered by an overhanging rock or some other shelter, and it will build up much more frost. This fact should be considered if you are having trouble with cold.

If camp is being made on a trip, try to make it early. Snow camping should be enjoyable, and it is more likely to be so if camp is made and sunset can be watched with a hot drink in hand, perhaps from the sleeping bag. I hope the reader does not need to be told to balance the earlier considerations (except avalanche danger) against the view. Melting snow may be worth the improved view from the ridge.

Finally, the campsite should be situated with consideration of the route of your trip. It should be far enough along so that not too much distance is left for the next day. More important, consider what happens if you have to retreat. For example, if there is danger of a storm in the mountains, you must not only pick a campsite free of avalanche danger, but try to avoid having your escape route pass over the avalanche slope.

If firewood is available, a fire can save fuel and provide an instinctive feeling of comfort that no stove can equal. If an open shelter or tent is being used, the fire will, of course, be built in front of it. With any sort of shelter, much more warmth will be got from the fire if any reflecting surfaces available are used. Placing the tent between the fire and a large rock, with some logs on the other side of the fire used as a second reflector, is an example.

SETTING UP CAMP

It is wise to lie around in the afternoon sun after camp is set up, rather than before. The duties of collecting water and wood should be taken up by some one or two. Everyone else should first stamp out platforms in the snow for the tent or tents. These should be a bit larger than the tents themselves. One begins by packing with skis or snowshoes and progresses to boots when the snow is sufficiently compacted. If the forest is not heavily used or situated at high altitude, the tent can be made warmer by laying out a layer of small evergreen boughs under the tent floor. Be careful of large

The first step in making camp is to stamp out a platform.

spears which will puncture the floor and your anatomy. It is worth some effort to get the platform fairly smooth and flat. The surface will soon freeze, and it will be more comfortable if mounds and troughs are kept to a minimum.

The tent is then staked out on the platform using one of several methods. Stakes may be carried. This is often necessary for camping above timberline, and other places where natural materials may not be available. Where locally available materials can be used, it is usually easier and more effective in snow to use some sort of dead-man arrangement rather than true stakes. For this method, it is best to have a two-foot length of parachute cord tied to each stake loop in advance. This loop is passed around a stick, rock, or pole, which is then buried and stamped into the snow. One long pole or stick may be used for the stake on a whole side of the tent. Remember that the dead men will be well frozen by morning; try to plan for this eventuality. If the cords are simply passed around the dead men, with the knot tied above the snow, the lines can often be pulled out after untying them without digging out the anchors.

Tent poles may also be carried, but if ski poles are being used, these can often be modified at home to double as tent poles. For a mountain tent, all that is usually necessary is to make the baskets easily removable. With a Logan-type tent, which requires a long pole, brackets to attach two ski poles rigidly together are necessary. Some types of hose clamps work quite well. The only difficulty in using ski poles for the tent, is that the tent must be dropped if it is to be left in place while the occupants make a day trip. This is not usually a problem, but the location of the tent *must* be well marked in some way if it is dropped. A fairly light snowfall during the day can hide it when the poles are removed.

After the platform is stamped, one person should normally begin to melt snow, unless liquid water is available. Sleeping equipment should be unrolled and fluffed when the tent is up, to allow it to gain full loft. If the sun is still high in the sky any damp clothing should be spread out to dry. Sunlight can also be used to melt snow if dark material is spread out and covered with a thin layer of snow; it can be arranged to drip into a pan. Drips from rocks should also be utilized. Even a small quantity of water can be helpful in melting snow over a stove because the first few inches of water require continuous care to avoid burning the bottom of the pan. The snow will wick up moisture as it is melted,

The following sequence shows the step-by-step erection of a tent. Different tents will vary somewhat, but the basic set-up procedure will probably be similar.

First, a level, solid platform is stamped in the snow, large enough for the tent.

All the necessary anchors should be assembled first, whether stakes have been carried or local material is used. Skis, poles, and snowshoes can substitute.

Unpack the tent, but hold the roll together if it is windy.

Setting up camp

Stake down the tent, pulling the floor tight. In the wind, kneel on the tent while you do this, and stake the windward end first.

Stamp down the snow around all the anchors.

Fix the guy lines to anchors, and pull them fairly tight.

If the snow is soft, deadmen can be used for anchors—stones, sticks, or stakes buried in the snow. First dig a hole, perhaps with a ski, cup, or ice ax.

Next tie the guy line or the cord from the stake loop around the anchor.

Bury the anchor.

Stamp the snow down on the anchor.

Setting up camp

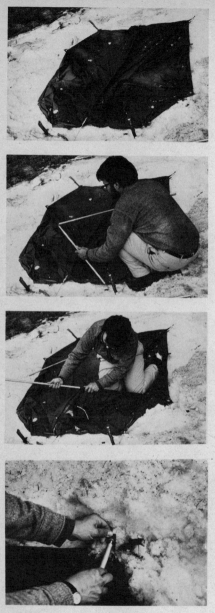

All the anchors of the tent are now fixed.

Assemble the poles.

Insert the poles in the sleeves.

The lower point of the pole fits into the grommet, so the pole won't sink in the snow.

CAMPING ON SNOW

The tops of the poles fit together with the guy line running over them. The guy line has to be loosened to raise the front.

Pull the front guy tight.

Insert the rear pole, which goes under the vent and fits into grommets.

Setting up camp 67

All the guys are then tightened and adjusted.

Once your camp is set up and things are set out to dry, if there is still sun, you can relax. A late winter ski-mountaineering camp. Tent is all-nylon with a fly and has entrances at both ends. Pack at the left is a packframe; in front is a rucksack.

CAMPING ON SNOW   68

as explained in the next chapter. A few inches of water in the pan at the beginning will allow the cook to toss a cupful of snow at a time into the melting pot while he pays attention to other things.

When you climb into the tent at night, it is best to take your gear in with you, but this is not always possible. If not, it is easy to forget mittens and other equipment strewn around the pack. Everything should be packed securely together and put in a place that you can absolutely locate, in the pack beside skis stuck vertically in the snow, for example. A storm during the night can bury even snowshoes and packs so that they can't be found. Mittens will be covered by a bit of wind-drifted powder. You may "know" where things are at night, but don't bet that you will the next morning.

TOILET MATTERS

A path should also be stamped out to a suitable spot to answer calls of nature without having to don skis or snowshoes. In choosing a spot the winter camper should recall that things melt in the spring and are well preserved until then. Pick a place that would not otherwise be an ideal campsite for spring or a water supply for other winter campers. When possible toilet paper should be burned. If the snow cover is light a hole can be dug to the ground, but this is not generally possible. In any case, your latrine should be well buried before you leave. The good wilderness traveler in any season takes pride in leaving as few signs of his passage as possible. The night will be more pleasant if toilet matters are anticipated and taken care of before bedding down.

IMPROVISED SHELTERS

No one should consider himself a qualified winter traveler until he has acquired the skill of finding shelter in any sort of snowy terrain that he frequents. Tents can be damaged, and parties can be forced to separate by accidents or other exigencies. Most common of all, you can be caught away from the tent on a day tour because of storm, injury, or just plain getting lost. If some skills are practiced in making improvised shelters before they are needed, these occasions can become pleasant challenges.

There are other reasons for using improvised shelters. Many experienced snow campers prefer to travel light without a tent when conditions are good for constructing snow shelters. Others, mostly forest travelers, carry only light tarps or plastic sheets to aid them in building shelters. In extremely high winds in the mountains a snow cave is more comfortable than a tent.

The first principle of improvised winter shelters is that *snow is a good insulator*. A shelter made entirely of snow will screen out the wind, and the inside temperature will rarely be much below freezing even soon after it is occupied. The main ingredient for any snow shelter is ingenuity; you must use the terrain and snow immediately around you to construct a shelter. You cannot cut blocks for an igloo from powder snow, but many other possibilities may be easier, anyway. General principles and examples will be given in this section. There are many other designs, some better and some worse than the ones described and shown here.

Lean-tos and all-night fires. The traditional method of the lean-to shelter with an all-night fire has certain virtues. The greatest, and one not to be shunned when it can be indulged, is the esthetic appeal of this fine arrangement. One goes to sleep with the stars shining in over the flickering fire. If the night is cold enough so that the fire is really required, it is necessary to get up a couple of times to stack a few more logs on the pile, but this, too, has its attractions. If the warmth is not really needed, and the lean-to is providing only a roof, sleep should be undisturbed.

Unfortunately, the vices of the lean-to often rule it out. It can only be used effectively in forested areas. It takes a long time and a lot of effort to construct a lean-to from natural materials. A tarp greatly eases the job, but this adds weight, and when storms come up, windbreaks must still be built. A lot of good wood must be gathered for an all-night fire, which requires time and usually necessitates carrying an ax or saw. Small sticks are all right for a cooking fire, but it would take a truckload of them to keep you warm all night, and you'd have to stay awake feeding the fire. You have to have sound logs to keep an all-night fire going. Finally, if you are not using a tarp, you will have to get a lot of boughs to shingle the pole roof of your lean-to. If the woods where you are camping can take it, fine, but in areas of heavy use, or at high altitudes, breaking live branches is criminal, except in a true emergency. In a true emergency a snow hole is probably better, anyway.

A tarp pitched over your sleeping bag to prevent radiational cooling or shed moderate snow is different from a full lean-to with a rigid roof and fire. It is akin to sleeping out with the bag alone and is done when only minimal shelter is needed.

To build a lean-to, you will need to arrange a number of poles into a shed roof over a tramped out floor. The poles are then either covered with a tarp or shingled with boughs. When a tarp is used, cover it with a layer of snow to hold it down and provide insulation. Snow is banked up on the sides to provide wind protection and in front beyond where the fire will be built for wind protection and reflection of the fire. Collect all the wood needed for the fire before it gets dark. If you have not built an all-night fire before, collect about five times as much as you think you can possibly use. You'll need it all.

Tree hollows. In forested areas with heavy snow, there are often deep hollows around the bases of large trees, caused partly because of melting and partly by the shelter of the branches above. A judicious choice of one of these hollows will give you a comfortable shelter with a minimum of excavation. The best ones are formed by conifers when the snow level reaches the lower branches. These form a fine roof over the hollow below. Stairs or a ramp are cut down into the chamber, which must usually be enlarged and tramped down a bit. A small fire can often be built on the floor for warmth, cooking, and cheer. Sleeping platforms should be cut or stamped above the lowest level of the chamber, for even a few feet of elevation will make for a warmer bed. Cold air sinks, and this disadvantage will be felt in the tree hollow even with raised sleeping platforms.

Brush shelters. When there is only a small snow cover, snow holes are impossible and other snow shelters tedious to build. In brushy areas quick shelter may often be found by burrowing into a thicket. When a reasonable chamber (the smaller, the better) is found, the walls and roof should be tightened as much as possible with broken brush. When the walls are tight enough, snow can be heaped on the top of the shelter for wind protection and insula-

Improvised shelters 71

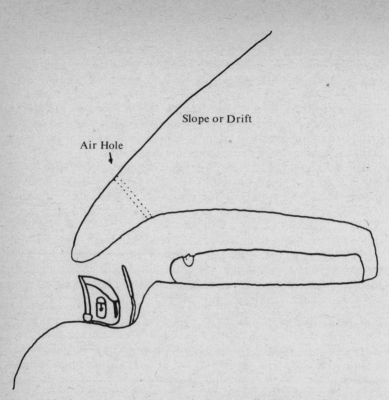

Slope or Drift

Air Hole

The standard snow cave, and the easiest type to dig. The cave is dug into a drift or slope, with the entrance lower than the floor. The pack seals the door, and as with all snow shelters the shovel should be kept inside in case of collapse or drifting.

tion. A plastic sheet or tarp can be used to advantage in forming the roof, but is not essential.

Snow holes and caves. The standard improvised winter shelter is the snow hole or cave, a form which merges into hybrids with igloos, brush shelters, lean-tos, and so on. Snow is full of air, and so it makes a fine insulator. A chamber in the snow is what is wanted, and the trick is simply to choose the easiest construction method for given circumstances. The size of the chamber should be as small as tolerable for the number of people to be housed; small size greatly increases warmth and decreases difficulty in construction.

CAMPING ON SNOW   72

When the snow is well enough consolidated, one of the best methods of making a shelter is the snow cave. This also requires a fairly steep slope of deep snow. All these conditions may prevail only in the immediate area of the cave. A deep, well-packed drift on one side of a little rise may be ideal, even though there are no large slopes or deep snow anywhere around it. One simply tunnels into this slope, cutting out blocks of snow with whatever tool is available. Two-man sleeping holes can be cut on either side of a central corridor, a couple of feet above the floor level. Blocks that remain intact are used after the cave is cut out to close off the upper part of the entrance tunnel and to build a wall around the front for wind protection.

When making a cave into a hillside for several people, it is good to have the entrance tunnel slant somewhat; the entrance should be lower than the central corridor, which should be lower than the sleeping platforms, giving the cold air a channel for escape. A smaller cave for one or two men will probably have only a small chamber, but the entrance can still be made lower. The entrance is cut large while the cave is being dug, and the upper part is blocked in after the digging is finished. Part of the entrance may be closed with a removable block, but the lower part should be left open for ventilation. A wall in front of the entrance helps reduce drafts. Another small ventilation hole an inch or two in diameter should be punched up from the front roof of the cave to the outside.

You may not have much choice in picking a spot to dig your snow cave, but there are some special considerations. The steeper the slope, the easier it will be to dig into, but the lower part of an avalanche slope is not a desirable site for your snow castle. Ideally, the wind should blow across the front of your entrance. The beginner is tempted to pick the sheltered downwind side of a ridge or hill, especially since this is the most likely spot to find a deep, steep drift. It is sometimes necessary to use this fact for the location of a site, but this is the least desirable position for a cave, especially when a strong storm is in progress or expected. The reason is that this is the place where all the storm's drifting snow will be deposited. You will only need to dig your way out through a twenty-foot drift once to recognize the great advantage of having the wind blow *across* your entrance tunnel, or even into it.

When a steep slope is not available for caving, some other type of snow hole or shelter must be chosen, a choice that will vary

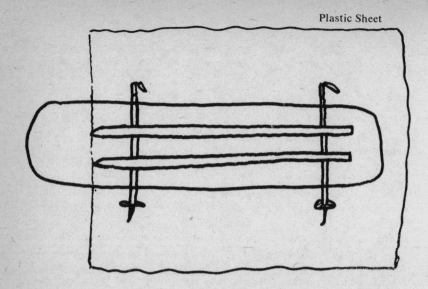

Plastic Sheet

Another trench shelter. The trench is dug first, then the poles and skis are laid as shown. These are covered with a tarp or plastic sheet. The edges of the sheet are weighted with rocks and snow, and then the whole sheet is covered with snow. The entrance can be covered with the pack.

with snow consistency. When consolidated snow is available on the surface or reasonably close to it, an igloo or a combination hole-igloo may be built. This requires snow that can be cut into blocks. In deep, unconsolidated snow a trench shelter can be stamped out fairly quickly, and the only problem is roofing it. If a tarp or plastic sheet is available, it can be supported by branches, poles, skis, snowshoes, packframes, etc. and can then be covered with snow. Boughs may be used like the tarp, though they are less effective. If none of these are available, enough blocks to form a roof can be made by one of the methods described in the paragraphs on igloo building.

In forested areas deep with snow, the long hump is frequently seen, covering a bent-over sapling. This sapling will form excellent structural support for the roof of a one or two-man snow hole. Just burrow underneath the tree and bed down for the night. Many other natural roofs can be used equally well: overhanging rocks, fallen trees, and so on.

CAMPING ON SNOW   74

Blocks of Snow Leaned Against One Another

A type of trench shelter. The trench is dug, and then blocks of snow are cut and leaned against one another to form a roof. Joints between the blocks are sealed with snow. Skis, pack, or snowshoes are used to cover the entrance.

It should be obvious from what has already been said that the structure and consistency of the snow are critical in decisions about what kind of shelter is most appropriate for a particular situation. Don't forget that the condition of the top layer tells you very little about what is underneath; lower layers may be much better consolidated. Slopes with different exposures may also exhibit great variations in snow structure, even when they are quite close together.

In emergencies, the winter traveler will have to fashion his shelter with whatever tools are available. Snow blocks can be cut with the heel of a ski, but never pried out with it. That's one of the best known methods for breaking a ski. Blocks may also be cut with branches and mittened hands. Snowshoes, pots, cups, and

Snowshoes

A cave dug under a bent tree. This is a good shelter in soft snow, when the roof of an unsupported cave would fall in. Snowshoes, pack, and skis can be used to protect the entrance from drifting snow.

Improvised shelters 75

.tute for a shovel. These methods should all be
.nergency procedures only. If you are planning to
.vith natural materials or it is likely you may have to
.iould always carry a shovel, a tool for cutting blocks,

.are a number of lightweight aluminum snow shovels
av.   .e from mountaineering and backpacking stores. The handles a.e removable, and if an ice ax is being carried, the handle
can usually be left at home. Appreciation of the value of a shovel
can be developed simply by spending an afternoon digging two
snow caves: one with a shovel and one with a pot.

Consolidated snow is handled more easily by cutting out blocks,
even if you are digging a cave. A tool for doing this may be purchased specially; igloo-cutting tools with aluminum blades can be
purchased from several suppliers. A cheaper and more versatile
alternative is a folding pruning saw, which can also be used for
cutting firewood. My own choice for a light-weight emergency tool
is a hacksaw blade, broken to form a point on one end, with a removable handle made from the end of a broomstick. This can be
used for cutting snow blocks or wood, but a more rigid tool is better if you know you'll be cutting a lot of snow blocks. Some people like a bread knife for cutting blocks.

Igloos. An igloo is a very comfortable shelter, and, contrary to
many opinions, it is easy to build when the snow has the right
consistency. Unconsolidated snow can be packed and allowed to
harden, but this is hard work, and under such conditions another
type of structure should be chosen, if possible. Hybrids between
snow holes and igloos are very practical, especially for one- and
two-man shelters. The igloo structure forms only the roof over the
hole, so that less work is involved. Most blocks are cut inside the
hole, lowering the floor and raising the roof at the same time.

Snow for the blocks should be hard enough so that the foot
sinks very little when standing without skis or snowshoes, and the
snow must be of the same consistency throughout the block, not
just crusted on top. Often, good snow for blocks can be found in a
layer below the surface where the snow has had more time to consolidate. Packing, first with skis or snowshoes and then with boots,
will usually form a good layer, but this is a measure of last resort.
Allow the snow to sit for a few minutes after packing. It will
harden as a result of both the increased density and the mechani-

cal disturbance. With shallow snow, balls can be rolled for snowmen and igloos, but igloos take a lot of rolling.

BUILDING AN IGLOO

Beginning the first row of blocks, cut from the floor inside to reduce the necessary height. Here we had to dig out 18″ before reaching snow adequate for blocks.

An inside bottom diameter of eight or nine feet will make an igloo large enough for four, and this is the largest size which should be attempted by any but true experts. Larger sizes require very accurately shaped domes to prevent collapse, and they should be practiced on occasions when their failure will be amusing.

Blocks for the igloo should be about two and a half feet by one and a half feet by half a foot. They should be cut out on the bottom as well as the sides, otherwise the inside of the igloo will be irregular and will drip. Each block is then beveled on the bottom, so that the wall will tilt inward at the proper angle, and on each side, so that each block is kept from falling by the preceding block, as shown in the illustration.

The diameter of the igloo should be marked out on the snow at the beginning. The first row of blocks is then placed and all joints chinked with snow. This chinking should be continued as construction proceeds, since it will help stabilize the structure. The next step is to make a diagonal cut from top to bottom across three blocks, which forms a ramp to begin the next layer. The first block of the next layer is put at the bottom of this ramp, and the

Improvised shelters   77

rest of the igloo is a continuous spiral. One person working inside puts up the blocks cut by his companions. When the dome is complete, loose snow is used to smooth the surface, especially on the inside. A smooth inside will prevent drips. An entrance tunnel should be dug under the wall; the entrance below floor level makes a much warmer igloo. The entrance tunnel is covered by a small arch. This tunnel should be perpendicular to the direction of the prevailing wind—that is, the wind should blow across the entrance. Finally, a vent hole should be punched in the roof opposite the entrance. The entrance may be partly blocked, but both the vent hole and some ventilation space at the entrance must be left open whenever the igloo is occupied, and ventilation must be increased when a stove or fire is in use.

When the first row is finished, the tops are smoothed and a ramp cut for the beginning of the next layer.

Each block in the upper rows must be beveled so that it is held by the one before and holds the one after.

The second row half-finished. Cracks must be filled as each block goes in. This snow here is barely consolidated enough for igloo-building.

Each layer tilts in farther. This igloo would be comfortable for four.

Each block must be held in place until the cracks are chinked well. Note the beveled edges.

Once cracks are chinked the blocks will stay in place.

Improvised shelters

The igloo nearly finished. Entrance is dug under the side to prevent warm air escaping.

Coming in through the tunnel. A comfortable shelter, but too long a job for an overnight camp, unless snow is perfect for blocks.

LIVING IN SNOW SHELTERS

The warmth of a good snow shelter is surprising to anyone who has not experienced it. A winter sleeping bag is often too warm in a well-built igloo, and even a quickly dug snow hole can be quite snug. Even more important, these shelters provide much better protection against wind than a tent. They also present certain special problems, however. Some ventilation holes should be left open at all times, especially when a stove is being used. Stoves and fires use as much oxygen as dozens of resting men, and they produce carbon monoxide as well. When a stove is not being used, enough air will normally filter through the snow for breathing, but when a

CAMPING ON SNOW   80

shelter becomes warm it will ice up, and the ice layer which is formed prevents air circulation. The heat inside a shelter can be regulated by the size of the vents. If the interior of the cave or igloo is smooth and rounded, dripping will not occur, but if smoothing is impossible, lower temperature will help prevent dripping.

Igloos that are too warm without uncomfortably large ventilation holes can be improved by scraping some snow off the outside. In very cold weather, when hoarfrost forms inside the igloo, the walls should be made thicker by piling snow on the outside. Igloos should not be used in thawing weather, since they have a tendency to collapse. High winds will tend to cut into the windward side of the igloo, and a small wall should be built at the base on this side if winds are strong.

Snow shelters obviously require the use of waterproof ground protection, as well as the usual insulation. When boughs are available for a floor, they make any snow shelter more comfortable. Some also use them for walls and floor, but this tends to increase dripping. In emergencies, anything available should be used for ground insulation.

The biggest problem in snow shelters is condensation, particularly when cooking is being done. Down clothing and sleeping bags should be kept in plastic bags when they are not being used, to prevent their becoming wet. Though snow shelters can be made quite warm, they are usually humid, so that drying gear out in them is practically impossible. On long trips using snow shelters, it is particularly important to use any good weather for drying out equipment.

With all shelters it is advisable to have equipment inside with you, but this is particularly applicable to snow caves, where drifting in front of the cave is common. When you dig out through a large drift, it is distinctly unpleasant to realize that your snowshoes are still underneath it, near the former entrance to the cave. In particular, *always take your digging tools into the shelter with you*. After the storm is over you may want to get out.

Some care should be taken when calls of nature are answered at night. Snow shelters, being made of snow, do not stand out so well as tents. They are also soundproof, and if you call out for directions, your friends inside will not hear you. A midnight expedition wearing long johns in search of the igloo or hole is an educational experience well worth avoiding.

Living in snow shelters   81

CAR CAMPING IN WINTER

The discussion of lightweight camping techniques is applicable with obvious modifications to winter car camping. Many prefer to begin their winter experience by camping near the car and taking short ski tours or snowshoes hikes during the day. Since weight is not a consideration, a heavy tent can be used—either a special double-walled model or an umbrella or similar tent borrowed from summer use. Less expensive types of insulation can be used for sleeping bags if cost is an obstacle, since weight and bulk are not so important.

The biggest problem is the car. Most campgrounds in snow country close in winter, so that it's hard to park your car near a good spot. Beware of backroads when the big snows are still to come. Will you be able to get out if they come while you're there?

I won't try to go into all the gadgets that are available for the car camper, summer and winter. There are a few that deserve special consideration, though. Folding cots are of considerable use in the winter, when the tent floor is wetter and colder than summer. Some insulation, such as a foam pad, is still needed on top of the cot, since air circulating under the cot makes a cold bed.

A catalytic heater may make your tent comfortable and may be more economical than buying heavier sleeping bags. Those using white gas are cheaper to run, but the propane models are more convenient. The catalytic heaters don't produce carbon monoxide, but they still use oxygen, so don't forget to ventilate your tent adequately.

When the weather is decent and your sleeping gear is adequate, it is often pleasant to sleep without a tent. When a camp is made for long periods in cold weather, the tent can be made warmer by surrounding it with snow walls and perhaps pitching a tarp over the top.

If you plan on having fires, don't forget to bring a saw, an ax, or both. In really cold weather, warm your cutting tools before use, or they may be damaged. Low temperatures make the metal brittle and easily broken.

CARS

Whether you're car camping or simply driving to a take-off point in snow country, don't forget to take the usual precautions for snowy driving. One recent serious case of frostbite occurred because of difficulty and delay in starting the car after the chilled victim reached it. Besides chains, shovel, sand, etc., it is worth leaving a dry, warm change of clothes and some extra food in the car. A key should be left at the car, and each member of the party should know its location. Try to leave the car where it will be neither snowed in nor plowed under. Remember that in case of accident someone may need it to get out for help. A more likely incentive is simply that one doesn't feel like digging out a car after coming down from the hills.

V

Cooking Out in the Snow

For anyone who has done a lot of cooking outdoors, cooking in winter will not be very hard to learn. A few things are a bit more difficult—finding dry wood, for example, Others present slightly different problems in the winter; the water situation is such a case. The principles of cooking on lightweight trips are essentially the same all year round, however. Proper planning and packaging at home is the key to an easy time at camp.

Still, what is easy after you have learned how is not always so simple for the novice. Get your first experiences cooking over backpacking stoves and campfires somewhere that's warm and dry. Then try your techniques out in the snow on a picnic. Save your first experience in a tent on a cold night until you are confident of your technique. One good method is to cook lunch a few times on day trips on skis or snowshoes. Supper on your first overnight trip will then come easily.

Successful cooking in winter camps begins at home. The ingredients for each meal should be measured out, placed in plastic bags along with any instructions necessary (such as the number of cups of water to add) and then packaged together with the rest of the meal. The principle is to leave no more work to do in camp than necessary. The planning of menus and nutritional principles will be discussed later in this chapter, but obviously where weight is a factor, the ingredients will contain as little water as possible.

The standard method of cooking for winter camps is the boiling of a "one-pot meal." This is the fire-top or stove-top version of some cross between a casserole, a stew, and a soup. The main reason for the one-pot meal is ease of preparation. If one is cooking on a stove, only one burner is available, and it is a waste of time to go through the struggle of preparing three or four courses. A well-planned one-pot meal can be very good, anyhow. A few of my more inspired creations have even been imported into our home menus. The technique results in meals that taste just right in a winter camp. Dehydration is a common problem in winter, and soupy meals help to provide the liquid and salt everyone needs.

Unless camp is made very early, one person usually starts getting food ready soon after the party stops, while the rest of the party sets up camp. This is especially true if the cooking is done over a fire. If the cooking is to be done over a stove, you may wait until camp is set up and everyone has settled down in his sleeping bag. Cooking is then done in front of the tent door or just inside it.

Cooking fires. A cooking fire is quite a different matter from an all-night warming fire. It can be much smaller, and needs only enough wood to last about an hour, with perhaps another pile for the next morning. You can make do with small sticks, usually dead tree branches, so that an ax or saw is not necessary, though handy. An all-night fire requires large chunks of wood, and an ax or saw is essential, unless you are burning down an old dead tree. Where the snow cover is light, it is probably easiest to scrape out a fireplace. Large rocks may also be used where they are available, but the standard method of building a fire on snow is to lay several green poles down and to build a fire on top of them. If the poles are somewhat longer than the fire, this arrangement will not

Wood-gathering tools for those planning cooking over fires. The saw is much preferred for packing. The ax is too heavy, and the saw is much more efficient than a light hatchet.

The same saw folded up. Other designs are available. On the left is an emergency expedient—a hacksaw blade and piece of wire carried in the tube of the packframe. Handles are picked up on the spot.

Cooking out in the snow

melt down into the snow; fireplaces built of small rocks generally melt down out of sight pretty quickly. If you have no ax or saw, you will have' to use a combination of smaller green boughs, stones, and wet wood.

Anyone depending on fires for cooking should acquire a good deal of skill in fire building before heading out in winter. This is a valuable skill for anyone, and one that can make the difference in a survival situation. Basic fire-building techniques are covered adequately in any book on woodcraft, but the principles are simple enough; putting them to use effectively requires some practical experience. The easiest way to gain experience is to force yourself to build fires without the use of paper and fire starters whenever you have a chance, on family picnics or just on a wet Sunday afternoon. The principles are to use dry fuel until the fire is going well, to start with small combustible material and work up to larger pieces, and to keep the distance between pieces just right; spaces that are too small prevent oxygen from feeding the flame, while spaces that are too large do not form combustion chambers. A combustion chamber traps gases and reflects heat so that a fire will burn; most wood won't continue to burn in single sticks even after a fire is started.

The key to all this lies in those casual words "dry fuel" and "combustible material." Some forests are always wet, and after a lot of rain or during spring thaws they all are. To add to the problem, a fire is usually needed most when the wood is wettest. There is no single answer to this problem, though experience is the most helpful guide. In addition to the practice suggested, one good method of learning winter fire building is to use a stove at first but to build one fire on each trip, preferably when the weather is worst. In winter, fire starters should be carried, even if you don't use them. Several adequate ones are available commercially. Candles also work fairly well, or you can impregnate wads of tissue paper with paraffin. In birch country, birchbark makes an adequate fire starter, but don't strip a live tree. Stripping the bark all the way around will kill the tree, and there are always plenty of dead trees.

"Squaw wood," the dead twigs still on the tree under the live branches, is often dry when everything else is wet, and it is just the right size for kindling. I won't go through the usual list of the best woods, since you will usually have to make do with what is available; knowledge of the virtues of hickory and oak is small consolation in a lodgepole-pine forest. Quite a few emergency matches should always be carried, but don't forget to take lots of extras if you are doing your cooking on campfires.

Unless there is plenty of burnable wood, it is usually a good idea to start collecting kindling about the time you start looking for a campsite. Knots from rotten conifers should be watched for; they are full of pitch and burn well. Once a fire is going properly, you may be able to dry wood out around the fire. In a really wet softwood forest, though, keeping a fire going can sometimes be an almost impossible chore. Usually this will not be a problem in really cold weather, but when temperatures go above freezing in the day, this problem should be anticipated. If you are camped in one place, you can usually dry out some wood and keep it dry, but if you are moving every day, it is best to use a stove in very wet conditions. One should stop traveling early enough to gather wood and cook before dark when using cooking fires. It gets cold when the sun goes down.

Cooking over a fire in winter is about the same as in summer, and there's not much of a trick if you're boiling the food. Soot is generally left on, and the pots should be packed in a bag which will keep other things in the pack clean. Pots with bails that snap into place are easiest to handle, and if chain or wire hangers are brought, such pots can be suspended over the fire from skis, poles, or sticks stuck in the snow.

Cooking with stoves. Despite the extra weight involved, many winter campers make a regular practice of doing all or most of their cooking with small, lightweight single-burner stoves. If you are going to do much camping above timberline in the mountains, you don't have much choice in the matter: you have to either use a stove or eat uncooked food. Eating cold food is a possibility for the really hardy, but there is a story about the great California mountaineer, John Salanthé, that is instructive in this respect. Salanthé swore by a diet consisting mainly of fruit, and when he took his first winter trip, he scorned the need for a stove, swearing that it was merely another proof of the bad eating habits of his companions. He was forced to eat his words before being allowed use of the stove to thaw his frozen fruit.

The stove has great time-saving advantages, allows food to be cooked from the sleeping bag, and makes cooking possible under storm conditions that sometimes preclude the use of a fire. Finally, it eliminates the conservation problems that are often attendant on the use of fires, and these are many, especially in the mountains. The winter camper should remember that in mountain regions, small trees are often very old, their size reflecting their precarious existence. The cutting of live trees in such areas is criminal. A less important problem attends fire building on rocks; the fire scars endure, and in heavily used areas they can become unsightly enough for the wilderness lover to consider other ways to heat his food.

Which stove? There are two main types of lightweight stoves that merit consideration, those that are fueled by gasoline and those using pressurized butane gas cannisters. The lightweight gasoline stoves are usually self-priming, which means that the pressure driving the fuel from the tank to the burner is provided by the stove's own heat. This is a very satisfactory arrangement, except that lighting the stove is tricky and requires some practice. Once the knack is acquired, not much bother is involved. The gas cannister stoves have the advantage of lighting in a less arcane manner: you just light a match and open the valve, and it's done.

Disadvantages of the gasoline stoves are that liquid gasoline must be carried, and care must be taken that it does not leak on food, nor on the hands in cold weather. Gasoline stoves without insulation melt down into the snow while burning, and they must be allowed to cool a short time before refueling.

The disadvantages of the gas-cannister stoves are higher fuel costs, lower burning temperature, less readily available fuel, the fact that the cannisters run at lower pressure in cold weather, the impossibility of filling a half-empty cannister at the beginning of a trip, the greater weight of fuel, the necessity of carrying out empty cannisters, the decreasing intensity of the flame as the tank pressure lowers, and the height and instability of the butane stove, an important factor when cooking in a tent. A newly available propane stove eliminates the instability and the additional problem that butane doesn't vaporize at sub-freezing temperatures. The other disadvantages are retained.

Both types of stoves function more efficiently with certain accessories. A wind shield is made for the cannister stove, which should be standard equipment. Of the gasoline types, a low-profile model with the fuel tank on the side offers extra stability, but if the upright model is purchased, a stacking cooker is available

Three types of gasoline cookers. The one in the center is very efficient, but bent pots stick together. The side tank on the right-hand cooker adds welcome stability.

which improves the efficiency of the stove. Gasoline stoves should also be insulated from the snow; otherwise, they tend to melt themselves downward. The butane stove doesn't have this disadvantage.

Each type of stove has its advocates. The author prefers the gasoline stove. Two points of caution—unleaded (white) gasoline *must* be used to prevent poisoning. Handle gasoline with extreme care, especially at low temperatures. A gasoline can left outside at night may be at 40 degrees below zero, and if it is spilled on your hand it will cause additional cooling by evaporation. Serious frostbite can result. The fire hazard presented by gasoline should be obvious and respected.

Cooking in the tent. The standard procedure mentioned earlier for really cold weather is to cook from a sleeping bag. This requires a certain finesse, since the crowded quarters of a mountain tent make spilling the soup an easy thing to do. One night in a soupy sleeping bag generally induces the necessary care. If the tent has two entrances, the cooking can begin as soon as it is set up, but if there is only one, it is usually best either to wait until everyone is settled or to start melting snow outside and move the stove in after everyone but the cook has arranged himself.

Cooking out in the snow 89

The water problem. The difficulty of obtaining water is decreased in the winter when snow is all around, but then one is faced with the new problem of how to use it. If liquid water is available, it should be used, since melting snow consumes time, effort, and fuel. Usually, one is faced with the necessity of melting snow, however, and there are a few tricks to remember. If wet snow is available, it is preferred, and the second choice is ice or crusty snow. Powder snow is worst, since a large volume is required to make a small amount of water. When you are melting snow, start with a small amount and add more slowly until there is plenty of water in the pan. Don't start with a pot full of snow—especially powder snow—over a high flame. The snow will act like a blotter, soaking up water as it is melted and keeping the bottom of the pan dry. The result will be a scorched taste in whatever is cooked with that water.

Another trick to remember is the maintenance of a snow supply as close as possible to the cook. If the tent has a vestibule or cooking hole, that may serve as a snow supply. If you are getting your snow near the front door, make sure to keep it clean. A toilet area should be designated, and if the tent has two entrances, the second one should be used. The sanitary reasons for this are obvious, but friendships are also saved: it's harder to kick over the stew pot if you enter at the foot of the tent.

Planning food. Food tastes vary, and there is plenty of room for individual preferences. The main requirements that must be satisfied for lightweight winter camping are high caloric content per unit weight and ease of preparation. Spoilage is not generally a problem in cold-weather camping, so that some tastes can be indulged in winter that cannot in warmer weather.

Nutritional requirements are somewhat different in winter camping than they are in daily life in the city. Vitamin requirements can generally be ignored on short trips, though they should be considered if you are heading away for two weeks or more. A working understanding of some facts about the three main food categories is very helpful, however; they are fats, proteins, and carbohydrates.

Carbohydrates are the sugars and starches. They are easily and quickly digested, and they are therefore the best foods for quick energy and for fuel while the body is working and cannot afford any more blood for digestion than necessary. Thus, candy, sweet drinks, biscuits, and such are good trail snacks.

COOKING OUT IN THE SNOW

Proteins have about the same number of calories per pound as carbohydrates. They are used to rebuild tissue in the body, and some should be included with each meal. The digestion of protein also liberates more heat than that of carbohydrates, making it a good bedtime food to help prevent chilliness at night. Proteins take more time to digest than carbohydrates, so that they tend to stave off hunger for a longer period, but produce less quick energy.

Fats provide over twice as many calories per pound as either carbohydrates or proteins and are therefore valuable as a light-weight food. They also have the same value as protein in taking more time to digest and liberating more heat in digestion than sugars and starches. It has been my experience that people working outside in the cold have a far greater appetite for fats than they would in other circumstances; food that would be excessively greasy is suddenly just what is wanted. For this reason I always add a lot of fats to my winter menus. Because of their long digestion time, the fats also help to provide energy later in the day when they are eaten at meals, but carbohydrates should be emphasized for quick-energy snacks.

All these considerations should be thought of as merely introductory. Various people adjust best to various foods. This is particularly true on weekend trips, where the body is in a transition state and never gets a chance to acclimatize completely. Before going on, two other details should be mentioned. If you are going to high altitudes, be wary of fats. Many people cannot digest them at high altitudes, and carbohydrates should be emphasized unless all members of the party have had experience with fats at the altitude where you plan to go. Vegetable proteins do not have all the ingredients of animal proteins, and they cannot be used as effectively by the body unless their combination is carefully planned. The easiest way to avoid this problem is to include some animal protein—milk, cheese, jerky, etc.—in a meal relying on vegetable protein. The quality of the latter is effectively improved by the combination with small amounts of animal protein. Those wishing to rely on vegetable protein can purchase meat substitutes or use combinations like those suggested in *Diet for a Small Planet* by Frances Lappé.

Meals. Decisions about meals are again partly a matter of experimentation. The question of whether or not to have a cooked breakfast, for example, is a matter to be decided by compromise

Cooking out in the snow

among the various members of a group. A lot of friction on trips can be saved if the member planning the food makes sure to find out the prejudices of all the members beforehand. The black-coffee drinker who doesn't bring a cream substitute will not be a popular man.

The one-pot meal for supper has already been recommended. A starch base, such as noodles, macaroni, rice, beans, bulgur wheat, or instant potatoes, is usual. Other ingredients are then added for proteins, fats, and flavor. The only limit to these meals is your imagination. Water content should be low in foods that are to be carried, and heavy, bulky containers should be discarded; the food should be repacked in lightweight plastic bags and containers. Enough dried foods are now available in the supermarket so that the beginner can use this as the source for most food. Backpacking stores carry excellent, well-packaged, expensive foods. These may ease some of the pains of planning and packaging on the first few trips, but beware of menus that are too elaborate. That dried cheesecake (I'm not kidding; there is one) is best saved for some other time than your first cramped meal in a mountain tent—unless, of course you want to lick it from your companion's elbow. One more defect to the backpackers' packages is that they are almost all packed for groups of four; if you have two or six, that's too bad. My own method is to buy all my camp food at once—every six months or so. I keep it in a couple of boxes, and I get it out and make up my meals sometime during the week before a trip (actually, almost always the night before the trip, but this is not recommended). This method avoids the last-minute rushes to the market, and it enables me to save money by getting my dehydrated food in bulk. It is much cheaper that way, and the supermarket stuff almost always has to be repackaged anyway.

After a few trips the beginner will have no problem devising his own meals, as long as a systematic method is followed.

Freeze-dried meals are generally easy to prepare and excellent, if one allows for their usually being too small after a hard day. Their defects are high cost and high bulk. The bulk can usually be accommodated on shorter trips. The other problem is between the reader and his wallet.

Breakfasts are a matter of taste and the amount of effort to which you are willing to go. Some people can't start the day without a hot breakfast. Most will want at least a hot drink, but a lot of us prefer cold food and a quick start. Some combination of biscuits, fruit bars, nuts, meat bars with a cup of hot cocoa, tea, or coffee gets us off and serves as the first installment on our all-day lunch. A possible compromise is a pot of hot water that can be mixed with instant cereal in the cup and used for the drinks. For those who want full-scale breakfasts, cooked cereal with butter, sugar and dried fruit added, or dried eggs mixed with cheese or dried meat are the most common choices.

Lunches are almost always eaten cold, and are usually composed of a long series of snacks on the trail. A lot of small meals keep warmth and energy flowing, and they avoid the competition for blood between the stomach and the legs that follows a large meal. Trail foods are a matter of taste. The variety of possibilities is immense. Even with cold lunch, a party can indulge in a hot drink if the stove and pot are carried near the top of the pack.

Planning. With a small party camping in a single tent, meals are best planned by one delegated person. The most experienced person should be chosen by a group of beginners. This applies to all supplies for cooked meals. Snacks, lunches, and trail food are usually left to the individual. Larger groups should usually plan and cook their food by tent. That is, a party of nine carrying three tents would usually carry three stoves and cook their meals separately. This arrangement is usually the most practical when using small stoves. Swapping is in order, of course, and for groups planning on using a campfire, menus may be planned for larger numbers. Those who do a lot of camping together may work out other arrangements, each man planning certain meals, for instance, but assigning things to one man per tent eliminates confusion over who was to bring the stove, the butter, or the salt.

Until you have developed another system, the best method is the checklist. Write down all the general supplies that need to go —salt, etc.—then list all the meals that must be planned. When you have decided what is to go into each meal, write it down. Package each of the meals together; the meat for Tuesday's stew should not be buried under Saturday's oatmeal. Then check off each meal as you pack. Make sure that everything is well-labeled, and that any necessary instructions are included.

In considering cooking time, don't forget that the boiling point of water decreases with increasing altitude. A thirty-minute cooking time is a bit long even in New England, but in the Rockies it means that you will eat the food still half-raw after boiling it for

Cooking out in the snow   93

an hour or two. Foods for high altitudes should be "instant." Cooking time should be kept as short as possible if you are cooking inside. Boiling creates a lot of condensation in a tent or snow hole.

Emergency food. In planning the food for any trip, allowance should be made for various unpleasant possibilities: bad storms, injuries, nonfunctioning stoves, and so on. Emergency reserves should be of a type that can be eaten cold if necessary, in case of the useless stove or the necessity of splitting the party. Extra trail food may be the best solution.

Fuel. In planning the amount of fuel to be carried on a trip much more must be allowed for a winter trip, when snow is to be melted for water. It takes almost as much fuel to melt the snow as it does to heat water all the way to boiling. It also takes just as long. The beginner should allow about one to one and a half pints of gasoline per stove per day. Three-quarters of a tank per day may be allowed for butane stoves, and one-third of a tank per day for stoves using standard propane cylinders.

Dishwashing. The best way to solve this problem on winter trips is to avoid it altogether. With a two-pot cookset one pot can be used for cooking food, the other for storing, melting, and heating water only. Fuel shouldn't be wasted heating water for dishes. The food pan and personal bowls or cups can be cleaned adequately with snow, especially if it is crusty. There will be no danger from this procedure in winter temperatures, especially since the pan will be heated at every meal. A few calories carried over from one meal to the next do no harm.

It should be emphasized that it is unwise to use soap in cleaning pans and dishes in winter camping. Unless enough hot water and energy are available to rinse the cooking gear thoroughly, the soap is likely to mix with grease in the pots, forming a bad-tasting contribution to the next meal. This soap residue will cause the digestive upsets that leftover food will not. If you insist on hot-water washing, it is best to use just water with a scrub pad that does not contain soap.

PROVISIONING SUGGESTIONS

For summer backpacking, dehydrated foods have become the method preferred to achieve the objective of maximum food value coupled with minimum weight and bulk. While this is often true in winter as well, the problems of obtaining water and the need for emergency food that can be eaten without melting snow modify winter menus somewhat. Each camper will probably find his own solutions, but a few suggestions are made here for the beginner.

On short trips I often carry canned meat or fish for economy. Canned tuna (packed in oil—more calories than water), canned salmon, or canned meat makes a good one-pot meal combined with margarine or butter, seasonings, noodles, spaghetti, instant mashed potato, or rice. In an emergency the fish or meat can be eaten without preparation. On longer trips, when weight and bulk become more important, Wilson's meat and bacon bars take the place of the canned meat.

For very cold weather the meat or fish can be removed from the can at home and frozen in heavy plastic bags, eliminating the problem and weight of the cans.

Cheese is one of the best sources of fat and protein. No heavy containers are needed, and the cheese can be used in one-pot meals or eaten alone. Salami and sausages fall in the same category.

So called multi-purpose food, a nutritionally well-planned combination of vegetable protein, makes a good addition to one-pot meals. It is now available both in unflavored form and in various synthetic meat flavors.

The easiest starch to use in suppers is instant mashed potato. I mix it with dried powdered milk, margarine, and seasonings before a trip. At camp, hot water and meat, fish, or cheese are added and the whole thing is edible after sitting five minutes and stirring. No further cooking is needed, and the remaining hot water can be used for drinks. No burned pan results.

Many dried soups make good bases for stews. Add some extra protein, noodles, margarine, and seasoning and a good meal will result.

TUNA WITH NOODLES AND SOUR CREAM
(serves four; for two, reduce amounts of noodles, cheese, margarine)

At home, put two large handfuls of egg noodles in a plastic bag. In another bag empty a package of dried sour cream sauce, a half-cup of dried milk, a teaspoon each of paprika, oregano, sage, and marjoram, a half-teaspoon of pepper, and about four ounces of grated Parmesan cheese. Put these two bags in a larger bag with an eighth of a pound of margarine and a six- or seven-oz. can of tuna.

In camp, melt snow in a pan, or get a panful of water. Pour the mixture bag into a pan or bowl, add about a cup of water, and stir for a minute. The remaining water should be brought to a boil. About six cups of boiling water are needed. Add about a teaspoon of salt to the boiling water. Add the noodles to the boiling water and stir. When the noodles are cooked (about eight minutes), add the tuna, the margarine, and the mixture. Stir, heat, and salt to taste. Eat.

Many other one-pot meals are made in this fashion using different starches, meats, cheeses, and substituting gravies, soup mixes and such for sour cream.

VI

On the Trail

The main requisite for enjoying the white wilderness is to get out into it—away from your car, house, ski lodge, and highway. You have to escape the sound and stench of gasoline motors to hear and smell the world of snow. It helps to go for at least a couple of days; that allows enough time for the sounds of civilization to die away in your ears and its smells to fade from your nose.

Of course, getting away from that noise can be a problem when snow lies on the ground to a depth of six feet. In that case you'll need skis or snowshoes to hold you up, and these special tools are discussed in the next two chapters. Sometimes, when the snow isn't very deep, or at higher altitudes in spring and summer when it is well-consolidated, you can walk into the white wilderness with nothing more on your feet than a sturdy pair of boots. Whatever your means of staying on top of the snow, the general techniques of travel don't vary too much.

PLANNING YOUR TRIP

Whether you are starting off on a weekend snow-camping jaunt in the mountains or a half-day tour in the woods around home, it is important to remember that the winter wilderness is a somewhat harsher place than the summer woods. A certain amount of planning and care is essential if you are to avoid unpleasant experiences. Planning in this case includes means of transportation, clothing, food, cooking gear, shelter, certain essential personal items, the means to find your way and cope with any emergencies, and the capacity to handle the trip you have in mind. By "planning" I don't mean that you have to have all these things written down or that certain set rules of organization have to be followed, but none of these items should be overlooked or left to chance. The winter traveler must have a system to insure that essentials are not forgotten. The beginner obviously has to consciously plan more of them than does the expert, who has learned to take care of some details automatically.

Several of these subjects are discussed at greater length in other chapters, but there is always a danger that the novice will forget that they apply to him, even at the most elementary level. Getting lost is one of the most obvious examples. You don't have to be on a week-long expedition to get lost; it can be done in ten minutes by a perfect amateur with no trouble at all. There are plenty of ways to keep yourself oriented other than by map and compass— you might follow a power line on an afternoon ski tour, for example—but if you trust your "natural sense of direction," you will be making a mistake. You don't have one. The tricks you really use have to be modified to cope with the winter landscape. For instance, your morning tracks won't do you much good in the afternoon when they are filled with drifted snow.

These same sorts of considerations apply to the other items on the list. You don't need a written menu for a day-long snowshoe hike, but good planning does include some extra trail food in case of the unexpected.

The last item, the capacity to handle the trip you are undertaking, is the trickiest. It's best to plan trips conservatively until you develop the experience to judge their difficulty in advance with some accuracy. This doesn't mean you shouldn't hope to get a lot farther than you may be able to travel, just that you shouldn't bet your life that you will. Don't, for example, plan on getting to a wilderness hut your party may not be able to reach and leave yourself unprepared for snow camping. With luck in weather and snow conditions, you might make it, but only by exceeding your capacity and courting disaster. A more experienced group might spend a cold night in a snow cave after running into bad weather but would not have taken unnecessary risks if preparations were made for a night out.

As you gain experience, you will learn the limits of your equipment and ability, enabling you to approach the limits of safety if you wish, but the experience is necessary to find out just where those limits are. The novice must be more cautious and allow a larger margin for error.

Some risks may also be worth taking, if they are outweighed by advantages. The experienced traveler may want to try some solo trips, for instance. A man with good sense may choose to take a calculated risk walking under an avalanche gully, perhaps, but the innocent who wanders by without even being aware of the possibility of a slide is not taking a calculated risk nor being brave. He's merely being foolish.

Planning in the narrower sense is also necessary, and the longer the trip the more it is needed. Food and equipment are best handled by checklists. Forgetting one item can make a trip impossible. It can also lose you some friends if you've just driven a few hundred miles for the big weekend and you discover at the trailhead that you forgot the tent. Other slips of memory can have more serious consequences; if you forget the first-aid kit, you probably won't cancel the trip, but later you may wish you had. As you gain experience, you may develop some system to substitute for lists, such as keeping your rucksack packed with the items you need.

Community equipment should be carefully arranged in advance to avoid the "But I thought you were bringing the tent!" scenes. The passage of a good deal of time is often required to enable one to appreciate the humor of such situations. The reverse of this type of planning is also required of groups. The weight of each pack is everyone's concern, and unnecessary duplication of community items has to be avoided. Four complete cooksets are not needed to cook for a party of five.

PACE

The importance of pace in wilderness travel was brought home to me when I was hiking in the Swiss Alps. Every Sunday many of the villagers go for walks in the mountains. Young and old, still dressed for church, they climb steadily up the trails. The tourists go zipping past them and then sit panting on rocks by the side of the trail, while the little old ladies in their black dresses climb steadily by, always keeping the same slow, ground-covering rhythm. It is an amusing and educational experience, though it may cause some reddening around the ears of those impressed with their own *machismo*. The little old ladies are in fairly good condition, of course, but more important, they know how to pace themselves.

Pace is even more important in winter than summer, because of the need to avoid perspiration. The trick of pacing oneself or a party is to try to set a rhythm that can be maintained for long periods with few stops or none at all. The start should be slow, and during the first half three-quarters of an hour there are always numerous brief stops for adjusting equipment and removing clothing. After this, you should try to keep your pace adjusted so that one ten-minute break each hour is adequate. Better yet it is not to stop at all except for food and adjusting clothing or equipment. Long stops should be avoided; muscles stiffen and rhythm is broken. The necessity for frequent short stops is a sign that the party is going too fast.

There is nothing wrong with a leisurely trip, if that is what is wanted, or with photography and gawking at the scenery. The point here is simply that you should try to set a pace you can maintain, rather than spurting up a hill for a few hundred yards and then collapsing by the side of the trail for fifteen minutes. There are several important reasons for pacing yourself or your party.

The first reason is a consequence of the physiology of muscular action. If you force your muscles to work beyond the capacity they can maintain steadily, waste products accumulate in the muscles, and pretty soon you have to stop to allow the waste products to be carried away by the blood, and to allow the oxygen deficit of the muscles to be made up. The muscles are inherently less efficient when they are operated this way than when they operate within their normal capacity. Fatigue occurs quickly with this start-and-stop traveling. The sign that you are going too fast is that you begin to pant; when you do or someone in your party does, *slow down*. Your circulatory system will also adjust itself to your physcal activity much better if your pace is fairly steady. This adjustment is the familiar experience of the "second wind." If you go too fast, you will be exhausted before ever catching your second wind.

The second reason for pacing a party properly is primarily a winter problem, that of perspiration. The need to avoid sweating whenever possible has already been stressed. To do this, it is necessary to regulate your body's heat loss by removing clothing as you get warmer from exercise. This is fairly easy to do when a steady pace is maintained. If you go by spurts and stops, it is almost impossible. You will have soaked your shirt before you realize that you are warmed up, and yet you will already be stopped for a rest and beginning to shiver with cold.

Another reason for pacing is psychological, and it is especially important for groups of uneven strength. A common mistake you should avoid is the familiar pattern of the strong members of the group rushing ahead for twenty minutes and then sitting down to wait for the stragglers. The slower members are usually pushed too hard, because they feel they are holding back the group, and they go faster than they should. When they catch up they are tired and panting. By this time the speed demons have already rested and are impatient to be off again, so that the stragglers feel compelled to go before they are ready, and the cycle repeats itself. The result of this sort of foolishness is that the group only gets about half as far as it would have if a proper pace had been set in the first place.

As a final word on pace, I would simply remind you of the tortoise, the hare, and the little old Swiss ladies.

CARRYING YOUR GEAR

Even on short showshoe hikes, it is usually necessary to carry more equipment in the winter than one would on a hike of similar duration in the summer. Extra clothing and food are normally required in winter even for half-day trips. The cross-country ski runner may travel a long way keeping warm just with exercise, but if he plans on stopping he is likely to need extra clothing. If his trail is not well-traveled, he should also picture the consequences of a broken ski tip before leaving the extra sweater, candy bar, and repair kit in the pack at home.

On trips that last overnight, the winter traveler must carry his food, shelter, and emergency equipment on his back. Since travel in snow is generally more demanding than travel on bare ground, he must also try to keep this weight to a minimum. Extra ounces must be pared off ruthlessly. This is another function of planning. Without it you will find yourself with an eighty-pound pack and still discover you have forgotten something important.

The problem of weight actually boils down to a question of what to take. The winter traveler must get as much use as possible out of each item. Multiple uses can often help cut down on weight. Items that are not either necessary for emergency gear or definitely needed for the level of comfort you consider essential are left behind. If the best reason you can think of for bringing an item is that it "might come in handy," leave it at home or in the car.

Weight is also a function of equipment design, and here it is sometimes necessary to make a few compromises in the interests of economy or durability. Most of the best equipment made these days is also very lightweight. Long-range economy dictates the purchase of the best equipment possible, but most of us cannot always afford this, so we have to make do with the best compromise possible. Fairly good compromises *are* possible, though. In fact,

Carrying your gear   101

the budget-minded traveler has some advantages over his wealthy counterpart, since he will be inclined to stick to essentials, which is the main secret to keeping weight at a minimum. It's hard to leave an expensive gadget at home once you've bought it.

A party as a whole must be just as concerned with keeping its weight down as the individual. Duplication should be avoided where it is not necessary, and even the strongest member of the party should be tactfully told to leave his frivolous junk at the car. His strength may be needed for more important duties.

MAKING UP THE PARTY

Generally, recreational winter travelers have better criteria for making up parties than organizers of expeditions; considerations of friendship and convenience are usually foremost, as they should be. There are a few special points to be kept in mind, however, especially for large parties. If no one in the group has had much experience, everyone will be learning together. This is an enjoyable way to do things, but in this case the group size should be kept fairly small; the occupants of two tents make a good party. Large groups of relatively inexperienced people can turn emergency situations into disasters. A party of four inexperienced people is stronger than a party of two, but a group of twelve neophytes is much weaker than either. At least a few experienced winter travelers should be included in any large group of novices.

All parties should be made up with consideration of both the prospective trip and the relative strengths of the members. It is common sense that no one should be asked on a trip that is too much for him; he will feel like a drag on the party rather than enjoy himself. A more subtle mistake is made by the relatively experienced person who takes a group of beginners on a trip they would have the good sense never to undertake alone. Don't forget: *you* may be the one who breaks his leg. If no one else has the ability to find his way back out or the stamina to break trail, how are you going to get out? Under these circumstances, the leader is undertaking a solo trip with other people.

Assuming roughly equal ability, a group of three or more is safer than a party of two. In case of injury, this leaves at least one person to go for help and one to stay with the injured person. Most other problems of making up and handling a group are matters of common sense and goodwill. Weight should be divided equitably, though in parties where there are great disparities in skill and strength, it often helps to give more weight to the strongest members of the party. One essential party item that should be carried by everyone is a sense of humor. There's nothing like a good laugh in a cramped mountain tent when the stew gets tipped over.

SOLO TRIPS

Traveling alone in the winter wilderness has been frequently condemned, for no particularly good reason. The fine companionship that is the virtue of group travel is lost, but there are many unique attractions to occasional solo trips. Obviously, traveling alone is riskier than traveling with others, so it is only prudent not to undertake solo trips until you know what you are doing. Once you understand the risks, the choice of whether or not they are worth taking is a personal matter.

Since the safety margin is quite a bit thinner on a solo trip, other safety matters should be given more attention. One of the advantages to group travel is that one does not have to be so conservative as when traveling alone. An injury is always serious in winter. If you are alone, it is much more so. The difficulties of survival with a badly sprained ankle under winter conditions should not be underestimated. The importance of leaving word of your plans with a responsible person is much greater for a lone traveler. With proper foresight you can survive most injuries for quite a while, but there is a good chance you will not be able to travel. If no one knows where you are or when you expect to be back, a broken leg may well be fatal.

ROUTE FINDING

The subject of finding your way is discussed in detail in another chapter, but in addition to the larger problems of route finding, the winter traveler is faced with hundreds of smaller decisions during the day, and the cumulative results can make the difference of many miles of progress. Intelligent route finding requires an observant eye and a consideration of your equipment and that of your party. The best route for the skier is not always the same as the best one for the snowshoer. If the lead skier is wearing skins, he should remember to choose an angle of ascent which can be followed by his companion using climbing waxes, or the effort of trail breaking will have to be duplicated. Many small details like these are the stuff of making a winter trail, and the observant beginner will not be long in picking up the most important tricks.

One of the most important considerations of small-scale route finding is the condition of the snow. Some snow conditions are very tiring, but it may be possible to avoid them by small changes in route, and the careful observer will not only reap the pleasures of seeing a few more of nature's patterns but may also save himself a good deal of unnecessary travail. For example, one side of a ridge may be deep in heavy powder snow, requiring hard plowing to make headway, while the other side is hard windboard, a highway for the skier or snowshoer. In late afternoon, the breakable crust on the south-facing side of a valley may not exist on the north-facing side, which received less sun during the day. At one time of the day the wooded portion of a slope may make much easier traveling than the open part, while a few hours later the reverse may be true. It would be impossible to catalogue this sort of thing here, but the novice can rapidly build up his own fund of knowledge about the way the snow conditions change in the areas he frequents.

Obstacles and dangers along the route should be anticipated when possible from your examination of the map or previous experience in an area. Avalanche slopes are discussed in some detail in Chapter XI, but it can't be overemphasized that these present an important and unfamiliar danger to the novice wilderness traveler. Streams and rivers also present special winter problems. Large rivers that are not frozen over should generally be crossed by bridge, since they otherwise present expeditionary problems, requiring rafts and wide detours.

In the North, rivers freeze over to a safe depth, but if your trip involves a crossing you should check to see that the river is safe before leaving, if possible. Except in the far North, it is usually best to plan to use a bridge for large rivers. Great care should be exercised in crossing, if a bridge is not used, since rivers have very uneven layers of ice. Skis or snowshoes should be worn to distribute weight over a larger area, unless the ice is very thick, but bindings should be adjusted so that they can be kicked off in the event of breaking through. A long pole will help in case of accidents, and so will a safety rope between members of the party. Wide spacing should be observed on any lake or river.

Rivers that freeze over to great depth have a peculiar hazard in the spring when break-up is approaching. The ice, while still thick, becomes very unstable, forming long vertical crystals called candle ice, which will support very little weight. At this time of year it is best to stay off the ice, but a pole should be used for probing when a crossing is unavoidable. Another common phenomenon on rivers with thick ice is the overflow of water on top of the ice. The feet can be quickly wet by this condition, which sometimes occurs in very cold weather, when waterproof footwear is not usually worn.

Lakes generally form safer crossings than rivers, because their quieter water freezes to a safe depth more quickly, and there are less likely to be thin spots and places where the water has sunk below the level of the ice, making an unstable bridge. The same general precautions should be observed on lakes as rivers, though crossings can usually be undertaken with more confidence. When the weather is cold for long periods, lakes are often preferred routes, offering flat highways free of obstacles. Thin spots are more likely to occur near shore, especially where streams and rivers enter or leave the lake. In guessing the thickness of the ice when planning a trip, the history of the winter should be considered. When heavy snows come early in the winter, the ice sometimes remains thin despite very cold weather because of a thick insulating blanket of snow. A long period of freezing weather before the first deep snow produces thick ice much earlier in the year. Chopping a hole is the most reliable way of assuring the safety of the ice layer when you reach a crossing.

Streams are more likely to be encountered by the weekend traveler than rivers, and stream crossings are often quite difficult. Unless the stream is completely and deeply covered over, a man-made or natural bridge must be found. A good deal of care should be exercised in approaching a stream, because the water tends to undercut the snow on the sides, so that an unsupported bench of

Snow often overhangs streams and requires finding a snowbridge to cross. Late winter in the California Sierra.

snow overhangs the stream. In the event of its collapse the unwary traveler will be precipitated into water that is at freezing temperatures with overhanging snowbanks in all directions. If he is unroped, his chances of survival in a deep stream will be quite slim. When streams are well-bridged, this problem does not occur, but crossings should not be attempted unless you are sure of the safety of your snow bridge. Mountaineers may use rope techniques to extend their safety margin. Bridges are more likely to be safe early in the morning than on a sunny afternoon. When in doubt, follow the stream course to a safe crossing.

The crests of ridges present a problem similar to the overhanging sides of stream beds. The wind blowing snow across the ridge often forms an overhanging structure of snow called a cornice. These are often impossible to detect from above, until the traveler is already standing out over space. The cornice appears from above as a convex slope, and the observer may not realize that, instead of sloping off continuously, the cornice drops off into thin air. Cornices form a particular hazard in stormy weather, when the traveler is likely to be so anxious to get across a pass and out of the wind that he does not even think of the possibility of a

Summer snow like this easily supports hikers without snowshoes or skis. The depressions in the snow are called suncups.

Route finding 107

cornice. The rule to follow is simply not to go out onto anything that might be a cornice. On a curving ridge, a look can often be got farther down the ridge. Cornices also present a great avalanche hazard, which is taken up in Chapter XI.

More mundane route-finding problems simply involve the best angles at which to climb slopes that present no hazards. A long angling climb is usually best, especially on skis. Sometimes such a traverse on a steep slope is uncomfortable on snowshoes, and a direct climb is preferred if it can be handled. A traversing ascent helps the party to maintain pace, and a traversing descent is often nearly effortless on skis. The snowshoer again sometimes prefers a short direct descent, followed by a distance on the flat.

WALKING IN WINTER

When the snow is not very deep, snowshoes and skis are neither necessary nor practical, and winter travel consists merely of walking. This same method can sometimes be used when the snow is very well-consolidated, so that one walks on top of what may be a very deep layer of snow. In either case, there is no particular problem of technique, except when the snow becomes steep, a subject introduced in Chapter X. The main differences between winter walking and backpacking in other seasons are that progress is slowed considerably and that special attention must be paid to footwear. One must also remain aware of the possibility of being caught by a heavy snowfall or softening snow. An easy walk in can become a nightmare going out. For this reason, it is often necessary to carry snowshoes or skis on longer trips. Unless they will definitely be used, at higher altitudes, for example, skis are inferior to snowshoes for this purpose, since they are much more difficult to pack.

BOOTS

Footwear is a problem at any time of the year, but winter exacerbates every difficulty in choosing boots. Waterproofing is needed more at the same time that better breathing qualities are important—two contradictory requirements. Much more insulation is needed, because even when the upper body is baking in the sun, the feet may be surrounded by snow at sub-zero temperatures. Thus, these essential parts of the body with their poor circulation are subject to the most severe cold. They are also more likely to get wet than the rest of the body. It is more of a problem to provide insulation for the feet, because the body's weight rests on them, so that compressible insulation cannot be used. Finally, in winter travel, the special demands of footwear for skiing, snowshoeing, climbing steep snow and ice, or all of these must often be met.

The first thing to remember in choosing winter boots is that the winter foot traveler is a generalist, whether he is a skier, a snowshoer, or a climber. His boots or other footwear must serve many functions. Any boot that he wears will be a compromise between the many conflicting demands that will be made on it. There are many excellent types of winter footwear on the market that are completely useless to him. The modern downhill ski boot is excellent for its purpose, but it is hard to walk in it from the door of the lodge to the bar, much less through twenty miles of rough-country. The same thing applies to many types of footwear designed for snowmobiling, ice fishing, duck hunting, and sentry duty.

There are particular types of boots that are preferred for skiing on various types of terrain, and these are discussed in the chapter on skiing. Snowshoeing is a bit more versatile in the types of footwear that can be used, and some types are also discussed in that chapter. Very wet weather, when there is as much water as snow, coupled with easy terrain may call for the rubber-footed boots mentioned in the snowshoe chapter. The most versatile footwear for the rough terrain that most of the readers of this book will encounter is the heavy-duty mountain boot.

A good general-purpose mountaineering boot can be used for hiking, climbing steep slopes, slogging through powder snow or mud, snowshoeing, and skiing. It is generally the best compromise available. Softer footwear is more comfortable if conditions are just right for it, but a heavy pack and a little rough terrain will make you curse it. It is impossible for skiing or for steep slopes.

A good winter mountaineering boot must be fairly heavy with a rubber-lug sole. The uppers should be of a double-layer construction with no seams sewn through from the outside to the inside. Seams in the outer and inner layers are placed in different places in well-made mountain boots. The tongue should open widely without too much difficulty, or the boots will be impossible to put on when they are frozen. It should also be gusseted, so that snow and water can't get into the boot around the sides. The best boots are lined with glove leather.

Double boots are good for extreme conditions, especially for mountaineering, but they are more expensive and not at all essential for most conditions. True double boots have one or more pairs of removable inner boots, which are worn inside heavy outer ones and which can be worn separately in the tent. They are very warm. An alternative to regular double boots has been offered recently, an inner boot insulated with fiber glass, which can be used inside a regular mountaineering boot. Whether regular socks or these inner boots are used, boots for winter use should be bought somewhat larger than those that are used exclusively in milder seasons. Room should be allowed for the inner boot or for two pairs of heavy socks, and one pair of lighter socks without cramp-

Boots for winter use in moderate conditions. Left to right: heavy- and medium-weight mountaineering boots with smooth side out for water-repellency, rubber-bottom boots. In very cold weather these must be supplemented by overboots or replaced with double or vapor-barrier boots.

ing the foot. The heel should then be snug but not tight, and it should be easy to wiggle the toes. Cold feet have poor circulation without any extra constriction from the boots. Tight footwear is the cause of many cases of frostbite.

Your summer mountain boots will be perfectly good for winter use, provided they are not too light or too tight. Light and medium-weight mountain boots do not generally provide enough insulation or water repellency for winter use. For snowshoeing they may be adequate if worn with a pair of overboots. These fabric covers will extend the temperature range of any boot, especially if they have pockets for closed-cell foam insulation pads. Plans for making them are included in one of the books mentioned in the do-it-yourself section. They can also be purchased from a number of suppliers listed in the appendix.

CARE OF THE BOOTS AND THE FEET

A good pair of mountain boots will last through several pairs of soles, but only if they are properly cared for. Water will ruin leather if it is not treated regularly with good preservatives. The silicon-based waxes are usually the best, since they preserve the leather with less tendency to soften it. Rough-side-out leathers should be treated with liquid silicon repellents first and then with the wax. The best thickness for the wax layer depends on the conditions prevailing at the time. For wet conditions—in fall and spring and all winter in some areas—a thick layer of wax worked into the boot will make it completely waterproof, but it will also prevent the leather from breathing. In colder weather, a thinner layer of wax will give enough water repellency without completely closing the pores of the leather.

The boots should be taken care of after you return from each trip. They should be cleaned, using saddle soap if necessary, and then allowed to dry at room temperature (excessive heat will ruin leather as fast as it will your skin.) The boots should be warmed slightly to open the pores, and then the wax should be applied. Work the preservative into the leather, paying particular attention to seams. Several coats may be necessary at twenty-four-hour intervals if the leather is dried out. When enough wax has been applied and dried, polish the boots with a cloth and put them away. On long trips it may be necessary to apply wax on the trail, but this is much less effective on cold, wet boots. If preservatives have to be applied on trips, try to do it on a sunny day during a lunch stop, when the boots can be warmed and partially dried.

Care of the feet is a particular problem on any backpacking trip, but it is much greater under winter conditions, when cold and circulation problems are added to dampness and friction. The first couple of rules of foot care have already been mentioned: proper socks and adequate room in the boots. The latter point is difficult to overemphasize. Tight boots can cause difficulty and discomfort on any winter trip, and they are likely to cause frostbite in a survival situation. Nails should be trimmed before the trip, and special problems like bunions or corns should be taken care of well in advance.

On the trail the traveler will always have adequate warning of foot troubles, and the main trick is simply to heed these warnings when they occur, rather than waiting until it is convenient and too late. Gaiters, anklets, or overboots should be put on when they are needed to keep snow and wet out of the boots. Otherwise you will have to change your socks a little later, which will be more time-consuming. The upper body has to be kept reasonably warm for the feet to be warm; circulation to the feet will be cut down if the trunk is chilled, and once the blood supply to cold feet is reduced, insulation will not warm the feet.

Blisters are often a particular problem in winter. Socks become damp and friction increases, while skis and snowshoes often cause more rubbing at the heel than would occur with summer walking. If you feel uncomfortable friction at some point on the foot, stop and take care of it, otherwise, you will soon have a blister. Moleskin, a felt backed with adhesive, is excellent for covering trouble spots. It should be carried somewhere that is readily accessible. If a blister has already appeared, moleskin should still be applied, preferably without breaking the blister. If the blister has already broken, or if its size makes draining necessary, clean it as well as possible, leaving the skin layer over the affected area, apply an antiseptic to the whole area and apply moleskin. Draining should be done from one side with a sterilized point and as little disturbance of the skin layer as possible. In the case of a large blister with the skin already pulled off, you will probably have to apply a dressing of either plastic or gauze covered with a slippery antiseptic cream and then cover the whole thing with moleskin. Adhesive tape can be used for any of these purposes instead of moleskin, but will not work quite so well. Remember that the best time to apply the cover is *before* the blister forms.

When you stop for a snack or a rest, try to get your feet up out of the snow. It is sometimes amazing how great a difference in temperature can exist between the top of the snow and the layer a few inches down, which is often much colder because it is insulated by the top layer. Your feet will be warmer if you prop them out of the snow. This is also the time to change your socks if they need it. If the stop is to last more than a few minutes it is a good idea to loosen the laces of your boots to improve circulation.

During travel, frequent wiggling of the toes will help improve circulation in cold feet. If your feet are painfully cold and the discomfort stops, you should stop immediately and warm the feet. This numbness is a prelude to frostbite. A more detailed discussion of frostbite and related problems is included in Chapter XII.

EQUIPMENT

When you are carrying your gear on your back, you'll first have to put it all in a pack, so we might as well start off with that. If you've done much mild-season backpacking, you probably already have one or more packs, and they will generally be adequate for winter use as well, at least for a start. Various types of packs will be discussed in this section with some recommendations for the best uses of each, but don't immediately go out and buy a new one unless the pack you have is completely inadequate for the first trip you have in mind. You may find that you like your old pack just as well even if it's not the "ideal" one for this or that type of trip.

Contoured frames. The contoured aluminum and magnesium frame packs, invented by A. I. Kelty a few years ago, have rapidly become almost universally accepted as the standard pack for the backpacker. Most snowshoe travelers will find that these packs suit them well, too. Many ski tourers use them also, especially on very long trips or difficult ski-mountaineering trips that require packing brutal loads.

Frames of various sorts have been around for quite a while, and they have always had the advantages of keeping the load away from the back, of providing ventilation while preventing gouges in the anatomy, of allowing all sorts of odd parcels to be packed comfortably, of getting the load fairly high and close to the body so that less forward lean is required, and of controlling the shape of the load. The new contoured frames do all these things, generally better than the old frames like the Trapper Nelson, but the main innovation that they provide is a design that enables the packer to carry most of the load on his hips. Most weekend wilderness travelers have a hard time with older-type packs, not only because the center of gravity is often far behind the wearer, forcing him to lean forward against the load, but also because his back and shoulder muscles just aren't in good enough shape to carry the load comfortably even if the center of gravity is right over his shoulders. The contoured frame gets the center of gravity very close to the back, so that it is over the hips with a very slight lean, and then the load is transferred to the hips by means of a broad waist belt attached to the bottom of the frame. The weight of the pack then rests on the strong muscles of the legs directly, instead of being transmitted through the back.

This waist belt is often not well-understood by novices (or by some pack manufacturers). Lots of packs have waist belts, but many of them are designed just to keep the pack from flopping. With a properly designed contour frame the belt can be used to carry most of the load. Sometimes a wide front belt in combination with the bands on the frame itself serves to transmit the weight to the hips. On many newer models a full belt going all the way around the waist is used, and the lower part of the pack is then hung on a couple of side tabs, which are attached to the belt. Either arrangement is all right if it is well designed, but the second is better for really heavy loads (the kind you shouldn't carry unless you're going in for at least a week). When you try a pack frame on, you'll never be able to tell if the waist strap will do its job if you only wear the empty pack. Load it up with thirty or forty pounds of stuff and then adjust the pack so that all the weight rides on the hips, the shoulders merely balancing the pack.

Snowshoer with a rigid-frame rucksack. A good pack, but it does not have the load capacity of a contoured frame.

Equipment 115

Walk around and imagine carrying the thing over ten miles of rough country. Bounce up and down. You'll be able to feel the difference between well-designed waist bands and poor imitations pretty quickly.

There are several big disadvantages to the contoured frames, and they are felt more in winter than at other times. The main problem is that by getting the center of gravity high the wearer is made more unstable, which is a disadvantage in snow, especially to skiers. For this reason rucksacks are preferred by many ski tourers and mountaineers, at least for weekend trips where loads are reasonable.

The rigidity of frames tends to cramp body movement, which again troubles the skier more than other wilderness travelers. This disadvantage is also strongly felt by the mountaineer, who also dislikes the extension of the frame behind his head, making it difficult to look up. Despite these annoyances, the contour frames are so much superior to any other packs for carrying heavy loads that they are almost universally used by mountaineers and skiers on long trips that demand heavy packing.

Rucksacks with rigid frames. Rucksacks with rigid frames are next to contour frames in their load capacity. As with the pack frames, the load is attached to the frame to which the carrying straps are fixed. This rigid frame holds the pack in shape, keeps sharp objects from poking you, allows ventilation of the back, and in a properly designed pack even allows some of the weight to be transferred to the hips. Most of the load is now carried by the shoulders. Both the volume and the weight that can be comfortably carried in a frame rucksack are quite a bit less than comparable figures for a contour frame, but the pack is less constraining on body movements. With heavy loads, the wearer is forced to lean forward to balance the backward pull of the pack, but with reasonable loads, the lower center of gravity makes the combination of the traveler and his pack much more stable than the wearer of a contour frame. Rucksacks of this type make good packs for touring of a few days duration, especially on skis.

Rucksacks with flexible frames. In the last few years some very good flexible-framed rucksacks have been designed, which are lighter and feel more a part of the body than the rigid-frame rucksacks, while offering some of their load-carrying capacity. The

A light, flexible-frame pack. Good for day trips or ultra-light weekend jaunts.

Equipment 117

flexible frames are often removable for easy storage and for use of the pack with very light loads. The loads that can be carried in this type of pack vary a great deal with pack design and the wearer, but the best ones are not normally comfortable with over thirty pounds, even if you are in good shape. Larger loads are possible but not advisable for most people.

The biggest problem with the flexible-frame rucksacks for many winter campers is the problem of bulk. The frames of most of these packs are not designed to hold the load in shape, and for this reason the pack tends to assume a cylindrical shape if it is overstuffed, and becomes uncomfortable to carry. Weight is increased in winter camping, but volume goes up even faster because more clothes are needed. Before you buy a pack of this type for your main hauling duties try packing everything in it that you plan to carry, and make sure that you won't need two packs instead of one. For the mountaineer or other camper who has learned to go light, this makes an ideal pack for weekend or slightly longer use. It is particularly fine for ski touring and ski mountaineering.

Frameless rucksacks. Frameless rucksacks will serve primarily as day packs for snowshoe hikes, ski tours, and side trips from a camp. Lightweight specialists who are bivouacking sometimes like to use this type of pack exclusively, but the best of the rucksacks with flexible frames are tending to replace them. There is one common use for the longer varieties of this type of pack: a frameless rucksack is used on a contour packframe instead of the regular packbag. This pack can then be detached and carried by itself as a summit pack for mountaineering or for day trips. Regular packbags can be converted to the same purpose by attaching straps.

Which pack? The choice of a pack will depend on the considerations mentioned above, budget matters, and personal taste. There are a few special considerations to be pointed out, though. Volume is important. Packs should not be overstuffed, and this is especially true of rucksacks. The bulk of the extra insulation that is carried in winter will usually not fit into a pack barely large enough for summer. A pack that is too large is better than one that is too small, though it tempts one to toss in unnecessary trivia.

Load-carrying capacity is relative. A 170-pound athlete may comfortably tote a 35-pound load in an Army ski-mountaineering pack, but his 105-pound spouse will not find this quite so simple, even if she is in very good shape. Her legs may be strong as iron, but she will have to lean too far forward to balance the load. She will need a contour frame to carry this much weight comfortably. Despite the advantages of rucksacks for skiing, many skiers who like mountain backpacking still prefer to use the frame because it makes load carrying easier. It is not at all impossible to ski with a frame.

The shape of a pack is very important: the slimmer the profile of the pack, the closer the center of gravity will be to the body, and the easier the carrying will be. This is why you should not buy a frame bag much larger than the one you need; you will lose some of the closeness of profile that makes the frame so advantageous. The best rucksacks are designed as much as possible to bring the load in close to the back.

Next to basic design, the quality of materials and construction are most important in the choice of a pack, well ahead of special frills. Basic pack material should be strong, seams should be sewn with nylon thread, and all hardware and hanging arrangements should be sturdy and well-made. A waist strap is desirable, especially for skiers and climbers, so that the pack can be prevented from flopping. Any pack should be tried out either in the store or at home while it can still be returned. You should test it with the load and bulk you expect to carry in it. If it is uncomfortable in five minutes in the store it will be unbearable on the trail. If it is comfortable with a load and is well-made, it will make a good pack.

Packing is as important as the shape of the pack itself in determining what characteristics the pack will have when it is being carried. Heavy objects should be kept close to the back (with proper care for the anatomy) so that they will not pull the pack backwards. Two techniques can be used to keep them there. The pack can be compartmentalized, a method that also has the great advantage of holding it in a desired shape but the disadvantage of always seeming to have a small compartment just where you want to put a large object. The other method is simply to stuff your light, bulky gear in the places where you don't want the heavy objects to go. For example, with the older-style frame rucksacks like the economical U.S. Army ski-mountaineering pack, extra clothes are stuffed in the backward projecting area, while stove, flashlight, fuel and food are kept near to the back. The same technique is used with flexible-frame and frameless rucksacks, except that more care must be exercised to make sure that pointed objects will not be grinding their way into the spine after a few miles.

There are some very nice, fancy, small packs for day trips, but if you are economizing, this is a good place to do it. Adequate and inexpensive packs are carried by some suppliers, and I have even used a pillowcase tied at the top and two lower corners with webbing for straps. For lunches on a day excursion from camp, a sleeping bag stuffsack can be used the same way. The trick is not to overpack it; that makes it uncomfortable.

Lights. For most purposes in winter, battery-operated flashlights or headlamps are standard lightweight gear. A headlamp has great advantages when the hands are needed for other things, such as cooking, gathering wood, or making midnight repairs on a guy line. The separate battery pack of the headlamp also enables one to get the batteries close to the body, where they will stay warm and hence operate efficiently. As any car owner in a cold area knows, batteries become progressively less powerful as the temperature drops. Because of their greater temperature range, longer life, and superiority in heavy use, alkaline batteries or one of the more exotic types of long-life cells should be used in preference to standard flashlight cells. Some of the truly rechargeable types are excellent, but there is an advantage in the alkaline type that they are now readily available at drugstores anywhere. A good combination of lights for two people is one headlamp and one small Mallory flashlight operating on penlight cells. This latter gives amazing light for its size and weight. With a fresh set of alkaline batteries in each light, spare batteries need not usually be carried for a weekend but should be taken on a longer trip. An extra bulb of each type being used should be taken. I carry mine taped inside the headlamp.

Any battery lasts for a longer total period if it is operated intermittently, so when two or more flashlights are available, their use should be alternated. If spare batteries are carried, the same principle applies: when a light is used for more than an hour, switch the batteries. When they are being carried in the pack, flashlights should be disabled in some way to prevent accidental current drain: tape the switch, reverse the direction of half the batteries, or insert an insulator in the circuit somewhere. At night, remember to keep your batteries warm so that the light will work well if you need it.

Sun protection. It seems rather contradictory that in winter when the sun is lowest, the danger of sunburn can be particularly great. Snow is an almost perfect reflector of light in the ranges that burn the skin and eyes. In a large snow bowl, you may consider yourself to be the focal point of a giant reflector oven. Cloudy days can be most deceptive, since visible light is shut out to a large degree, but this is not always the case for the burning ultra-violet portion of the spectrum. Skin and eye protection should always be carried, unless you know you won't need them. In high mountains, everyone must carry sun protection, since the danger there is much greater. Much of the ultra-violet that is filtered out before reaching sea level is still present in the light of the mountains.

At lower altitudes, most people will find conventional sun-tan preparations satisfactory. At higher altitudes, a special cream should be carried, and it may be wanted by people with sensitive skin at all times. Several good preparations are available in mountaineering shops. The budget-minded can use mineral oil for the milder sort of protection, and the zinc oxide ointment usually marketed for baby's diaper rash gives complete protection against high-altitude burning rays.

Sun glasses or goggles do not have to be expensive, but they must be of good quality. Some types of cheap plastic glasses can do more harm than good, since they cut out visible rays, thus making the pupils dilate, while allowing the ultra-violet rays that do the damage to pass through. Snow blindness is disabling and very painful, and it must be avoided by foresight and care, since the victim rarely feels pain until the damage has been done. Lenses of glasses for use in snow should be darker than conventional sunglasses, and they should be good enough optically so that they do not produce eyestrain after a few hours. Climbing shops and some ski stores have excellent models, some of which are not too expensive. Glare from the side should be cut out by some means, but as much ventilation as possible is desirable to prevent fogging.

For some reason, most of the manufacturers of goggles and sunglasses seem to believe that all mountaineers and winter travelers possess perfect vision because they generally pay little attention to the needs of eyeglass wearers. Some goggles will fit over eyeglasses, but if they aren't well-ventilated you will have a lot of trouble with fogging. Even with those that are well-ventilated, you will probably need some anti-fogging compound to smear on the lenses of your goggles and glasses. The double set of lenses causes far more trouble than a single set. Probably the best alternative for the wearer of eyeglasses who can afford them is a set of prescription sunglasses with large dark lenses and colored or opaque side visors to cut glare.

Two other special needs of the eyeglass wearer are a spare set of glasses and some sort of holder to prevent him from losing his specs in a tumble. A piece of cord and a pair of rubber bands will do if nothing else is available.

Toilet articles. A small piece of hand soap, or, better, a tiny tube of liquid hand soap will take care of washing needs. Washing the face and hands more often than necessary should be avoided, since the removal of the skin's protective oils will aid chapping and sunburn. Those who don't possess weather-toughened skin are well advised to carry a small container of oil-based skin lotion for chapping. A tiny tube of petroleum jelly takes care of chafed spots, and can be carried in a pocket of the clothing or pack. Everyone should have a special stick or cream for the lips, which are particularly prone to cracking and chapping. For high altitudes a special opaque cream to protect the lips from sunburn may be desirable, since the protection used for the rest of the face often comes off the lips too easily.

Toothbrushes are a necessity for some, while others never bother with them on a trip. Suit yourself, but remember that a little plastic bag of tooth powder attached to the toothbrush with a rubber band is a lot lighter than a tube of toothpaste and is less messy if it gets broken.

Don't forget to take the toilet paper! Rerolled into small bundles, it will fit into convenient spots in your pocket and pack.

Tools and repair kit. A knife is needed for many purposes, and one should be carried by each member of a party. A sharp pocket knife is usually adequate, though a small sheath knife may be justified if you are building fires but not carrying a saw or ax. The knife should be kept sharp. A small whetstone may be worthwhile on longer trips. If you are building fires to keep you warm, you will need a saw or an ax. A saw is much lighter than any adequate ax. A Hudson Bay ax with a one-and-a-half-pound head is about the smallest practical size. There are several folding saws that are fairly light and compact. Some of these can also be used for cutting snow blocks. For a lightweight emergency saw, a hacksaw blade can be carried or a lightweight wire saw can be purchased.

A repair kit will vary with your own experience. Wilderness tourers, like armies, tend always to be prepared for the last war rather than the next one. Aside from this personal aspect, your repair kit will depend on your equipment. Skiers, who might have to repair the hardware of bindings, may want to carry a plier-screwdriver-crescent wrench combination tool and any spare parts that seem appropriate. An emergency ski tip should be carried by skiers with wooden skis. I prefer to carry most emergency equipment together in one small package, including spare matches in a waterproof container, fire starter, and medical supplies, which are covered in Chapter XII. Some items like adhesive tape serve for repairs of both equipment and people. Other items like parachute cord serve many ordinary camping uses as well as being useful for emergency repairs, and they will usually be carried in the pack or a pocket. Any repair kit should include a needle and some nylon thread for mending clothing; ripstop nylon tape is also handy for fabric repairs. About a yard of wire is very useful for some kinds of repairs on skis and snowshoes. For quick repairs a few safety pins should be carried somewhere; I leave mine on one of the belt loops of my trousers, where they are handy.

If an emergency kit is to do any good, it must be available when it is needed, and this means that it should be light and compact. If it is too complete it is likely to be left in the tent when you go off on a day trip. One kit will do for a small party, if there are no plans of splitting the group for day trips or on the trail.

If you plan to split into smaller groups at some point, one emergency kit must be carried for each group. Some experienced travelers carry their emergency items in two packages. Medicine, extra bandages, and other items are left with the tent, while a lighter kit is carried at all times. The items left at the tent can serve a large party, and the smaller kit is duplicated for each small group that is going off by itself. Detailed lists for suggested emergency kits are included in Appendix D.

Containers and utensils. It is important to have a container in which you can carry liquid water after finding or melting it. Such a container has innumerable other uses in the jugglery of camp cooking. The most serviceable type I know is a strong polyethylene flask with a wide mouth. Marks can be made on the side with a hot knife for measuring water in cooking. The wide mouth is essential so that snow can be added to already melted water. Pick a bottle that doesn't leak.

Whatever type of water bottle you have, remember to fill it whenever there is an opportunity. If you have extra hot water at breakfast, you can make a hot drink for lunch and wrap the bottle in the middle of your sleeping bag to keep it warm. If you like a fast start in the morning, make some sort of nourishing drink at night and wrap the bottle in some clothing to keep it from freezing overnight. This can be combined with normal trail food for a fast breakfast.

For eating, I usually carry one plastic cup and one light plastic bowl for each person. These are easier to use in a crowded tent than metal dishes, since they don't get so hot that people burn their hands and spill things on the floor and sleeping bags. Plastic dishes are light, and the flexible ones are quite strong. Make sure that the ones you get are shaped so that you can pack them easily. One tablespoon per person is usually adequate for a utensil, together with personal penknives. One or two clamp potholders are very useful for handling hot pans. When held they grip the pot like a saucepan. If you plan to fry anything in the thin cook kit covers that double as frying pans, it helps to bring a light spatula, since it is nearly impossible to keep things from sticking to these pans.

If you are using a gasoline stove for cooking, you will need a gasoline container. The best type is the rectangular metal kind with a narrow pouring spout on one side and a vent spout on the other. Test the container at home to make sure it doesn't leak. Pack it in a plastic bag for extra safety, and then put it somewhere in the pack as far away from food as possible, to prevent any accidental leaks from doing too much damage. Gasoline, even used in small quantities, gives food a very distinctive flavor. (Mountaineers should also take care to pack the gasoline away from nylon climbing ropes and slings, which are attacked by gasoline.) In testing the can at home, make sure you can pour easily into the stove from a full can without much spilling. If you can't, carry a small plastic funnel for filling the stove. A pricker for the jet should also be carried by the gasoline stove user. Don't forget that you must use white (unleaded) gasoline or the special fuel sold in camping stores. For buying white gas, you will need a gallon or larger size metal container. Gas station attendants are understandably reluctant to start their pumps to fill pint containers.

Miscellaneous items. Maps and compasses are discussed in Chapter IX. They are essential, and so is the knowledge of how to use them. Other instruments for navigation are fascinating but are rarely needed on short trips. On trips to the mountains, an altimeter is an interesting luxury item that is useful in navigation and weather forecasting.

Other gadgets will be considered essential by different people, but remember to be stingy both in the store and at the trailhead. Will you really use it? Is it really worth the price and the weight? Photographic equipment is the most commonly carried gadgetry. If you take it, make sure it is accessible enough so that you use it. A camera buried in the pack will be left there with the thought of getting that picture tomorrow. Only tomorrow it usually snows! A light and inexpensive camera often gets the pictures missed with a heavy *SLR,* which can't be carried in a convenient position.

ALONG THE WINTER TRAIL

The main reason for being on the trail in winter is to have a good time, and the need for too much attention to details and worry about problems will spoil your trip. Leave yourself enough time and energy to enjoy the company of your companions and the beauty around you. You are more likely to have a good time if you limit your objectives at first. It's fine to end the day tired, but the slower members of the party shouldn't be shoved along on a forced march, except under unusual circumstances.

Normal procedure is to alternate regularly in the trailbreaking position, which is very tiring in some kinds of snow, especially on snowshoes. Weaker members of the party may be spared this work, but you should be wary of letting the strongest member of the party do all the work. His stamina may be needed later, and the necessity for reliance on one person should indicate to you that the party's strength is being stretched out a little too much. What happens if the bull breaks his leg? If there is a heavy fall of new snow? Parties of uneven strength should keep their goals on the conservative side.

With larger parties, it is common to go into camp and then split up for day trips. This sort of arrangement is fine, but groups should always be aware of the dangers of dividing the party. Each separate party must have the capacity for handling any emergencies and problems they may encounter.

A dangerous and common mistake is for all the strong members of the party to go on a hard trip, while the beginners take a trip of their own in country in which they are not competent to travel. The only emergency kit is taken by one group, and is not available to the other. The same will be true of the map, if only one is carried. This sort of situation has all the makings of disaster, and that fact is obvious when it is presented in this way, but otherwise sensible people still make this type of mistake rather frequently.

Parties should never be split up in dangerous situations except in the specific circumstances discussed in the chapter on emergencies. The most common mistake of this kind is to allow the party to separate in whiteout conditions when blowing snow reduces visibility to a few yards: a few members of the party may stop to rest, while their companions proceed out of calling range in the howling winds, or two groups may split to investigate different routes, losing each other before they realize what they are doing. In any case, the result is that they are soon looking for each other as well as the trail. When a group is in any difficulty, special efforts must be made to keep it together, and even during normal trail travel, morale will be higher if the group does not spread out too far because of uneven pace. Experienced parties made up of members of equal strength who want a little of the silence afforded by a ten-minute spacing can indulge themselves as long as there is no danger of skiing down different valleys. In good conditions this does not pose any danger, but as soon as tracks start drifting in rapidly, the party should get together and stay that way.

CHILDREN ON THE TRAIL

Taking children on winter trips can be quite enjoyable, but some special attention is needed in planning, and ambitions will have to be scaled down somewhat. With children of about ten years and over, there aren't many differences from planning a tour for adults, except for appropriate evaluations of strength and the length of the trip.

One thing you should remember is that children generally do not have the reserve strength of adults, either physically or emotionally. A very strong and energetic child will still usually be nearly spent once he is tired. The transition from incredible energy to exhaustion and collapse is quick. This is especially true in cold weather. Special care is necessary in guarding against the effects of cold. Children also cannot usually be expected to pace themselves, and it is important that some care be exercised, especially with large groups of young people. Those who are used to the outdoors and have developed some habits of foresight and self-reliance may have better judgment than their adult companions, but most boys and girls have not had a chance to develop that kind of maturity.

Children between the ages of five and ten can also undertake trips on their own power, with objectives appropriate to their size and stamina. Older members of the party will have to carry some or all of the supplies for this age group.

Below the age of five, children usually have to be carried, along with their clothing and regular equipment. Older children are rather heavy, and with younger ones the problem of bulk is considerable due to diapers and changes of clothing. The frame carriers in which the child faces forward are effective, though not as durable as they should be. These carriers can also be lashed high

Children can be taken on winter trips with proper clothing and easy itineraries.

on a packframe equipped with an extension bar, and a packbag will fit below.

A child who is riding should be dressed very warmly; he is not climbing a hill to generate heat. The problem of insulation is not too great, however, since the child is sitting in one place and is easily padded.

The biggest problem in snow camping with small children is that they can't play around the tent or lunch spot in deep snow, since the packed platform doesn't extend very far. This means they don't get any real break from the monotony of sitting, and they become understandably bored and cranky. Another real difficulty of winter weekends with small children is the changing of diapers and clothes.

With small children the most enjoyable alternative is usually to take day trips from a car camp or cabin. Most of the difficulties are manageable on day jaunts. On longer trips they can be handled, but in winter they are likely to turn your trip into more of an ordeal than a pleasure. Overnight backpacking with small children is best saved for milder seasons.

STAYING ON TOP OF THE SNOW

Skis and snowshoes are dealt with in the next two chapters. Besides the choice between these two methods of staying atop the snow, there are many types of skis and many snowshoe patterns. If you already have a pair of webs or skis, you can use them, at least for a while, without worrying about whether they are perfect for the conditions you expect. You may also be able to try out different types of equipment by renting them.

However, if you have to put down the money to purchase skis or snowshoes you will want to study the different types with care, and these are discussed in some detail in the following chapter. The basics are easy. In mountainous country, heavier skis are used and some skill at managing them must be acquired in advance. Thus, the non-skier who wants to head for the high country right away will probably choose snowshoes. Technique with touring skis for easier terrain is not hard to learn, and the beginner needn't worry about starting right off with skis.

Mountains that don't usually get a heavy cover of snow often require snowshoes for winter climbing, since a deep snow cover is necessary for skiing in really rough terrain. In the Northeast, for example, ski tourers are often confined to gentler trails. In the high Western mountains, the skier can manage terrain as difficult as any that can be traversed by snowshoe, since the snow cover is usually deep. In fact, skis are generally easier to use on open difficult terrain when snow depth is adequate.

On steep terrain snowshoes are somewhat safer than skis, but skiers admit few other advantages to the plodding webs. In flatter country, where light cross-country ski equipment is used, skis are as safe as snowshoes. They are always faster.

Whatever sort of equipment you already have or decide to buy, you'll be able to handle a wide variety of terrain from snowy beaches to mountain peaks. Though each ski and snowshoe design is best in one type of terrain, it can be used in a much wider range of situations. Picking equipment simply amounts to choosing the best compromise for your purposes.

VII

Snowshoeing: Walking on the Drifts

When winter really settles in and the drifts begin to pile up, slogging through the snow can become impossible unless you spread your weight over a larger area than the soles of your boots. The easiest way to do this, the one requiring the least practice, the cheapest, the traditional American way, is with snowshoes. It is the traditional American way because snowshoes were invented by indigenous Americans, the Indians, and there have been no significant improvements in design since.

The greatest advantage of snowshoes over skis is that you can learn to walk on them in about five minutes. Using skis requires that you learn to ski. This advantage is not nearly so great if the country where you plan to tour is flat or rolling, since Nordic-style ski touring is fairly easy to learn. Mountain-touring technique with skis takes some time to master, however. The snowshoer needs to learn only the fine points of technique, not the basics, because he already knows how to walk. This means that he can learn on trips rather than practice slopes, a great boon.

There have always been myriad patterns of snowshoes, for each Indian tribe that used them had its own distinctive design. The features of a particular type were dictated by tradition and available materials, but most of all by the snow conditions prevailing in the area where they were used and the activities for which they were designed. The same conditions govern the design and choice of snowshoes today.

There are a few additional advantages to snowshoes that should be mentioned. Snowshoes are superior to skis for many jobs in the woods, that is, for work rather than travel. Felling trees and hauling loads is easier on snowshoes than skis. Almost any footwear suitable for winter wear can be worn with snowshoes. This can save money and be of considerable advantage on a trip where some particular type of shoe or boot is needed for other reasons. Finally, on trips with terrain alternating between soft snow and walking or climbing conditions when only boots are needed, snowshoes are much easier than skis to carry between drifts.

Snowshoes are simply webs of thin, strong material stretched over a rigid frame that are attached to the feet and spread the wearer's weight over a wide area of snow. The snowshoes are held to the foot in such a way that the foot pivots forward freely but is held fairly strongly from sideways motion. The standard snowshoe is made of varnished strips of cowhide on a curved wooden frame. Some attempts have been made to use modern industrial materials for snowshoes—plastics, metal, and rubberized nylon—but these have made few converts, except for neoprene-nylon strapping, which has been used successfully for both bindings and webbing.

Walking technique on webs varies somewhat with design and terrain, but basically, a long, gliding gait is used when possible. The feet are a bit farther apart than in normal walking, but not so

Some types of snowshoes: left to right, modified bearpaw with H binding, a Maine shoe with ties for a squaw hitch, a modified bearpaw with a Howe binding, and a standard bearpaw with an army sandal binding.

Snowshoeing: walking on the drifts 131

far apart as one would think from looking at a pair of snowshoes sitting side-by-side on the floor. The widest part of the shoe is beside the foot, with the frame tapering in both forward and backward directions. In walking, the wide parts are not placed beside one another; instead, the forward curve of the rear shoe fits beside the back curve of the leading shoe, as shown in the illustration. In walking, the rear shoe is lifted just enough to clear the front one as it comes forward. The legs are just far enough apart so that the shoe doesn't strike the opposite leg as it comes forward.

The design of snowshoes is supremely functional, and choosing the right type is fairly simple if you know the conditions that prevail where they will be used. How much do you weigh, and how big a pack do you normally carry? Does deep, dry, light powder cover the woods in the part of the country where you live, or is heavy, wet snow or breakable crust the rule? Will you be traveling mostly in brushy, dense country or in the wide, open spaces? Are you thinking of steep mountains, flat plains, or rolling country? Or do you have some special use in mind, such as utility shoes for use around a cabin where the main transportation will be on skis?

The main features of design are: length, width, general shape, tail, and upturn of the toe. Many other differences, such as rounded or pointed toes, are relatively unimportant. Models are more standardized than they once were. The features mentioned above will be discussed, and then the general types of shoe will be listed with the conditions where they are preferred. The main types each have a number of practically synonymous names. Niceties such as the differences between Michigan and Maine shoes will be left for the interested reader to find for himself.

The larger the area of the snowshoe, the more weight it will support without sinking too much into the snow. The smallest shoe that will do the job for you is the best. Every extra ounce on the feet is tiring, and larger sizes are more awkward as well. Where hard snow conditions prevail, smaller shoes than normal may suffice. The designs that are suitable for areas with deep, soft snow are usually made with fairly large areas. The recommended sizes below are for general use.

Width tends to increase the general awkwardness of snowshoes and makes them slower because the legs must be kept wide. Fourteen inches should be a maximum shoe width. Where long shoes are not a disadvantage, area is increased with length rather than width, but where maneuverability is more important than speed, width is increased. The general shape of a shoe will be dictated both by the area needed for adequate support and by handling characteristics.

A tail is always desirable for hiking, but it makes the shoe slightly less maneuverable. The tail makes the snowshoe somewhat heavier to the rear of the pivot axis. When the foot is lifted, the tail remains on the snow, supporting some of the weight of the shoe, and the toe turns up out of the snow. A tail-less snowshoe can be made either with the weight to the rear of the pivot, like the tailed variety, or with the weight approximately balanced. If the weight is balanced, more weight has to be lifted by the leg, because no weight is supported by the tail, and it must be lifted higher, because the toe is not pulled up by the heavier tail. A tail-less snowshoe with a heavy pack also slows the wearer, because the rear of the shoe drags badly on the snow. Instead of a narrow width of smooth wood, one drags a small snowplow. The great advantage of the tail-less shoes is their maneuverability. They are also very convenient to carry on a pack due to their reduced length.

An upturned toe is another essential feature of snowshoes made for the trail. A straight toe tends to dive into the snow or at least to act like a snow shovel, especially in downhill travel. Shoveling a ten-mile path with your legs is rather tiring. One compensates for this defect by stepping very high, and this is almost as tiring as shoveling. With an upturned toe and a heavier tail, deep snow can be handled without excessively high steps. The amount of upturn depends on the conditions for which the snowshoe is designed. Too high and long a toe merely adds weight to the shoe without increasing its carrying capacity. Extra weight must also be added to the heel for balance. The additional length makes the shoe more awkward to handle. Ideally, the toe should be long enough and with just enough upturn to handle the depth of snow expected.

The Maine or Michigan snowshoe. This is the standard all-purpose snowshoe and the one against which the performance of other types should be measured. The toe is tapered and turned up slightly, and the tail insures good tracking. Standard sizes are available that will provide enough flotation to handle just about any snow conditions and load. The pattern of the shoes is such that the legs do not have to be spread too far for a stride to be maintained. The shoes are reasonably maneuverable, and they are

Tracks of Maine shoes. The feet need not be kept very far apart, because the shoes are shaped so that the curves fit together. In walking, the edge of the moving shoe just clears the stationary one. Note the tail tracks. The tail drags behind, carrying some of the weight of the shoe.

SNOWSHOEING: WALKING ON THE DRIFTS   134

not impossible in bushy country. The standard lengths of forty-eight inches or less are short enough to carry on a pack without being terribly awkward. This is the snowshoe that most beginners should buy. The following are recommended sizes:

Usual weight with pack up to 125 lbs.—12″ x 42″
up to 170 lbs.—13″ x 48″
up to 225 lbs.—14″ x 48″

Some Canadian varieties with pointed toes will be a bit longer in each size.

The Pickerel snowshoe. This name is a descriptive one for the long narrow shoe also known as the Alaskan trail shoe and the Yukon trail shoe. It is designed for fast going on open ground. The standard size is about ten inches wide and forty-eight to sixty inches long. The tips of these shoes are turned high to clear deep snow, and the narrow track enables the experienced user to attain good speed. Shoes of this design were originally used for running down game. Their large area gives good flotation in deep, soft snow. For the beginner who plans to do a lot of hiking in open country with deep, powdery snow, a pickerel design is a good choice. It is even more inconvenient to carry on a pack than the Michigan shoe and is a horror in heavy brush. Like the Michigan it is poor for steep, soft slopes.

The pickerel and Yukon trail-type shoes are best made with a fairly pointed front and the toe hole placed well forward of the center of gravity. Some badly designed models with a wide front and centrally spaced toe hole pick up a great deal of snow on the front. The extra weight of the snow is very tiresome. The sizes of pickerel type shoes are generally ten by forty-eight inches for light people with packs, ten by fifty-six inches for most men, and twelve by sixty inches for heavy men with packs.

Cross-country snowshoes. These are similar to the pickerel type, but they taper less and are a bit shorter. The toe hole is closer to the front of the shoe, which turns up more sharply. These features make the cross-country shoe somewhat more maneuverable than the pickerel and reduce the possibility of snow piling up on the front of the shoe. Overlapping is not quite so good, however. Generally speaking, the cross-country model is good and bad in the same conditions as the pickerel. Ten by forty-six inches is the standard size, and it is adequate for most people. The shorter length makes it easier to pack than the longer pickerel.

Bearpaws. There are several types of bearpaw snowshoe, the standard bearpaw and variations that modify both its defects and advantages. The standard bearpaw is flat; it has no upturn at the toe. It is roughly oval-shaped, usually with a slight taper toward the heel, and the foot hole is far forward. There is no tail. Bearpaws are very maneuverable in areas where uncovered brush and obstacles cause the wearer of long, tailed shoes to tear his hair. On steep slopes that are soft enough to require snowshoes, bearpaws are excellent. The straight toe can be kicked into the slope, giving the climber a flat surface to stand on, a feat that is almost impossible with long curved toes. The foot rests in the step even when it is not kicked deeply, because the foot is well forward on the shoe. Bearpaws are excellent for doing chores, because of their maneuverability and because the toes do not stick far in front of you, keeping you from your work. They are easy to pack.

The list of vices for the bearpaw is not long, but it is convincing for anyone who does not absolutely require its virtues. The straight toe, excessive width, and wide, dragging heel make it a tiresome curse on the trail, especially in soft snow. If you need a bearpaw, check to see if one of its modifications will suit you as well, while ameliorating a few of its vices.

The modified bearpaw tapers more to the front and rear, adding some length to maintain area. The toe is raised somewhat to reduce diving, and the foot is placed farther back. There is still no tail, but the rear of the shoe is narrower than that of the true bearpaw, reducing the drag. The modified bearpaw retains the maneuverability of the original, while being a bit more feasible for trail use. Feet do not have to be quite so far apart, since the tapering allows the shoes to fit together when one is placed ahead. The modified design is still a poor trail snowshoe, but it is much better than the original. It is just as good in brush and generally rough terrain, and it is almost as good for utility uses around a cabin or camp. It is inferior to the standard bearpaw in steep snow, however, for the upturned front, which sticks out farther in front of the toe hole, is harder to kick into the slope. The modified bearpaw is generally preferable to the standard for all-around use in brushy areas, except where the straight toes are definitely needed for kicking steps. Even on steep slopes, the straight toes become an annoyance on the descent, when they dive under the snow with every step.

The Green Mountain bearpaw is another modification of the standard design. It is not tapered, but the toe is turned up, and the oval shape is longer and narrower. The tail-less design assures maneuverability, and the narrowness and upturned toe make it fairly good on the trail. It is not as good as other bearpaws for kicking up steep slopes and not as good as the tailed varieties for the trails, but it makes a good compromise in brushy areas that are not too mountainous.

Recommended sizes of the different types of bearpaws are listed below for the maximum weights of the wearer and pack.

Weight of wearer with pack up to	Standard bearpaw	Modified bearpaw	Green Mountain bearpaw
100 lbs.	12" x 26"		
125 lbs.	12" x 30"		
150 lbs.	13" x 28"		
200 lbs.	13" x 33", 14" x 30"	13" x 33"	10" x 36"
250 lbs.	15" x 30"	14" x 36"	

CHOOSING SNOWSHOES

If all the endless advantages and disadvantages just listed sound a bit confusing, don't worry about it. Just about any snowshoe will do what it's supposed to do—hold you up in the snow. Obviously, it's a good idea to get a type that will be most likely to suit the terrain where you'll be traveling if you're going to plunk down thirty or forty dollars for a pair. If you already have access to snowshoes, though, don't worry if they're the right type. As long as they are of reasonable size and are sturdy, they will serve well enough to get you started.

One inexpensive alternative that is sometimes available is the Army bearpaw, which can sometimes be found in surplus stores or basements. Those kept in dry places are usually still in good condition, and they're cheap. The design is that of the regular bearpaw.

Plastic snowshoes called Snow Treads have been on the market for a few years now. They are cheaper than regular shoes and much lighter. They are made in the shape of a modified bearpaw. Unfortunately, they are too small to be practical for most people except for emergency use. They might be worth trying for light women or children. They should also be good for a long trip when there is only light snow and conditions are good for walking, but snowshoes need to be carried in case the snows come while you are in the back country. Various breakage problems have occurred. Last year a larger version appeared but these weigh and cost as much as conventional designs, leaving little, if any, apparent advantage.

The standard filler for snowshoes is varnished rawhide. The best frames are made of ash. Neoprene-nylon material is now being used as a substitute filler by at least one manufacturer. Snow does not stick to this material, and it is extremely strong. Experiments with materials other than wood for frames have not yet resulted in any widely available snowshoes.

The size recommendations made above are general indications. Varying snow conditions and individual preferences can modify them, and obviously you will not always carry a pack of the same weight. A smaller shoe will tend to sink deeper, but one that is only slightly too small according to the charts will not make much difference. One that is much smaller should be used only on fairly hard snow or for emergency and auxiliary purposes. All the sizes listed can be purchased from at least one of the suppliers listed in Appendix C. Other sizes are available from these and other suppliers. It should be fairly simple for the reader to evaluate other sizes and designs from what has already been said.

HITCHES AND BINDINGS

The traditional method of attaching snowshoes to the feet was the lampwicking snowshoe hitch. Aside from the difficulty of finding lampwicking these days, the main difficulty with this hitch is its floppiness and absence of control. Some people still like it, some for its virtues and some for its snob appeal. It is worth trying for

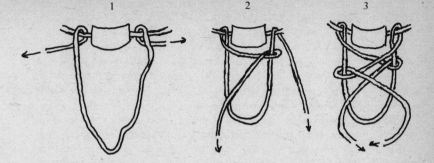

How to tie a squaw hitch. Some sort of soft webbing makes the best squaw hitch. The one shown is tied on a snowshoe with a permanent toe strap, which is always preferable, and which is essential with hard-toed boots. The same squaw hitch can be tied without a toe strap, or a separate toe strap can be tied. Finish the hitch off with a square knot behind the heel.

fun and learning for emergency use, anyway, and a drawing is included. Soft nylon webbing will work well as a substitute for lampwicking, but rope is not satisfactory and should be reserved for emergencies.

The bindings that have gradually replaced hitches give good control when they are well-designed. The normal material is leather, and this is satisfactory, but the new neoprene-nylon types are much better. They don't freeze, and snow and ice don't stick to them. They will also wear longer than leather bindings. Best of all, the neoprene-nylon material doesn't stretch, so that the curse of tightening your bindings a dozen times a day is gone. Somehow, the adjustment was always needed just when you were halfway across a barbed wire fence. Neoprene-nylon is more expensive, however.

Aside from the material, there are several types of bindings, the main difference being in rigidity and control. There is no best type, and you should pick according to the type of terrain on which you will travel and the footwear you will use. It is silly to pay in money and comfort for a very stable binding if you won't need it. With soft footwear on moderate terrain the sandal-type

Hitches and bindings   139

binding is adequate and comfortable. This consists of a very wide strap into which the toe is inserted. A heel strap holds the foot in the toe piece. Both the heel strap and the attachments to the shoe are connected with the toe piece. More control is gained and flexibility lost when an extra strap is added over the instep to hold the heel strap in place. The H-type with heel strap going directly to the shoe is next in control, and finally a piece going over the toe is added in the Howe binding to prevent the boot from sliding forward in steep downhill going. The last two types are good in rough country, because they give the strong lateral control that is desirable on steep terrain. You will be happy with the sandal-type for snowshoeing across gentle fields. You may even be happy with lampwicking!

FOOTWEAR

What you wear between your foot and your snowshoe will depend on the terrain you will frequent, the temperatures that are likely, and what you may already have. If you are going into the mountains and you plan to climb up steep slopes, you will have to have some kind of mountaineering boot. For gentle terrain, lighter and more flexible footwear is cheaper and more comfortable. In any case, lightweight hiking or work boots are inadequate for winter conditions.

Moderate terrain, moderate temperatures. The biggest problem in these conditions is the wetting of the boots and socks, which then lose all their insulating qualities. Wet or melted snow can rapidly soak through lightweight boots, and the snow then chills the feet thoroughly, with subsequent frostbite becoming a distinct possibility.

Probably the best footwear in these conditions are the rubber-bottom boots with leather tops. These are completely waterproof on the bottom, and proper care keeps the tops very water-repellent. They are much more comfortable to wear than all-rubber pacs; they are lighter and do not present nearly so much of a condensation problem. Insoles should be worn with them for insula-

Cheap, light footwear. An overshoe with buckles cut off and left open for ventilation, wool felt liner, and long gaiter to keep snow out. Spare liners must be carried in case these get wet.

tion and to absorb moisture, and several pairs of spare insoles should be carried. The bottoms may be insulated, and the insulated models can be worn in quite cold temperatures. The best insulation for this purpose is closed-cell foam, such as Ensolite, the cells of which cannot absorb water. Some rubber-bottom boots are now becoming available with Vibram lug soles, which wear longer and give better footing and insulation to the bottom of the foot but I have not yet found a pair that fits. Also, none are yet available with Vibram soles which are also insulated throughout the boot.

Insulated rubber pacs are adequate for these conditions, though they are not very comfortable. If they are used, however, they *must* be either the Korean double-vapor barrier type or use closed-cell foam for insulation. The double-vapor barrier seals the insulation between two completely waterproof layers and prevents its getting wet. Tight-fitting rubber pacs with insulation that can become wet should not be used, since it will be wet very quickly by perspiration from the feet.

One inexpensive type of alternative footwear for these conditions is a normal rubberized fabric overshoe. I have used these fairly successfully with wool felt liners and heavy wool socks by

Footwear 141

cutting off all but the bottom buckle and wearing long nylon gaiters overlapping the top to keep the snow out. No shoes are worn, so the combination is light and comfortable. The overshoes open widely enough to allow quite a bit of air circulation while walking, so that the condensation problem is reduced. Even so, an extra pair of felt liners should be carried, and they can also be used to keep the feet warm in the sleeping bag. For trips longer than three or four days, you should make a pair of closed-cell foam liners to the same pattern as the felt liners. These can not accidentally be wet through as the open-cell foam-type can.

With any rubberized footwear, no matter how well it is designed, the condensation problem will plague you, and you should plan for it by carrying more socks and inner soles than you would with other footwear.

Moderate terrain, cold temperatures. Under these conditions, the classical footwear of the North—high-topped moccasin shoe pacs —is the most practical and comfortable footgear. The pacs are high-topped moccasins with flexible leather soles. They are very light. They should be large enough for several pairs of heavy socks to be worn inside. Sokkets, low felt socks that are worn over a regular pair of heavy socks, can also be used. This combination is light and warm—a joy to wear.

The temperature range of moccasin pacs can be greatly extended with the use of a pair of fabric overboots, not the normal heavy overshoe, but a pair like the type described in the previous chapter. These are light, adding hardly any weight to the foot, even when an insulation layer is included. They extend the lower temperature range of moccasins down to anything you are likely to encounter, and if they are made of coated fabric, they will also enable you to use this type of footwear in wet conditions where running water is not present. You can make overboots fairly easily, or you can obtain them from one of the suppliers listed in Appendix C.

Steep or rough terrain. In mountainous areas where a lot of steep terrain will be encountered, mountaineering boots are necessary, as discussed in the preceeding chapter. Occasional steep slopes can be handled with the footwear described above, if snowshoe crampons are used, and if all climbing is on moderate slopes that are well-covered with snow, boots may not be necessary in the mountains. Really rough terrain often requires carrying snow-shoes, however, and footwear with rigid soles is necessary. Mountaineering boots are also adaptable to wet or cold conditions, using the methods described earlier.

GETTING AROUND ON SNOWSHOES

Snowshoeing is, as stated in the beginning of the chapter, fairly easy to learn, and the techniques can be practiced on real trips. Most snowshoers carry one or two ski poles as an aid to balance and a particular help in righting themselves after spills. Some mountaineers, who carry ice axes, use the ice axes for the same purpose after attaching a removable ski-pole basket on the bottom. Ski-pole length does not much matter, but the basket width should be six inches or so, rather than the narrow sort now preferred by downhill skiers. This is to your budgetary advantage, since many of the older types can now be got cheaply second-hand.

Poles are of even more advantage in rough country, when they serve as props during awkward maneuvers over and around obstacles and as aids for climbing slopes. Snowshoe crampons of some sort are necessary in steep terrain and are often very useful on slippery crusted snow at any angle. Many types have been improvised, and what is needed is simply a few points about an inch long attached to the snowshoe just under the ball of the foot. They should be easily removable, and almost any device that satisfies these requirements will do the trick. My own preference is for a pair of aluminum-alloy instep crampons that can be attached to either snowshoes or boots. It is hard to find instep crampons that can be attached rigidly to snowshoes without removing the side tabs, but there are some available, and the versatility of the dual purpose makes them worthwhile. Almost any instep crampons will work after the tabs are broken or sawed off. A cross-strapping arrangement that will hold the crampons securely should be devised and tested ahead of time. Sections of T-shaped aluminium rod can also be used to make effective snowshoe crampons. See Gene Prater's book, listed in the appendix.

Climbing in steep soft snow. Weight shifting to left foot on the platform made by the horizontal snowshoe.

SNOWSHOEING: WALKING ON THE DRIFTS   144

The right foot comes up and back.

Right shoe is kicked straight into the slope.

Getting around on snowshoes 145

Climbing slopes with snowshoes is fairly easy to learn after a little practice. It is not always easy, but the beginner will do as well as the expert before too long. On moderate slopes and on steep, hard slopes when crampons are being used, the shoe is simply stamped flat on the slope, while the toe of the boot protrudes through the toe hole. The toe gains some purchase on the snow itself, and the ball of the foot rests on the snowshoe thongs. With straight-toed bearpaws on steep, soft slopes, the shoe is kicked straight into the snow.

Descent is somewhat trickier, and in soft snow or breakable crust it can be just as tiring, since the toe of the shoe tends to drive under the snow. The only real trick is to stand up fairly straight. Sometimes a slide or a sliding step can be achieved, similar to skiing. In this case the poles are usually held together, and they can then be used for braking. Be careful not to slide where there is a dangerous drop-off below or where it is so slippery that you may not be able to control the slide. A shuffling step keeps the toes from diving under.

Changing direction on steep slopes and crossing obstacles such as fences are both accomplished by a maneuver similar to that

A helpful binding in slippery spots. This sandal binding has prongs protruding from the bottom. Really steep hard slopes require longer removable crampons.

used by skiers, the kick turn. It is hard to describe and to learn, but is fairly easy after you have done it a few times. Study the illustrations in the next chapter and then go out and try it a few times on flat ground. Try crossing the barbed wire fence *after* you have mastered it.

VIII

Skiing the White Wilderness

Skis are unquestionably the most elegant way to stay atop the snow, and under the right circumstances they are much more than that, for they give the skier the feeling of soaring flight. Even on flat terrain, the skier has the great advantage of being able to glide with each step. When the depth of snow is adequate, the skier can do just about everything that the snowshoer can, and a good deal more, besides.

The skier's only problem is the depth of the snow cover. Skis tend to require somewhat deeper snow than snowshoes, especially on rough terrain. Once the snow lies deep enough to cover most of the small brush and rocks, this disadvantage is unimportant. In the Western mountains, where the snow lies heavy all winter long, it is rarely a disadvantage at all. In some other regions, such as New England, where the brush is heavy and snow is sometimes light, snowshoes often have an edge over skis except on prepared tracks. Skis can be used on a golf course with only a few inches of snow, but fighting through brushy country with only a few feet of snow is easier with just boots or with bearpaw snowshoes; long skis or long snowshoes are a nuisance.

Once the snow is deep enough, skiers have most of the advantages. On little bumps or big hills, they can slide down the downhill sides, while snowshoers must keep on walking. Skis are easier to use on steep slopes, because the edges can be dug into the slope. On the flat, a gliding step can be developed that eats up the miles

The heavy snow in places like Yosemite National Park covers underbrush and small trees, making skiing easy even in wooded areas.

more quickly and pleasantly than can ever be managed with snowshoes.

The main objections to skiing as a way to get into the wilderness are that it is more dangerous than snowshoeing and that a lot of skills have to be acquired before one can get off. These criticisms have some validity, but they really apply mainly to one kind of skiing.

Skiing equipment is made in a wide variety to meet very different requirements. The best-known ski equipment is downhill gear —the type of skis, bindings, and boots that are used by skiers on prepared mountain slopes who are carried to the top by lifts. Skis for this type of skiing are heavy and wide for stability at high speeds; they are fairly stiff and have steel edges for control on hard steep slopes and for carving out turns. The boots are very heavy with flat, inflexible soles, and they are designed to provide a great deal of support to the ankles, allowing practically no movement to the side or rear. These boots are held rigidly to the ski by a binding that is designed to have no give at all, except for safety release features intended to prevent bad injuries in a fall.

At the opposite extreme is cross-country ski-racing equipment designed for use on a prepared track. Everything is very light and flexible. Skis are very narrow and springy and without steel edges. Boots are light and low-cut, resembling track shoes more than their downhill cousins. Bindings consist of a light arrangement that fastens the shoe to the ski only at the toe of the sole.

Neither one of these extremes is suitable for skiing into the wilderness for a few days or a few weeks, but the equipment that is suitable ranges from slightly modified downhill equipment to slightly sturdier cross-country gear. It all depends on what kind of country you'll be going to. The problem of safety and the amount of skill required to start are dependent on the same factor. The flexible ski bindings used on cross-country skis are no more likely to break your leg than a snowshoe binding, and that is pretty unlikely. On the other hand, any binding that can be made rigid enough to handle downhill skiing on steep mountain slopes does present some hazards: soaring like a bird sometimes ends with an undignified crash landing. Such equipment also takes some skill to use, and this skill must be learned on the practice slopes. The heavier equipment tends to cost a good deal more. Lightweight cross-country touring equipment doesn't cost any more than snowshoe gear, and it is not much more difficult to learn to use.

Ski mountaineering and mountain touring require relatively heavy equipment. The author in Yosemite.

The prospective wilderness skier in this country now has a fairly complete spectrum of equipment offered him, so that an adequate compromise can be got easily for almost any purpose. This is quite a change from the situation a few years ago, when wilderness skiers had to spend the summers improvising with old downhill equipment. The choice between the types of available equipment may seem a little complicated, but it really isn't. There is quite a bit of leeway in the use of various types of skis. Take a look at the chart presented later in the chapter. Any compatible combination of equipment listed as good for terrain fairly similar to yours should be all right. The chart should help the beginner get the best combination.

WHAT KIND OF TERRAIN?

Snow falls on all sorts of slopes, ranging from board-flat prairies to steep mountain faces. A very wide range of these are suitable for skiing, including slopes too steep to walk up without crampons, but it would be surprising if some kinds of skis were not more suitable for the prairies and some for the mountains. It shouldn't be very difficult to narrow down the choices quite a bit; just look out your window or glance through the pictures of your last few hiking trips. If there isn't a mountain to be seen anywhere, then don't get mountain-touring equipment. It might be very romantic to have skis that are capable of handling steep, icy slopes, but if there aren't any within 500 miles the steel edges will just get heavy and spoil your fun sliding across the fields. On the other hand, it's not much fun traversing one of those icy slopes with pin bindings and wooden-edged skis.

There is nothing esoteric involved in judging the terrain in which you will be skiing. Is it rough with small obstacles during the snowy seasons, or is it smooth? Is it flat; is it composed of rolling hills; is it very rough country with small hills, or is it mountainous? If it is mountainous, are the mountains gentle enough so that fairly easy routes can usually be found, or are they generally steep and precipitous? Is the vegetation on them relatively open or thick and heavy? If the cover is heavy, do you plan to follow trails through it, or beat your way through the bush?

What kind of terrain? 151

Downhill or mountain skis with steel edges are needed in alpine terrain like this to handle icy slopes.

SKIING THE WHITE WILDERNESS

152

Are the trails well-developed, like regular skiing trails, logging roads, or power-line right-of-ways, or are they narrow foot trails? Once you answer these questions, it should be a fairly simple matter to figure out a range of equipment that would be suitable, from the lightest to the heaviest that would be practical for the sort of terrain you will be skiing. Choice within this narrower range is largely a matter of personal preference.

TOURING ON SKIS

The technique of touring cross-country on skis doesn't vary much, whether one is using light touring skis or heavy, modified downhill equipment. The main difference is that the light equipment enables the skier on easy trails to make much faster progress with much less effort, while the heavier equipment makes it possible to handle more difficult terrain. A skier good with touring technique strides along with as much glide as possible, and this requires that the heel of his boot be free to lift off the ski. The more free play allowed the heel by the binding and the flexibility of the boot, the longer strides the skier will be able to take. For this reason, the tourer should pick the most flexible combination of boots and bindings that will also satisfy the other requirements of the terrain on which he will ski.

The technique of getting a glide at the end of each step is much easier to learn than to explain. The skier plants one ski and the opposite pole, leans forward slightly, and pushes with both the foot and the pole. The other leg comes forward rapidly to throw extra power into the stride and the skier's weight is shifted to this ski as the push is finished. There is a glide, and then the procedure is repeated with the other ski and pole. The amount of glide that can be achieved is quite variable. With light touring skis and a day pack, some glide can often be got even on uphill stretches, and the speed that can be reached on packed trails is phenomenal. On the other hand, with heavy skis, a heavy pack, and unbroken snow, the skier usually gets little glide even on the flat. Under such circumstances he settles for a walk or, better, a swinging stride.

The skier has to have some traction when he plants his ski, otherwise it will simply slip backward when he pushes forward, especially when he is climbing a hill. This traction is achieved by applying an appropriate wax to the bottom of the ski. Cross-country waxes are chosen to be soft enough at the temperature of the snow so that snow crystals will make tiny impressions in the surface of the wax, producing a high static friction. At the same time the wax must be hard enough to run forward in the snow. No one wax will satisfy these conditions for all types and temperatures of snow, so the tourer must carry a number of waxes. The technique of waxing will be discussed in more detail later in the chapter.

SKIS

In selecting equipment for wilderness skiing, the traveler must match his components with each other, as well as with the terrain and his particular requirements. He may, for example, want to use a pair of heavy mountaineering boots for skiing, in which case he will have to choose bindings and skis that can be used with those boots. A chart is included below to help the reader with this problem. If no special considerations dictate particular boots or bindings, the beginner may as well choose his skis first.

Length. The usual rule of thumb is for the tips of the skis to reach the wrist or palm of an upstretched hand. Shorter skis are not advisable if you will be carrying a weekend pack in soft snow, since they will not provide adequate flotation. Longer skis may be preferred by some experienced skiers; they give better flotation, especially for heavy people or packs, but they are more difficult to turn and clumsier in brush.

Types of skis. Unfortunately, though a good variety of skis are now available in this country, there is little uniformity in the use of names or descriptions. What one dealer describes as a standard touring ski will be another's wide touring ski. Dimensions are often not of much more help, since some catalogues will give the width under the foot, the narrowest part of the ski, while others use the widest part of the ski for a dimension. The names that are used here are not definitive, but the approximate dimensions given should enable the reader to compare them with various catalogue descriptions, as well as allowing the comparison of skis in catalogues that use different measurements. Weights are only indicative of what may be expected for average lengths.

	Approximate width at center	Approximate width at front	Approximate weight
Cross-country racing skis	48 mm. ($1\frac{7}{8}''$)	55 mm. ($2\frac{3}{16}''$)	$2\frac{1}{2}$–3 lbs.
Extra light touring skis	50 mm. ($1\frac{15}{16}''$)	60 mm. ($2\frac{3}{8}''$)	3–$4\frac{1}{2}$ lbs.
Light touring skis	52 mm. ($2\frac{1}{16}''$)	65 mm. ($2\frac{9}{16}''$)	$3\frac{3}{4}$–$4\frac{3}{4}$ lbs.
Standard touring skis	60 mm. ($2\frac{3}{8}''$)	72 mm. ($2\frac{13}{16}''$)	$4\frac{1}{2}$–$5\frac{1}{2}$ lbs.
Mountaineering skis	65 mm. ($2\frac{9}{16}''$)	75 mm. ($2\frac{15}{16}''$)	6–$7\frac{1}{2}$ lbs.
Downhill skis	70 mm. ($2\frac{3}{4}''$)	85 mm. ($3\frac{7}{16}''$)	$8\frac{1}{2}$–10 lbs.

Soles. In general, wooden soles are still best for touring skis, since they hold waxes better than the various plastic soles that have been tried so far. Some may prefer plastic soles anyway, because this eliminates the need of putting on base wax. The running waxes are applied directly to the plastic. Teflon soles are fine for downhill running, but wax will not adhere to them, so for touring they must be reserved for skis that will be used for climbing only with plush or sealskin climbers. Climbers will be discussed later in the chapter, but I would recommend against this choice for all-around back-country touring, even in the mountains. On rolling stretches, waxing is much preferable to the use of climbers, edging, or herringboning up the hills, and the tourer should choose a wooden or plastic base that will take wax, even if he also uses climbers on steep slopes.

Wooden soles on mountain skis should be made of hickory, which will wear much longer than birch or beech. Hickory soles are advisable on any skis for longer service, especially in areas with very rough, granular snow.

One new type of sole which will probably attract many is the "fish-scale" base on a line of fiberglass skis. Small semi-circular plastic scales run along the sole. These grip the snow when the skier pushes, but lie flat in forward running, eliminating most of the need for waxes and climbers. They should be excellent for wilderness use, though I personally don't like the noise they make or the slight slip at the beginning of the push.

Edges. Mountain and downhill skis must have steel edges, the only kind that will give control on the steep, icy slopes these skis are designed to handle, especially for a skier with a heavy pack. Steel edges are heavy, however, and they are undesirable when they are not needed. Skis lighter than the "mountaineering" category should not have steel edges. For rough country where steel edges are not required, lignostone edges can be used for extra control and better wearing qualities. Lignostone is a specially treated and compressed beech wood, which is quite hard but much lighter than steel. This type of edge is advisable except in very easy terrain. Aluminum or plastic edges have similar characteristics.

Stiffness. If you are buying touring skis, you should not have to worry too much about stiffness in your first pair. Touring skis are quite limber, and they should be. The amount of pressure you put on your skis will vary depending on the size of the pack you are carrying. If you plan to use downhill skis for touring, they should be more flexible than the standard downhill ski. Those hard-sprung slalom skis are a pain in the neck in the woods, since the tips always bury themselves when you are crossing small depressions. As long as the skis are fairly flexible, stiffness isn't too critical for touring, and the beginner shouldn't worry about it.

In general, skis for touring should have a lot of camber, but should not be too stiff. Heavier people and heavier packs call for stiffer skis. Skis made for touring are stiffer at the back to give the skis a forward spring. Mountain and downhill skis are equally stiff at front and back for better turning.

On the trail, touring skis that are too stiff will not give very good traction for the pushing ski because the sole under the foot is not pressing down on the snow. You can check to see if this is really the trouble by looking at the bottom of your ski. The wax should wear fairly evenly; if it all wears off the ends and doesn't seem to be wearing much at all in the middle, your skis are too stiff. Skis that are too limber feel draggy when you are sliding, haven't much spring, and the wax tends to wear off much faster in the middle than the ends.

WHICH SKI?

The descriptions below and the table that summarizes the discussion of equipment can be used as a rough guide to the appropriateness of various types of equipment. A few general considerations should be mentioned first, however. The first is that a fairly wide range of equipment *can* be used in various circumstances. No one should hesitate to undertake a trip in terrain different from that he frequents because his equipment isn't ideal. That is carrying specialization of equipment to a ridiculous extreme. Still, there are reasons why particular equipment is best for a particular sort of country, and certain limitations have to be observed.

These limitations apply much more to the wilderness traveler than the backyard tourer. Touring in wilderness areas requires stronger equipment than day touring on prepared trails. Packs increase the load on skis. Terrain is rougher, and the skis should stand up to it without breaking; even though contraction bands and ski tips are carried, it is much easier to get home with your skis intact. Trail must be broken, often through crusty snow, and this is rough on light skis. Boots have to be adequate to protect the feet in severe conditions, and the skis must be heavy enough for use with the boots required. As a rule, skis that are at the light extreme for the terrain you will ski should be avoided in wilderness backpacking. Touring in difficult country with very light equipment is best reserved for day trips, when the consequences of a broken ski would not be too serious.

Increasing the width of a ski improves stability, so that wider skis are easier for beginners to handle, are easier to ski on with packs, and are easier to manage in downhill running. Increasing the width also improves the flotation of the skis, but not nearly as much as one would expect. Width must be greatly increased to gain the same amount of flotation that a small increase in length will give. Narrower skis, while they require a bit more practice, are much nicer to tour with, *providing* they are adequate to the kind of skiing you will do. A light touring ski just will not suffice for long backpacking trips in mountainous terrain.

As equipment gets stronger, the trend is towards lighter equipment. Fiberglass is now being used both to reinforce the tips of wood skis and to make entire skis.

Cross-country racing skis are designed for use on prepared tracks. They are very light and quite fragile, and while they can be used for some light touring, they are not at all suitable for wilderness travel.

Extra-light touring skis are all right for touring with a lightweight and flexible boot and binding combination on good trails or open country that is not too rough. They should not be used for deep wilderness backpacking or for breaking trail in areas that have a lot of crusty snow. They might be a good choice for someone who wants to do a lot of day touring in easy country with an occasional overnight trip in the same sort of terrain.

Light touring skis are somewhat more rugged and stable skis for the same general conditions as the extra-light ones. For day trips, experienced tourers may want to use these on moderately difficult trails and rolling country. They are fine for easy backpacking trips, but they are not designed to stand up in backpacking on rough terrain or for much trailbreaking in heavy, crusted snow. They are poor for any sort of steep downhill running.

Standard touring skis are the best all-around skis for wilderness backpacking, when steep mountainous slopes won't be encountered. A good grade standard touring ski is very strong and quite stable, but it is still light enough to move along at a good clip without being too tiring. People who want to tour in the Midwest or the non-mountainous sections of the Northeast would do well with standard touring skis for long winter backpacking trips over summer foot trails.

Mountaineering skis are designed to give the control on steep slopes that downhill skis have, while retaining some of the flexibility and cross-country speed of touring skis. Mountain skis should always be equipped with steel edges and bindings that will provide downhill tension when it is needed. Without these features, the extra weight is wasted. Even with these features, mountain skis will only weigh half of what downhill skis often do. They are a little narrower than downhill skis, and they are still not designed for steep downhill skiing at high speeds. Mountaineering skis are stronger than touring skis, a mixed blessing. They also break more easily than downhill skis, and have to be treated with a little more care. Mountaineering skis are excellent for all kinds of touring in really difficult country and for mountain skiing with boots of moderate weight and stiffness, like heavy mountaineering boots or lightweight ski-mountaineering boots. Such boots do not have enough stiffness to really control downhill skis, but they are perfect in combination with mountain skis. Heavier ski-mountaineering boots give even more control.

Downhill skis, even when they are of the fairly light and flexible kind, are rather heavy for touring cross-country. They do have the advantage of providing all the control that is ever needed, and for this reason they are often preferred for touring in difficult mountainous terrain or when the objective is a downhill run on some wilderness mountain that must be reached by touring. The strength of downhill skis makes them less likely to break than lighter touring skis, especially when they are made of metal. This advantage has a double edge, however, since your leg might break, instead. Safety release bindings are essential on downhill skis that are used in the wilderness. Conservative skiing is still necessary, however. The fact that the safety binding prevents a bad sprain from becoming a fracture doesn't really make the task of getting home much easier. One of the advantages of the lighter skis and the bindings that go with them is that they will usually break before your legs are injured. It's still a lot easier to get home after breaking a ski than a leg.

BOOTS

Boots follow the same general pattern as skis, ranging from lightweight and very flexible cross-country racing shoes to the modern cast-plastic frames that encase the padded foot of many a modern downhill skier. The wilderness skier makes the same sort of compromise choice of a boot as he does with skis, except that for some travelers the boot must serve additional purposes to that of skiing. The skis, boots and bindings must be either chosen together or chosen to match equipment you already possess. All are complementary, and a badly matched set of equipment can possess all the vices and none of the virtues of the various components.

The basic situations in which particular types of skis excel have already been mentioned, and there is no point in repeating them all. Boots will be discussed in terms of the kinds of skis with which they are best used and their special characteristics for uses other than skiing. Naturally, your choice may go in either direction. If you are planning on skiing in to the base of a difficult mountain that you plan to climb using technical mountaineering skills, you will probably pick your boot first, and then find a binding and skis to match.

Touring boots are light, flexible boots designed for ski touring. The best ones are excellent, but many are not heavy enough for wilderness touring, where your feet are often plowing through deep, cold snow and where heavy packs and rough country may prevent you from going fast enough to keep your feet warm. Touring boots for wilderness use should be fully insulated and should have a construction that makes it possible to waterproof them effectively, without a lot of thin leather or sewn-through seams. Height is a matter of personal choice, providing your arrangement of pants, socks, and gaiters enables you to make a snowproof seal at the top of the boots. Low-top shoes are often used for touring with just knicker socks, but this practice is only suitable for prepared courses or well-consolidated snow. Deep powder will soon soak and freeze your feet if you use low shoes without gaiters or long pants under wilderness conditions. Higher tops give more ankle support, of course, which is desirable with heavier ski and binding arrangements.

You should make sure that whatever type of touring boot you are considering is compatible with the type of binding you want to use. Some touring boots will fit pin bindings and some will not. Finally, the boot *must* be adequate for the temperatures you expect to encounter. Light weight is desirable in touring equipment, and a lot of touring is done at high speeds for periods of a few hours, after which the tourer retires to warmer quarters. For wilderness touring, your boots will stay on your feet all day, while you climb hills, take rests, stop for food, and pitch camp. The boots must be heavy enough to protect your feet from the elements and large enough for sufficient socks or other insulators. For wilderness touring, especially in mountainous areas, it is often necessary to use a heavy winter-mountaineering boot or a ski-mountaineering boot, simply to protect the feet, especially if the skis may be removed for climbing steep slopes.

Mountaineering boots may be used for ski touring if they are heavy and sturdy. Either double boots or single ones, both discussed in Chapter VI, may be suitable. Luckily, with the introduction of the Silvretta binding, which will be discussed below, modern mountaineering boots are now much more suitable for use with touring skis than they were before, since this binding allows the foot to pivot almost as well as the pin binding, though with a bit less grace, even when stiff-soled winter climbing boots are used. Mountaineering boots may also be used with the several types of ski-mountaineering bindings on mountain and downhill skis and with some of the standard cable-type touring bindings for touring skis.

You should check to see that the binding and boot will fit each other and that the boot will be held positively. Mountaineering boots generally have a very narrow welt to reduce leverage on small holds, and this may not provide enough purchase for the bindings to hook over. Again the Silvretta is excellent, and I have found that it will fit some boots with very narrow welts. A groove can be filed in the heel of any boot to accommodate the cable.

Mountaineering boots are not ski boots, and even the heavier ones will not give you really good downhill control. If you are getting skis and bindings that will enable you to do fast downhill skiing, you will probably be better off with a heavy pair of ski-mountaineering boots.

Ski-mountaineering boots have a considerable range in weight and rigidity. The lightest ones are medium-weight mountaineering boots modified to accommodate cable bindings by cutting a cable groove in the heel and by extending the sole in front and squaring it off. The heavier ski-mountaineering boots are adequate for fairly rigorous downhill skiing but have soles that are flexible enough for touring. All these boots have Vibram-type soles, and they have sufficiently narrow welts to allow fairly severe technical climbing.

The lighter ski-mountaineering boots are subject to just about the same considerations as mountaineering boots, since that is what they are, except that they are better adapted to most touring bindings. Heavy ski-mountaineering boots should have enough padding to provide good insulation against the cold and good lateral support for the ankle when laced tightly, and they should be sturdy enough to withstand strong downhill tension. They should still be fairly comfortable for walking. The heavier varieties are suitable for use with mountain skis and downhill skis. Some of the best ones are also quite cheap, and they make quite good downhill skiing boots, besides being much more versatile.

Other boots. Ski tourers once used old leather downhill boots for touring, but this method has become increasingly less satisfactory as downhill boots have become heavier and more rigid. These days, just about any downhill boot that is flexible enough for touring is of such poor quality that you shouldn't use it, though you may have an older pair of flexible-soled downhill boots that is satisfactory for touring. If you are buying a new pair of boots to serve for touring and downhill skiing, a pair of heavy ski-mountaineering boots is the best compromise.

Boots for ski touring. On the left are light, low touring shoes, not well suited for extended tours in deep snow, nor for use with heavier skis. Next are standard-weight touring boots, good in all conditions with light skis, providing they have good insulation. Third is a pair of standard mountain boots, good with standard touring skis or mountain skis. On the right are pairs of light- and heavy-weight ski mountaineering boots.

Work boots are generally not satisfactory for wilderness touring, since they are too light to protect the feet from the cold, are difficult to fit to bindings, and are almost impossible to waterproof adequately.

Fitting boots. It is important for any ski boots to fit well, but a bad fit is much more serious in wilderness skiing than it is on commercial slopes. Boots should be tried on over all the socks or inner boots with which they will be worn. Fit should be snug around the heel, but there should be no binding or tight spots anywhere that may cramp circulation. There should be enough room at the front to permit curling and wiggling the toes. Walking should not cause the heels to slide up, since blisters are likely to result. Pull-on loops at the back of the ankle are helpful and with high, heavy boots they are almost essential; frozen boots can be very, very difficult to get on in the morning.

BINDINGS

Bindings range from light and flexible to heavy and rigid in the same way that skis and boots do, and the choice of a binding is fairly simple once the first two components have been selected.

Pin-type bindings are the type used for cross-country racing, and they are also excellent bindings for use with light or extra-light touring skis and touring boots. These bindings attach to the toe of the boot with a clamp pressing the toe of the boot down onto three or four pins that fit into the bottom of the toe of the sole. This clamp is attached to the ski, and the boot is not held at any other point so that it is almost completely free to move forward and back, while still retaining some lateral control of the light ski.

Pin bindings are well-suited to use on moderate terrain where edge control is not needed and loads are not too heavy—roughly the same conditions where light touring skis can be used effectively. Like the light skis, they are unsuited to hard trailbreaking, steep downhill running, or heavy backpacking. Boots must be mated to the bindings, so that usually only touring boots can be used with

Two types of light touring outfits. Below is a standard rat trap pin binding. Above is a variation on this type which fastens with a latch when the toe is kicked in.

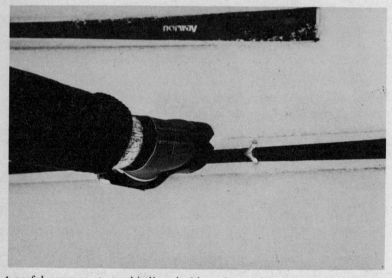

A useful accessory to toe bindings is this wedge, which gives the skier better edge control when the heel rests on the ski.

pin bindings. Not all touring boots are made to fit pin bindings, but you shouldn't have any difficulty finding a pair that is.

Many similar bindings to the pin-type are available, with the common characteristic that they fasten to the toe of the boot. They have the same advantages and disadvantages as a pin binding.

Cable-type bindings are more varied, and most touring bindings fall into this class. A metal cable runs behind the heel and holds the toe of the boot in the toepiece, which may be of several types. The cable may be attached directly to the toepiece or to the ski ahead of the toepiece. The Tempo binding has side-irons that hold the toe in place and a cable running back directly from the toe irons around the heel. This allows considerable flexibility and makes a good touring binding for standard-width touring skis when no difficult terrain or steep downhill running will be encountered. Either touring boots or some other boot with a squared toe that will fit the binding must be used. The heel cannot be clamped down to the ski for downhill or edge control with the Tempo binding.

Other types of cable bindings have cables that attach to the ski ahead of the toepiece. The most common, which is similar to the old beartrap binding, is made by a number of manufacturers and has front toe irons like the Tempo. When a cable binding of this sort is purchased, the front cable guides must be on the toe irons, not on the skis, so that the cable will not tend to hold the heel down. With the front-throw cable, hooks can be attached to the side of the ski that will hold the cable and the heel down for downhill runs or edge control on icy slopes. This arrangement is satisfactory for occasional use on difficult terrain where there is little danger of a bad fall on a downhill run, but this binding is too rigid to be safe for much use in downhill skiing. The pin and Tempo bindings are flexible enough so that when they are being used with light skis there is little danger of injuring a leg in a fall; the binding will come off or the ski will break first. With heavier skis and a beartrap binding, especially with the cable hooked down, the risk of injury is too high, especially since safer bindings are available that are more satisfactory in other respects as well.

The Silvretta binding is the most versatile binding available for wilderness touring. It uses a front-throw cable that passes under the toe of the boot before going around the heel. Shaped rods form a trap for the toe, and the whole trap pivots forward, giving more freedom of motion than any binding except the pin-type.

Bindings   165

Silvretta bindings in use with mountain skis and heavy double mountaineering boots—an excellent arrangement for mountain touring.

Two types of touring arrangements using regular alpine skis. Above is a triangular toepiece, cable binding, and removable side attachment for touring. Below is the preferable Ramy binding.

The cable can be hooked down on the sides for downhill use, and the binding has safety-release features that make it suitable for use on difficult terrain. The front trap can be used with touring boots, ski-mountaineering boots, and with a number of mountaineering boots that have welts too narrow to be used with most beartrap bindings. Silvrettas are well-suited for use with standard touring and mountain skis, and they are satisfactory for use with light touring skis when there is reason to use a mountaineering boot with very light skis. The binding is too light for use with standard downhill skis, except very light ones.

The Ramy and Eckel bindings are the best bindings for wilderness use when full downhill control is wanted with heavy boots and skis. These bindings look like standard beartrap bindings, but the side irons are held by a spring-loaded safety release, so that they will open in a bad fall. The use of a cable with hooks permits a reasonable amount of heel lift, making this type of binding good for ski mountaineering and touring on rough terrain with skis too heavy for the Silvretta bindings. These bindings do not allow nearly the heel lift of the Silvretta.

The most common downhill binding using a front-throw cable is the Marker-type triangular toepiece. This binding provides the

Bindings 167

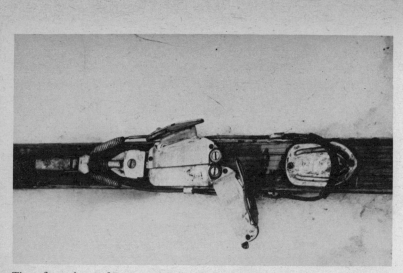

The safety release of Ramy and Eckel bindings allows half the toe iron to pivot out. No extra attachment is required for touring.

safety release that is necessary for downhill skiing, but when the cable is loose enough for touring, the toe of the boot tends to come out of the binding. Several attachments are available that prevent the boot toe from slipping to the side while touring. The attachments are removed or flipped out of the way when a downhill run is made. This arrangement is a bit awkward, and I definitely don't recommend it as an ideal binding. The dual purpose of a full downhill safety binding and touring binding is better served by the Ramy or Eckel. If you want to convert your present downhill equipment for mountain touring, though, and you already have this type of binding, the touring attachments are cheaper and less trouble to install than a new binding, and they will serve your purpose. I have used this arrangement on many mountain tours.

Several step-in bindings have been introduced in the last couple of years that include attachments for touring. The step-in heel, which has a safety release, holds the boot rigidly to the ski for downhill runs, and a hinged piece allows the heel to lift for touring. These bindings are heavier and much more expensive than those already mentioned and have no real advantages to offer the wilderness tourer. They are useful mainly for the downhill skier who wants a step-in binding but wishes to be able to climb a hill occasionally.

With any of these bindings except the step-ins, some sort of heel pop-up should be attached to the ski where the boot heel strikes it. These are used to prevent snow and ice from freezing between the boot and ski. They are usually made from plastic, rubber, metal, or linoleum. The best ones have rubber pop-ups in the center and metal teeth on the sides which give the heel purchase for making turns.

CHOOSING YOUR EQUIPMENT

The table gives a summary of appropriate combinations for different requirements, and the preceeding discussion should provide the additional information you may need. In general, you should pick equipment that is well-suited to the kind of skiing you will do most and that can also be made to serve for trips you will only make occasionally. Obviously, heavy equipment can always be made to serve for easier trips, and it carries a safety margin of strength with it, but beware of getting much heavier gear than you will need. Touring is much more pleasant when the lightest equipment that will do the job is used. With caution, a good skier on a day trip can take light touring skis over quite severe country. I sometimes use very light touring equipment for ski-mountaineering, carrying climbing boots in the pack. The light gear makes for a fast and enjoyable trip in.

Poles have not been mentioned previously, since there is not much complication in choosing them. The best poles are bamboo or fiber-glass touring poles that have wide baskets, adjustable straps, and tips that curve for easy placement and removal from the snow. Metal or fiber-glass downhill poles will do nicely, however, providing the baskets are of reasonably large diameter—not less than four inches. Large baskets may be attached to poles not originally equipped with them. Large baskets are particularly desirable when steep slopes must be climbed in soft snow. Touring points prevent an annoying kick and difficulty in removal from packed snow. The points of downhill poles can sometimes be modified to duplicate this curve. Ski poles that reach from the floor to your armpit are about the right length.

Choosing your equipment   169

SKIS	BINDINGS AND BOOTS	TERRAIN FOR WHICH EQUIPMENT COMBINATION IS:	
		GOOD	FEASIBLE
Extra light touring skis	Pin or equivalent toe bindings and light or standard touring boots.	Day touring on flat or rolling smooth ground or on other terrain with good trails.	Over night and weekend touring on easy terrain. Day touring on moderate terrain.
Light touring skis	As above.	As above. Satisfactory for terrain with some obstacles, but not for steep sections or much trail breaking in breakable crust.	As above. Somewhat more sturdy, but still too light for heavy packs or rough terrain. Not much control for down hill.
	Tempo bindings with touring, light mountaineering or ski mountaineering boots.	As above, slightly more control, but heavier boots reduce speed.	
Light touring skis with lignostone or aluminum edges	Cable bindings (touring type) or Silvretta with touring, light mountaineering, or ski mountaineering boots. Silvretta with heavy mountain or ski mountaineering boots.	As above, except capability for holding down heel allows agile skiers to *handle* occasional difficult spots. Note that these skis won't tolerate real downhill tension or much rough country.	
Standard touring skis	Tempo bindings with touring boots.	General touring over all but roughest terrain, providing there are no steep icy sections. Adequate for trail breaking in bad snow. Good for extended packing on moderate terrain. Not so pleasant for easy touring as lighter combinations.	Occasional steep spots, if skis have lignostone or aluminum edges.

SKIS	BINDINGS AND BOOTS	TERRAIN FOR WHICH EQUIPMENT COMBINATION IS:	
		GOOD	FEASIBLE
Standard touring skis with lignostone or aluminum edges.	Cable bindings with rear hooks and touring, light mountaineering, or ski mountaineering boots Silvretta bindings with heavy mountaineering or ski mountaineering boots.	As above, but also adequate for *coping* with occasional steep sections. Still not advisable for alpine routes.	Can be used for alpine routes following easy contours, but care must be taken, and flotation in deep snow is barely adequate for a heavy pack.
Mountain skis	Silvretta bindings with mountaineering or ski mountaineering boots.	Adequate for all touring conditions. Heavier boots improve downhill control and make moderate touring less enjoyable. Excellent compromise for alpine terrain.	Difficult downhill is feasible, but not really enjoyable. Adequate for general touring, but far from ideal on easy terrain.
Alpine ski	Ramy or Eckel bindings with mountaineering or ski mountaineering boots.	As above with better downhill control and worse touring characteristics.	
	Cable rear with Ramy or Eckel toepiece or triangular toe combined with touring attachment. Heavy mountaineering or ski mountaineering boots.	Difficult alpine touring with many steep slopes. Best combination for steep downhill —not so good anywhere else.	Possible but tedious for general touring.

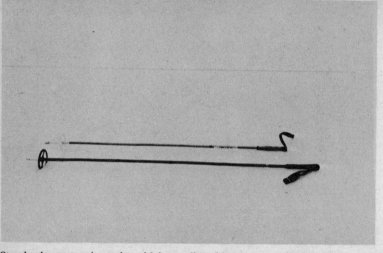

Standard cane touring poles with long adjustable straps and curved tips. Baskets on these models are a bit smaller than the best size for wilderness touring.

It is often possible to get excellent poles second-hand, since the characteristics desirable for wilderness use are out of fashion on commercial slopes. If you are careful to get a pair of ski poles with baskets that are easily removable or if you can modify a pair for the same result, the ski poles may also be used to hold up a tent.

WAXING YOUR SKIS

In touring, the purpose of wax is to provide enough traction so that you can push along, even up moderate slopes, while still allowing your skis to slide on the snow without sticking. These seemingly contradictory properties can be achieved if the wax layer is soft enough to allow the crystals of snow to form tiny indentations in the wax when the ski is planted, yet hard enough to melt a thin layer of snow into a water film with the friction of sliding. This water film forms the actual sliding surface. If the wax layer is too hard or too thin, the indentations will not be numerous enough or deep enough to hold your pushing ski. If, on the other hand, the wax layer is too soft or too thick, your skis will not slide forward, and clumps of snow will begin to stick to them.

These principles form the basis for waxing. Waxing is an art, since there are many varieties of snow and some mixed snow conditions are very tricky, but the essentials of waxing are not really too difficult to learn. The beginner should remember that the colder the snow for which he is waxing the harder his wax should be to produce the necessary friction. Warmer snow will require a softer wax to enable the skier to obtain purchase. Snow will never be warmer than 32° Fahrenheit, of course, since this is the freezing point of water. Under melting conditions, however, the snow layer will become wetter and better lubricated, and this requires a softer wax to develop adequate static friction between snow and ski.

The form of the snow, as well as its temperature, should influence your choice of a wax. Dry, starlike crystals with many fine points will make many more indentations in the wax than old, rounded pellets at the same temperature. Thus, fine crystals will require a harder wax or thinner wax layer than the pellets in order to allow the ski to slide properly, or, alternatively, a thicker wax layer or softer wax will be used to allow the rounded pellets to bite deeply enough. In general, a thicker layer of wax tends to have the effect of a slightly softer wax.

Types of wax. There are three main types of wax: base waxes, binders, and running waxes. The running waxes are the ones that we have just been discussing, waxes you apply to meet particular conditions. Base waxes are preparations that protect the bottoms of wooden-soled skis and form a surface to which the running waxes can bond. Binder waxes are special waxes used to provide a better bonding surface between base and running waxes so that the running waxes will wear longer. Base waxes need be applied only when the old coat begins to wear off, usually not more than a few times in a season. Binder waxes are not usually needed at all, except on plastic-soled skis.

Terminology. The beginner is likely to have more trouble coping with the various systems of labeling waxes and of describing the snow conditions for which they are used than he will have with the actual problem of waxing. Most modern development in touring has taken place in the Scandinavian countries, and most touring

Waxing your skis

equipment is made there, as are most touring waxes. Thus, many waxing terms have been borrowed from one or another of the Scandinavian languages, but the meaning of a borrowed term is often different for each user. I think the novice is best advised to stay away from all these complications until he has a basic familiarity with waxing.

In this book the only distinctions made are between *running waxes,* which provide the actual surface contacting the snow, *base waxes,* meaning any preparation intended to be applied on the bare surface of a wooden-soled ski, and *binder waxes,* which are intended for use between a base and the running wax. Running waxes are divided into two categories that can be easily separated by the beginner: *cake waxes,* which are packed in little cylinders and rubbed on, and *tube waxes,* which come packed in containers like toothpaste tubes, and are spread on the ski surface like peanut butter. Running waxes are also beginning to appear in aerosol cans.

Base waxes. There are several types of base waxes, each available in a number of forms. Most bases made by companies specializing in touring waxes are adequate for general use. The best ones are made with a tar base. The original tars had to be burned in with a blow torch, but tar bases are now available that can be painted or sprayed on. They still form a more durable surface if they are burned in after application. The blow torch should be moved back and forth over the wax until it just bubbles. Be careful not to burn the ski and hold a cloth in the opposite hand from the torch to smooth any rough spots while the tar is still hot. In using paint-on or spray-on tars, don't light the torch until the application has dried, and keep the container away from flame.

Lacquer bases are not so durable as tar, and they will not hold the running waxes as well. If there is no mention on the package that the wax can be burned it is probably a lacquer. Most downhill base waxes are of this type, though they are becoming uncommon because of the disappearance of wooden-soled downhill skis.

Whatever type of base is used, it should be applied at home whenever the skis show signs of needing it. Most touring skis these days come with a base already applied, and you won't need to apply your own until you have worn this first coat down. Scrape off any old wax before applying a new coat. Follow the instructions in allowing the wax to dry. If you try to apply running wax before the base is hard, you'll have to start over.

BASIC WAX KITS

The selections of waxes below are intended to give the beginner an idea of what he needs to buy in order to make a beginning at touring. Other brands will do as well, but those listed are the most commonly available in the United States. A kit from a manufacturer is also a good way of getting a starting selection. Before buying waxes, the beginner should look at the instructions on the packages and compare them with the conditions in his own area. Someone beginning touring in the Rockies in midwinter, for example, might wish to buy a couple of extra cold snow waxes and drop the wet snow ones. He should stay with one brand, though, and learn the characteristics of his basic waxes before gradually adding others.

The selections listed below are not quite equivalent, but any of them should enable the beginner to wax adequately, if not ideally, for most conditions. The cake waxes are listed first, then the tube waxes, each roughly in order from colder to warmer snow conditions.

SWIX   cake waxes: Green, Blue, Purple, Red
                tube waxes: Blue, Red

REX   cake waxes: Green, Blue, Purple, Red
                tube waxes: Blue, Violet

ØSTBYE   cake waxes: Mix (also in aerosol), Mixolinvox, Klistervox
                tube waxes: Skare, Klister

BRATLIE   cake waxes: Silke, Blandingsføre, Klistervox
                tube waxes: Skareklister, Våtsnø Klister

Binder waxes are used by cross-country racers under some conditions to make running waxes wear better in abrasive snow conditions. They may also be used in very cold weather instead of a base wax. These techniques are not of much interest to the novice tourer, who can spare ten minutes to rewax if necessary. If you use skis with plastic soles, to which running waxes do not bond well, it may be worth your while using a binder wax. Binder wax (often called *grundvax* and sometimes base wax) is a cake wax and is applied by rubbing on the ski. Use a very thin layer and rub well with a cork or foam waxing block to smooth and polish the wax.

Waxing your skis

Running waxes. The choice and application of the running waxes are the difficult part of waxing. Base waxes generally don't have to be applied more than a few times a season, but running wax must be chosen for every tour, and it may be necessary to rewax periodically through the day, especially in rapidly changing snow conditions.

It's not really too difficult to acquire a good basic waxing technique. Start off by buying a beginning kit of waxes from one manufacturer and stick with these same waxes until you know their characteristics well. Then you can start adding a few more waxes from the same manufacturer or trying a couple from another company. Don't do too much switching around at first, though. No two lines are quite the same, and if you change early in the game, you won't know whether differences in performance are due to your method of application, your skiing technique, the snow conditions, or the wax. Several manufacturers make up beginners' kits, and these are the easiest way to start. Typically, they include basic sets of waxes, a scraper-spreader, and a cork or foam rubbing block. The waxes can be replenished as you use them. Alternatively, if you can't find a made-up kit, choose one brand of wax, and get a basic selection like one of the ones discussed below.

Judging snow conditions. Since a particular wax is designed to handle a particular range of snow conditions, the first and most important thing you must learn about waxing is how to judge snow conditions. Directions on wax packages most often refer to "new" or "old" snow, to the air temperature, and sometimes to special characteristics—crust, powder, and so on. All these are necessarily subjective and imprecise ways of describing conditions. How old is "old"? Well, it depends on other circumstances. Even the temperature, which seems straightforward enough, is only an indication of what snow conditions are likely to be, since wind conditions and previous temperatures affect both falling snow and the cover already on the ground.

In general, the newer the snow, the more sharp points the crystals are likely to have, and the harder your wax will have to be to prevent sticking. Colder snow also calls for harder wax. As snow grows older, the points disappear and the snow crystals grow rounded, and a softer wax must be used. Wetter snow, which is better lubricated, makes softer wax necessary. Warm temperatures

Inland christens computer system for coal industry

SESSER, Ill. (AP) — When veteran miners first heard a production computer system would be installed in a mine near Sesser, they were skeptical.

But the miners are now convinced the computer system — installed by Inland Steel Coal Co. — works, and some are wondering how they ever got along without it.

Mine Supervisor John Prudent said he was a "little skeptical about that type of equipment being in the mine . . . about it possibly being too fragile or susceptible to dust." After seeing a similar system operate in the company's steel-making plant in Chicago, he changed his mind.

The system, he said, delivers what its developers promised — a precise, up-to-the-minute flow of information about what's happening in the mine. "It gives me a lot better handle on what's happening," he added.

Employees of Inland's general offices and two computer consultants have been working on the system for several months to coordinate what they say is the first production-oriented computer system in the American coal industry.

Currently operating with three programs, the computer keeps track of everything from inventories of spare parts for mine machinery to production records on a given section. Production foremen report their progress and reorder needed parts. Foremen can see what needs to be done, and when.

In one word, the computer system provides something vitally important to coal mining — communication — says a former miner who is now production systems coordinator.

"It's all communication," Roger Adkins said. "It's vital you know what's going on in that section of the mine. This helps establish better communication."

Before the computer, he said, production information passed from foreman to foreman would be at least eight hours old. That information would be passed in a 10-minute conversation shouted above the roar of man and machine at shift change.

The computer system consists of 18 cathode-ray terminals, nine of which are in constructed underground rooms. All are tied into a coordination center and linked with the central computer in Chicago, Adkins said.

"The name of the game is loading coal and you need to know what equipment is working, and how efficiently it operates, to get maximum production," said consultant Kurt Mueller.

So far, he added, the results of using a computer in a coal mine have been so good that plans already are under way to add another program, one dealing with mine safety, to the system in the near future.

ROPER 30" GAS RANGE WITH LIFT UP TOP. AUTOMATIC OVEN LIGHTING. REG. 379.95...... **$247**

30" EAGLE GAS RANGE CONTINUOUS CLEAN OVEN. CLOCK-TIMER. GLASS DOOR. DELUXE WITH TIMER. REG. 459.95 **$299**

PILOTLESS 30" GAS RANGE BLACK GLASS OVEN DOOR. REG. 469.95 .... **$338**

SHARP AM/FM STEREO WITH 8 TRACK PLAY & RECORD, BUILT-IN TURNTABLE & SPEAKERS. REG. 309.95 .... **$218**

SHARP AM/FM STEREO WITH CASSETTE PLAY & RECORD, CHANGER & DELUXE SPEAKERS. REG. 449.95 **$297**

PANASONIC AM/FM STEREO RECEIVER WITH BUILT-IN 8 TRK. PLAY & RECORD. 12 WATTS PER CHANNEL. REG. 359.95 ...... **$299**

FISHER-STUDIO STANDARD SEMI-AUTO D.C. SERVO BELT DRIVE TURNTABLE. REG. 149.95 .... **$109**

FISHER-PLAY & RECORD CASSETTE DECK WITH DUAL V.U. METERS & AUTO STOP. REG. 179.95 .... **$115**

PANASONIC 3 WAY DELUXE THRUSTER SPEAKER. DAMAGED AS IS. REG. 109.95 EA. ½ PRICE..........EA. **$54**

MICROWAVES & DISHWASHERS

E NOW ON ERATORS

HOTPOINT 2 DOOR REFRIGERATOR AUTOMATIC DEFROST. 5 YEAR WARRANTY. REG. 519.95.... **$344**

KELVINATOR 17 CU. FT. FROST FREE 2 DOOR REFRIGERATOR. HAS SMALL DENT. REG. 619.95 .... **$356**

HOTPOINT CUSTOM 18 CU. FT. FROST FREE REFRIGERATOR WITH GLASS ADJUSTABLE SHELVES. HOTPOINT'S BEST. WHITE. REG. 679.95 .... **$464**

ROPER MICROWAVE OVENS. LARGE CAPACITY. 10 POWER LEVELS.. **$329**

HOTPOINT DELUXE MICROWAVE WITH MEAT PROBE AND MULTI-POWER................ **$388**

SHARP MICROWAVE OVEN WITH "CAROUSEL." MEAT PROBE. VARIABLE COOKING CENTER..... **$469**

KELVINATOR BUILT-IN DISHWASHER WITH AUTOMATIC ENERGY SAVER. SAMPLE ONLY... **$188**

YOUR CHOICE ROPER CUSTOM OR HOTPOINT DELUXE PORTABLE DISHWASHERS WITH HARDWOOD CUTTING BOARD TOP.......... **$288**

E OF A KIND PLES—ALL BJECT TO R SALE

● **TONITE TILL 9 P.M.**
● **SATURDAY 10 A.M. TO 6 P.M.**
● **SUNDAY 11 A.M. TO 5 P.M.**

tend both to make the sharp points on snow crystals disappear more quickly and (if they are above freezing) to provide more of a lubricating film; cold temperatures have the opposite effect. Also, as I mentioned earlier in the chapter, thicker layers of wax tend to have the effect of a softer wax, thinner layers the effect of a harder wax.

Speaking of the hardness of a wax is an oversimplification, but it gives a good rough idea of the characteristics of different waxes. The novice should remember that "hardness" refers to the state of the wax in touring conditions, after it is applied to the ski and is at the temperature of the snow layer. Tube waxes designed for crusty snow, for example, are sticky fluids when squeezed from the tube, but they form very tough layers on the bottoms of the skis.

For practical purposes, there are a few simple tests that will tell you quite a bit about snow conditions. The first and most obvious question is: "Is it snowing?" If it is snowing, you are obviously faced with "new" snow. If snow is not falling, look at the snow, kick it, walk in it. If the snow has begun to consolidate and the layer holds together, either holding you up or leaving distinct footprints, which don't tend to collapse at the sides, it is becoming metamorphized "old" snow, and a softer wax will be called for than for new snow at the same temperatures. In very cold weather, the snow may remain powdery and fluffy for weeks, while in warmer weather metamorphosis takes place very quickly.

Next, scoop up some snow with mittens on. Look at it. Is it crusty, granular, powdery? Blow on it. Dry powder snow fluffs away like flour. Squeeze it into a snowball. Very cold, dry snow, whether it is powdery or granular, just won't stick together at all. Older dry snow that is not quite so cold but is not icy or granular will form snowballs with difficulty, but they fall apart if you squeeze the wrong way. Damp snow will form snowballs easily, and if the snow is really wet it will pack tightly and leave your mittens wet.

By this time you should know enough to wax for the snow condition that you have observed. You pull your wax kit out of the pack and set the skis up against the car and begin to puzzle through the descriptions on the labels. You will probably find that the store clerk placed the price sticker on the English directions, leaving you a choice of Norwegian, French, and Swahili.

Waxing your skis   177

Which wax? New snow generally calls for one of the cake waxes —the colder the snow, the harder the wax. A manufacturer will have one, two, or three waxes intended for dry, new snow, with the differences usually broken down by air temperature. As the snow gets older, the same wax change is required as for new snow of a higher temperature—a thicker coat or a softer wax. If, for example, you go out touring during a storm with temperatures of around 25 degrees, you may find that things go very well with Swix or Rex Green, which are fairly hard waxes. The next day, with temperatures about the same, you might find that the snow had settled enough to prevent your getting good grip with Green, and you would then go to Blue, which is somewhat softer.

After the wax or group of waxes intended for new dry snow, the manufacturer will have a group of softer cake waxes intended for damp or wet, new snow and for settled snow, ranging from dry snow near the freezing point to sopping wet. Each brand often includes quite a number of waxes in this category because these conditions are the most difficult for which to wax. The beginner should probably start by experimenting with only a couple of waxes in this group.

The tube waxes, or klisters, are intended almost exclusively for older snow. The method of application naturally produces a fairly thick layer of wax, so tube waxes cannot be used for dry powder snow, in which they would stick badly. Tube waxes follow the same range as the cake waxes, however there are some that form a hard layer for cold snow and progressively softer ones are used as the snow gets wetter. The hard tube waxes are very tough once they are applied. They are used for crusty, icy, and dry, hard, granular conditions, when the thin layer of a cake wax does not grip well and wears off rapidly. Softer tube waxes are used for old snow as it becomes progressively wetter. Occasionally, these soft tube waxes are useful for very wet, new-fallen snow.

After you have inspected the snow conditions and looked over the labels on your waxes you should have some idea which wax to use; you should at least have narrowed the possibilities down to two or three waxes. If the wind is whipping along at temperatures not much above zero and the new powder is lying on the ground to a depth of a couple of feet, you won't be considering any of your tube waxes or the cake waxes intended for thawing conditions. This will leave you no more than two or three waxes to choose from. There are a few general rules for choosing and applying these that save a lot of trouble.

The first rule in picking a wax is to start with a thin coat of the hardest wax you think will work. The reason for this method is simple: one can always apply a second coat of this wax or a coat of a softer wax over the first layer to give more grip, but if a harder wax is needed because of sticking, it is usually necessary to completely scrape the ski, a tedious business. The rule may not always be followed: if the weather is getting warmer, for instance, you may choose a wax that will maintain its grip in slightly warmer snow; but it is often best even in these circumstances to add a little soft wax for grip later in the morning than to risk sticking by using too soft a wax to start off.

The second rule is to test adequately before adding more wax. Don't expect the wax to grip properly until you have skied a quarter mile or so. The elasticity of the wax does not develop until you have skied some distance. You should get some grip right away, but you may find that a slight slip at the push in your stride disappears after you have gone a few hundred yards. If your skis are sticking badly, though, you may as well start over, since things will get worse rather than better.

After you have checked your first wax, you may want to add more to get a better grip. Unless you greatly misjudged the snow condition and found that your skis were not gripping at all, you should add more wax of the same or the next softer grade in the center of the ski only. This will give extra grip with less danger of causing sticking. If you find that you still need more grip, you may want to continue this second layer the length of the ski.

A third important rule is to learn to anticipate conditions. This is a matter of experience, attention to maps and weather forecasts, and luck. Some changes should be obvious. If you are starting before sunrise on a beautiful spring day, you may expect the air to get warmer and the snow softer. On the other hand, if you are starting up a climb of several thousand feet you should anticipate snow conditions generally reflecting the colder conditions and stronger winds that occur at high altitudes. In either case, it would be worthwhile to try to pick a wax that might work in both types of snow. You should look around the area before waxing, checking for variable snow conditions. In windy areas during cold snaps, you may find that conditions alternate between hard crust or windslab and drifted powder. In this situation, if you looked

Waxing your skis 179

only at the crust and used a tube wax, you would probably find yourself sticking in the powder. Waxing for changing conditions and anticipating those conditions is part of the art of waxing—it is a very tricky business—but the first step to mastery is to be alert to possible changes and watch for their signs.

Applying waxes. Waxes are usually most easily applied in warm rooms, preferably with accessories like solvents and blowtorches. All this is unfortunately not of much use to the wilderness tourer, who usually has no warm room available even at the beginning of the tour, when he is likely to be standing out in the early-morning cold beside some highway, anxious to get off before he freezes from standing around. In actual touring conditions, body warmth is usually the best available; any extra heat beyond that must be supplied by friction. Some tourers do carry a light blowtorch, a waxing iron that uses tablets for heating, or use their cooking stove to the same end, but usually the only fuel used is elbow grease. Cake waxes are rubbed on in a thin layer and then smoothed out by rubbing with a foam or cork block or with the heel of your hand. Care is necessary with the latter method, since a blister will be raised pretty quickly on a city-softened hand. Tube waxes should be spread on with the stick provided, with a spreader-scraper, or with a putty knife.

Application of the softer cake waxes and the tube waxes is easier if they are kept near the body for warmth. This is especially true of the tougher tube waxes, which are almost impossible to squeeze out when they are cold. If you forget to keep them warm you may have to get out the stove and heat the front of the tube. The harder cake waxes are usually easier to use when they are cold. Incidentally, if you are carrying the tube waxes in a pocket —or anywhere else, for that matter—keep them wrapped in a good plastic bag, since there is no stickier substance known to man, and the tubes always leak. The tube waxes are usually smoothed with the spreader or the heel of the hand, since bits of cork tend to stick in the wax if a rubbing block is used. The skis should be dry and free of any snow before they are waxed, and they should be allowed to stand a few minutes after waxing. Sticking problems are likely if snow gets mixed into the wax. If you do have a chance to wax the skis where it's warm, make sure they cool before use without getting snow on them; otherwise the bottoms will freeze up.

When you are going from a softer to a harder wax, it is almost always necessary to scrape the ski clean before applying the new wax. A combination scraper-spreader works, as do any number of individualistic instruments from putty knives to implements that look more like the tools of an assassin than a ski tourer. The job is easier if you use some solvent. Several are available where waxes are sold, though almost any solvent like gasoline will work. Lighter fluid is a handy wax solvent because it is cheap and comes in squirt cans that are just right for use without wasting solvent.

Whatever the wax, remember to spread it or rub it on in thin layers and to smooth it well. If you need a thicker layer for grip, use two or three thin layers instead of one thick one. Thick layers tend to be lumpy, and lumpy wax invites freezing and sticking. Hard waxes should be rubbed well until they are smooth. Squeeze soft waxes on before spreading, using about a quarter of a tube per ski.

Waxing problems. There are some conditions that are particularly tricky and a few that are just plain nightmares. I think the worst is a thin layer of very wet snow that has fallen over cold, dry powder. The skis get wet as you slide them over the top layer of snow, and when weight is put on them they sink into the cold powder and freeze up. After a few steps in this (you never do get a glide), each of your skis has about ten or fifteen pounds of snow stuck to the bottom. This is a difficult condition, and I know of no really satisfactory solution. If you have made the mistake of using a soft wax for the wet snow, this must first be removed. A downhill wax or plain paraffin should be applied for most of the length of the ski, with perhaps a thin layer of fairly hard climbing wax in the middle for grip. Try to use a stride that keeps the skis moving; they will have less chance of sticking if they don't stay in one spot on the snow very long. When the icing gets bad, stop and rub the iced spots with the downhill wax. You may be able to do this quickly without removing the ski.

Another difficult condition occurs when wet snow is falling because of a high layer of warm air, while the air temperature around you is below freezing. Skis tend to ice up in these conditions when they become wet and are chilled by the air. Try not to lift the skis off the snow at all in these conditions and keep them moving as much as possible.

The problem of anticipating changing conditions has already

been mentioned. There are far too many possibilities to discuss here, but one of the most common occurs in mountain touring, when one normally encounters colder snow with increasing altitude. A couple of thin layers of wax that is too hard for the condition at the lower altitude can be applied, with one thin layer of a softer wax to finish the job off. Much of the softer wax will probably have worn off when you reach colder snow and you have a good chance of not having to stop and rewax.

Another of the most common changing conditions is the softening of the snow during the day. This is an easy condition to wax for, since you simply have to add a bit of softer wax if your skis stop gripping.

Some of the uses of standard downhill wax or paraffin have been mentioned already, and the tourer should always carry a small lump. This can also be used to help prevent snow from sticking in various places under the heel, for example. It is most useful to help solve icing problems on the ski bottoms. Just rub the icing spots with the hard downhill wax. Finally, it can be used on top of many of the tougher touring waxes for a fast downhill run. It will tend to wear off by the end of a long downhill stretch. Don't try this over the softer touring waxes; the downhill wax is too hard to rub over them.

CLIMBERS

Where a tour involves a great deal of steep climbing, especially with heavy packs, it is useful to be able to climb steeper slopes than climbing waxes permit. Under these conditions, which occur mainly in mountain touring, it is useful to have a pair of climbers, also known as "skins," because they were originally made of sealskin. The sealskin variety is rather uncommon these days, though it has some advantages; climbers are now generally made of plush. In either case, the climber is a long strip of material covered on one side with fur-like hairs. It is attached to the bottom of the ski with the bristles running toward the tail of the ski. The ski will slide forward fairly easily with the grain of the fur but will not slide backward even on hills that are quite steep.

There are several ways to attach the climbers to the skis. One

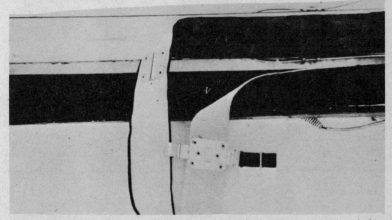

Two types of skins, actually made of plush. Top is the Trima rail type; below is the Vinersa rigid strap. These skis have the steel edges required in the high mountains.

of the best means is preferred by true lightweight experts: strips of sealskin, without backing, are glued to the skis with a climbing wax. It is quite difficult to obtain this type of climber, so most travelers will probably settle for one of the varieties made of plush sewn onto a canvas backing. Fittings for attaching the climbers to the skis are attached to the canvas. The old kind used canvas straps for attachment, a rather poor method, since the straps were cut by steel edges and the skins tended to roll off the skis on traverses.

The best plush climbers use rigid metal fittings, which hold the skins on the skis quite effectively. Two types are now widely available. Trima climbers use matching rails and grooves on the skis and climbers. This type has several great advantages: the skins are held on very well and will not tend to slip off; they are fairly simple to put on and can be taken off without removing the pack or skis; they will not slip from side to side; and the steel edges of the skis are completely free when they are needed for edging. The Trimas have the disadvantage of requiring that you install all the fittings on both climbers and skis and that holes be drilled in the skis.

Climbers   183

The second currently available climber with metal fittings is the Vinersa. It is fixed to the ski with straps like older climbers, but instead of being made of canvas the straps are metal. The metal straps are not cut by steel edges, of course, and their rigidity eliminates the tendency of the skins to roll off the skis. The Vinersas have an advantage over the Trimas in not requiring that your skis be drilled and in having fittings that are already attached. They are not held to the skis quite so rigidly, however, and you may find that the rear bracket tends to slip off your skis unless you make some modification. Finally, one of the straps on the Vinersa skin is placed in a spot that coincides with the position of some bindings, so it may not work on your skis. Make sure to check this before you bend the rear brackets to fit your skis, in case you want to return the skins.

Any type of climber will enable you to climb much steeper slopes than climbing waxes, but you cannot glide or sideslip with skins. For this reason, they never really replace climbing waxes. Even in mountain touring, a party equipped with skins may want to use touring waxes on long rolling sections of the trip or on long, gentle climbs. Waxing enables you to glide down short downhill sections and to slide your skis forward with much less effort than when you are wearing climbers.

SKIING TECHNIQUE

Skiing in the wilderness is quite different from either downhill skiing on commercial slopes or touring on well-used cross-country trails, though it is much closer to cross-country than it is to following the snow packer down a carefully manicured slope. You will have a pack, probably weighing around twenty or thirty pounds if you are out for the weekend. Even the accomplished downhill skier will find challenges he didn't know existed when he tries to make a downhill run with all that extra inertia strapped to his back. The snow will be unbroken and may change condition every few yards. To top it off, the ski patrol isn't waiting at the top of the hill to whisk you off if you take a flying somersault. You will quickly develop a conservative technique if you give a little thought to the consequences of a broken leg.

Touring stride. Weight is on right foot and skier pushes with right foot and left pole. Left foot and right pole are coming forward.

Push on right foot and left pole continue, while left foot and right pole reach forward.

Skier starts final kick on right foot and left pole; left ski is on the ground, but is unweighted.

Pressure on right pole and left ski are beginning.

Skiing technique   185

Push on right pole and left ski continue as the right foot and left pole come forward.

Let's start at the beginning, though. If the terrain is easy, moderate ski tours can be attempted even by a group of beginning skiers if they have already mastered the art of winter camping. The first thing to do after getting out of your car or cabin is to wax your skis. Chances are that the beginning of the tour is either flat or uphill, so you won't have to worry about warming up. Beginners should spend an hour or so getting used to the feel of walking on skis before putting the pack on. Bindings and boots should be adjusted so that there is plenty of heel lift. Push off with one ski and the opposite pole, and try to get as much glide as you can with each stride. Get your rear leg moving forward during the push; then as it comes forward it will put extra power behind your glide. When you put your weight down on the foot that is about to push, plant it on the snow and leave it there, pushing off with a smooth thrust. A jerky push will break the ski loose, especially going uphill. The position for touring is more like jogging than walking since your weight is a bit forward, but the tread is light, not heavy, and the glide is smooth, not choppy.

If you really aren't getting any traction when you plant your skis you may have to put on a softer wax. A soft wax can usually be put on right over the harder one. Start off by just putting some on in the middle, under your foot; this may be enough, and if it starts to stick, you won't have as much to scrape off. If your skis are sticking badly, you need a harder wax, and this cannot usually be put on over the soft one. Before you stop for scraping and rewaxing, make sure you can't prevent the sticking with just a steady pace. Snow will stick to the bottom of a ski much faster when you are standing still, and an even, slow rhythm will often solve the sticking problem. You should also check to see that the wax layer is smooth and thin; sticking will occur sooner on a thick, lumpy wax job.

Climbing. Touring waxes easily enable the skier to climb reasonable slopes. Practice without the aid of poles.

In actual climbing the poles are used just as they are on the level. The stride is somewhat shorter.

As soon as you feel comfortable on level terrain, try climbing some bumps, and experiment a little to find out how steep a slope you can climb. Vigorous use of the poles will increase the angle. Even a beginner can often manage a respectable slope with waxes, and improved climbing and waxing technique will help quite a bit. You cannot expect to climb the slopes that a cross-country racer would, however. Your pack will keep you back and so will a sensible conservation of energy and dry clothing; sweat and exhaustion are best saved for short training jaunts.

Turns. The most common turn used by the ski tourer is the step turn. The skier simply picks up the tip of the ski on the side toward which he wants to turn, points it over a comfortable distance, and follows with the other ski, repeating the operation as many times as necessary to achieve the turn. When the skier becomes more practiced, this operation is combined with a skating stride to achieve smooth turns without losing stride, especially in skiing downhill with touring bindings. This turn in its simplest form is easy to learn, being almost instinctive. It is a bit harder to perform while the skier is sliding downhill, the trick being to bring the second ski over quickly, before the two have traveled far in different directions.

Skiing technique 187

Step turn. In a step turn, the skier simply lifts the toe of his ski and moves it in the direction of the turn. The other ski follows.

A more difficult turn for one who has never learned it is the kick turn. This is a skill that should be mastered immediately by the beginner, since it is used to extract oneself from all kinds of difficulties from steep slopes to fence crossings. The turn is more easily illustrated than described, so the reader is referred to the pictures of the execution of the turn. It will take a few tries to get the knack of this turn, but the advantage is that once mastered it can be executed easily even on very steep slopes, allowing the skier to proceed down or up in a series of traverses linked by kick turns. Incidentally, you really don't have to wait until you're on the snow to learn a kick turn. It can be learned and practiced in your back yard on any surface that won't damage your skis; a good lawn or an old rug will do. A kick turn can be used to get over any obstacle up to crotch height.

With bindings in the touring position these are the only two turns that can normally be used by the beginner. Stem and parallel turns can be managed in good snow by experienced slicers, but practice will be required to get used to doing them with the heels free.

Kick turn to right. The skier faces right. Left pole is near the front of skis, right pole is behind and very close to skis.

Right foot is kicked up and the heel of the ski is planted well forward, close to the left ski.

Right ski is swung down parallel to the left and facing in the opposite direction.

Weight is transferred to the right ski.

Skiing technique 189

Left pole is replanted and the left ski brought around to complete the turn.

The skier ends facing in the opposite direction. On slopes the turn should be executed *away* from the slope.

Skating is a useful technique that may already be known by experienced downhill skiers. Practice it after you are fairly confident and stable on your skis. It is easiest to learn with a slight downhill slope that is not quite steep enough to allow you to slide down without an extra push. The pushing ski is angled out from the other at an angle of perhaps thirty degrees and is edged into the snow, while the poles are both planted as far ahead as the skier can reach and still get a good push. The skier pushes off with his poles and his foot at the same time, carrying the push as far as possible. At the end of the push the arms and the pushing leg will be well behind the skier and the body will be leaning well forward over the running ski to counterbalance the leg. The skier takes as much glide as possible and then brings his back ski, still in the air, forward next to his running ski. His weight then shifts as he pushes off with the second ski and both poles. At first, your skating stride will be rather anemic, but as you learn to lean out farther with a longer push, you will find that the skating stride can be very powerful.

The skating stride is generally only used for short stretches. The standard touring stride is just as effective over long stretches and is much less tiring, but the skating stride is quite useful for some special circumstances such as picking up speed on a gradual downhill section and maintaining speed over short hills, especially when rear hooks are used to hold the heels down for downhill skiing.

Climbing. As previously mentioned, the best way to climb a slope is to just ski up it, using the traction provided by your wax. The steepness of the slope you can go up in this way will increase as you gain experience, but the upper limit is somewhere around fifteen or twenty degrees. As long as the slope is open enough to permit traversing, the normal method of climbing is simply to cut across the slope going upward at the maximum angle that your wax and digging the edges of your skis into the slope will permit. Occasionally, the direction of the traverse is reversed by a kick turn.

On short, steep sections of narrow trails either a herringbone or a side-step may be used, the side-step being much less tiring. In the herringbone the skier faces straight up the slope, his skis in a V with the tails together, one slightly above the other, the inside edges of the skis dug into the slope and the poles dug in behind the skis for support. The herringboner then walks up the slope, maintaining the V. The steeper and more slippery the slope, the

Climbing using a combination of waxes, side stepping, and an upward traverse.

wider the V must be and the more the edges and the poles must be dug into the snow. An accidental slip while climbing with the herringbone is most undignified, unless you have mastered the art of skiing backwards.

The side-step is less tiring, and it is generally preferred by the tourer. The skier simply stands across the slope, his ski edges dug into the slope on the uphill side as much as necessary to prevent slipping. He steps up with the uphill ski and then brings the downhill ski up to meet it. This step is best used in combination with an uphill traverse if the width of the slope permits: the skier works up diagonally with both a side step and a forward slide. Occasional kick turns will change the direction of edging and provide relief for the feet as well as keeping the skier on course. When edging becomes tiring, the climber can rest his feet by planting his downhill pole and allowing the skis to slide down onto it, allowing a halt without edging.

For long, steep slopes, climbers and steel edges on the skis may be necessary. The procedures are similar to those described above, except that a much steeper angle may be pursued. When some members of the party are using climbers and others climbing on waxed skis, the member breaking trail should keep his angle of climb low enough for all to follow, otherwise the work of trail-breaking will have to be duplicated.

When steep slopes are encountered and regular climbers have not been brought, the best method of getting up is often to take off your skis and climb on foot. If the snow is too deep to permit this, you can make an improvised set of climbers by wrapping part of the length of the skis with parachute cord or rope. Keep the wrapping near the center of the skis if only part of the length is wrapped. Of course, the skis will no longer slide well with rope climbers, but these can be removed at the top of the hill. The skis will not drag so badly if only the centers are wrapped, and this is often effective for short, steep sections.

In the chapter on emergencies it is recommended that holes be drilled in the tips of the skis for easy conversion into a sled. This arrangement is also useful for climbing open slopes of hard snow when it is more convenient to remove the skis and walk up on foot. If the skis are drilled it is a simple matter to tie them onto the pack and tow them ten or fifteen feet behind. Under good circumstances this method is much easier than carrying the skis.

Skiing downhill on wilderness trips is different from anything one encounters on commercial slopes. It ranges from easy touring on slight downhill slopes to negotiation of precipitous and icy mountainsides where one worries about keeping body and soul together. Technique varies accordingly, but there is a natural division between the techniques used with bindings that can be adjusted to hold the heel down to the ski and the type that can't be used this way.

With light touring equipment designed for cross-country skiing over mild inclines the heel cannot usually be fastened down, a characteristic that can seem sometimes a curse and sometimes a blessing when running downhill. With the heels free to lift, it is impossible to lean forward, since you will fall on your face if you do. The preferred method of turning is the step turn, as long as the course is not too steep. The downhill skier new to touring equipment will find that some stemming and snowplowing are possible to slow down and change direction in reasonably soft snow, even without the edge control of downhill equipment. Later he may learn to use parallel techniques when snow conditions are right. The beginner should practice these maneuvers: stemming consists of pressing the heel of the boot and ski outward against the snow, while keeping the knees close. This presses the inside edge of the ski into the snow, tending to steer the skier and slow progress at the same time. Stemming with both skis at the same time is known as snowplowing.

Snowplow. In a snowplow the tails of the skis are pushed apart. The skier's knees are pushed in slightly, forcing the inside edges of the skis into the snow. Steered turns are easy to make.

Skiing technique 193

The telemark position and turn are so far out of fashion that most modern downhill skiers don't even know what they are, but the position still has some unique virtues for the wilderness skier. On ski slopes in the wilderness the skier is likely to find that snow conditions change radically as he travels from one part of a slope to another. He will run from hard windpack to breakable crust and then from good granular skiing to ice to sloggy powder, sometimes changing only a few feet from one another. The weight of the pack increases the difficulty of these conditions. The best way to keep from falling in terrain like this is to drop down and push one ski far ahead of the other. Lateral stability is reduced, but the skier is able to keep from pitching forward over his ski tips. This position çan be assumed very rapidly once it is learned. Weight should be on the rear ski in running from fast to slow snow and on the front ski in the opposite situation. If control is lost, fall to one side, which is easy to do from the telemark position.

A useful maneuver with the poles is their use as a brake. Both poles are held together with the grips in one hand and the other hand near the baskets. The skier bends low and puts weight on the poles with the lower hand, pressing the baskets into the snow. This brake is only effective on gentle slopes with soft snow, but it is an ideal method of slowing on a narrow trail that is just a little too steep for comfort.

Light touring bindings and the turns used with them are suitable only on easy slopes; steep hills require heavier equipment and some experience in using it. The skier whose bindings can provide downhill tension is better-equipped for handling downhill skiing, and he may use whatever repertoire of turns he has picked up on regular ski slopes, the stem christie, christie-into-the-hill, and the jump turns being the most useful. The beginner should still use the traverse and kick-turn method, practicing edging his skis and side-slipping as he goes. The expert will use the same method as the going gets steeper. Side-slipping is just what it sounds like, a controlled slip on a slope that is steep enough so that edging would be needed to stay in one place.

The experienced downhill skier who is new to skiing with a pack will soon find that he has to ski with his weight farther back than a slalom racer would consider to be good form. The turns that are safe under normal touring conditions would look rather prosaic on commercial slopes, but they can be exciting enough in the back country. A series of linked parallel turns with a heavy pack will be feasible only occasionally, and the skier will find that stem christianas are the most useful turn away from the hill. As the going gets harder, kick turns, traverses, and parallel turns into the hill will be resorted to. Often the easiest way down a really steep stretch is to just side-slip.

The skier with bindings that are rigid in downhill skiing must remain aware that such bindings hold the feet firmly to the ski during a fall as well. The skier with light touring bindings will rarely be hurt in a fall, but heavier equipment may prove more durable than your anatomy. Rigid bindings should always be equipped with safety releases, but these should never be trusted to prevent injury; they often only reduce its severity. The skier in the wilderness has to judge conditions conservatively and ski accordingly. Ski slowly enough to spot changing snow before you hit it. Many experienced wilderness skiers rarely attatch their cables to the rear hooks preferring to ski downhill with the heels free as a matter of safety.

Another precaution that should be observed is to remove ski pole wrist straps when running downhill in heavy brush or timber. This prevents dislocations in the event your pole should catch on a branch.

In most circumstances, the simplest way to handle a run that starts to get out of control, regardless of the type of equipment you are wearing, is to bail out: just sit down, falling backwards to one side. This is far better than taking a header a few seconds later when all control has been lost. In forest running, you may have to postpone your fall briefly to avoid collision with a tree. In ski mountaineering, slopes are sometimes skied that are steep and slippery enough so that the skier will just keep sliding if he falls, retaining even less control than if he had stayed up. It should go without saying that such a slope should never be attempted except by experienced ski mountaineers with steel-edged skis. A more or less controlled side-slip is usually the best way down.

Even from the vantage point of a sitzmark, though, wilderness skiing is a fantastic experience. Whether you are touring over flat fields or making the first track down in a mountain bowl, there is nothing quite like it for pure exhilaration. And it is certainly an improvement over standing in lift lines!

IX

Finding Your Way

A snowy landscape presents many route-finding problems that are not encountered by the summer traveler. Obviously, anyone who is going into wilderness areas in winter has to be skillful enough to find his way. This is true whether you are going on a two-week trip or an afternoon ramble; many fatal incidents involving lost men have occurred near roads and dwellings. It is quite possible for a man to wander for days within a mile of the nearest road. Short trips may require less elaborate preparation than long ones, but the winter traveler must still have some method of finding his way, particularly since a night in the open is a much more serious matter in winter than in summer.

Many experienced mild-weather backpackers are used to finding their way by simply following trails, using signposts or guidebooks as direction finders at intersections. In many areas this technique is so effective that there is no real need for walkers to develop the skill of finding their way without blazes, cairns, and tracks. This method is rarely adequate in winter, since snow often covers the familiar trail signs. Even when a summer trail can be followed for a time, it may be obscured a few miles farther on, or a fresh snow in the night may obliterate it. For example, you may successfully follow the line of a trail through thick woods but lose it completely above timberline.

The most common mistake made by novices in the winter is reliance on their own tracks as a means of finding the way back to their point of departure. The tracks make such an obvious and comforting line that one relies on them without even thinking about it. Unfortunately, fresh or windblown snow can completely cover them in minutes or even seconds, leaving the hiker at a complete loss concerning his whereabouts.

The way to avoid this problem is to develop the habit of always knowing where you are. This injunction may have different meanings in different situations. Sometimes it is essential to know exactly where you are at all times, keeping a record of compass bearings and distances. In another situation it suffices to know that you are in a certain valley or just to know the general direction and distance in traveling time you've gone from some sort of boundary. The important thing is the habit of constant awareness of your position and understanding of what you need to know in order to find your way in a particular area.

LEARNING TO LOOK

In order to find his way around the wilderness in winter, the beginner must first develop some skill in observing his surroundings. We all have this skill in some environments—we have learned, for example, where to look for street signs in the city—but navigation in snowy woods or mountains requires that we look for quite different things than most of us are used to noticing. In fact, different kinds of wilderness often require looking for different signposts.

Many routine tricks are part of keeping yourself oriented. One of them is looking backwards as you go along. Remembering landmarks as they look when you are going into the woods may do you no good in finding your way back out; the trail tends to look very different when you are looking at it from the opposite direction. Hence, you should develop the habit of looking back frequently, memorizing landmarks that might help you retrace your steps. This is worthwhile even if you are not planning on returning by the same route. You might have to go back the same way in the event of trouble.

The habit of looking backward is particularly important at various kinds of junctions. If, for instance, you are going up one of a number of gullies to a long ridge and then turning right, the intersection with the ridge is obvious when you are coming out of the gully, and you are likely to go on without giving further thought to the matter except for a feeling of gratitude that the hard climbing is over. Coming back, however, there are likely to be half a dozen gullies heading off to the left, and unless you have foreseen the problem you will have difficulty in deciding which one to follow. The time to meet the problem is on the way in, when you should carefully note the distinguishing features of the gully you came up.

Another similar trick of observation is to make your landmarks as weatherproof as possible. While this is only feasible to a limited degree, it is a method that should be kept constantly in mind. It is certainly a good idea to remember that you traveled a whole day in the direction of a certain peak and that you will want to keep it at your back on the return journey, but you will need alternative landmarks as well, since the mountain may be obscured by a cloud bank. The possibility of a blanket of snow or poor visibility should also be considered in choosing landmarks. The only method that can be used to find your way in really bad weather is with a compass, which will be discussed later in the chapter, but some care in picking different kinds of landmarks will save you a great deal of trouble.

No matter how well they are chosen, landmarks are of little use if your memory of them is fragmentary and confused. This is a good reason for writing down key landmarks as an aid to memory. There are many ways of doing this, though a rough map is usually the best. Everyone uses different systems in remembering things, and for this reason, there is no "best" way to remember, list, or map landmarks. Each person will develop his own methods, which will improve in accuracy and will require less effort as time goes on and he acquires experience. The important thing to remember in the beginning is that we all tend to flatter ourselves on the accuracy of our memories. You may think that you could not possibly mistake that distinctive-looking rock when you first see it, but you may find a dozen that look the same when you return a couple of days later, cold, tired, and confused. And was the rock before or after the pass? Develop your own system of mapping, observing, and memory jogging, but be realistic in your expectations of it. Your memory isn't as good as you think it is.

On short trips you may be able to guide yourself by landmarks alone, particularly if you are following some prominent line, whether it is a river, road, or power line. For longer trips and many shorter ones, you will have to use a map to orient yourself to the landscape, even if you draw the map yourself.

MAPS

A map is of little use unless you can read it. The map is a symbolic depiction of an area of land, and in order to use it effectively you will have to learn to read the symbols. This is less a matter of instruction than experience, since most of the symbols themselves are fairly simple. With a bit of practice you can learn to visualize the landscape that is represented by a particular map. Once this knack has been acquired, the map becomes a really helpful tool. With it you can plan trips in wilderness areas you have never seen, estimating with fair accuracy the time it will take to reach your destination. Once you are in the woods you can often find your own position quickly by relating the visible land- marks to those shown on a map.

Many types of maps are available. They are designed for many different purposes, and since any one map is limited in the number of things it can show, it may be more or less useful to you. It may, of course, be well or badly designed even for the purpose of which it was intended. You might be interested in a ski tour in coastal marshes, for example. Many nautical charts are probably available for the area in which you are interested, some good and some bad, but they would be of little use to you, since they are designed to aid someone traveling by water and not by land. The charts may show the location of sand bars but not jeep roads, when you want the opposite emphasis. Road maps are usually just as useless to the wilderness traveler, since they are generally drawn to the wrong scale and ignore the features in which the tourer is most interested.

Even the maps that are of help to the wilderness user are of many different types, and he may often need more than one to serve the several purposes he has in mind. One map may show trails, while it gives only a small number of reference points on the local landscape, for reasons of scale or economy. You may need to use a map like this, which will show you where trails have been cleared in the forest, in combination with a detailed map of the topography, which may not show the existing trails.

By far the most useful maps of most wilderness areas in the United States are those published by the U.S. Geological Survey. They are quite accurate and very cheap. Several series and types of maps are published by the Survey, including special sheets on the national parks. The series of most interest to the wilderness traveler are the seven-and-a-half-minute series and the fifteen-minute series. There are maps of the fifteen-minute series available for most of the United States, except for Alaska, where a different scale is used. These maps are detailed enough to be very useful. The scale is 1:62,500, which is very nearly one inch to the mile. The seven-and-a-half-minute series is even more useful; the maps are drawn to a 1:24,000 scale. Unfortunately, this series is not available for many wilderness areas.

The Geological Survey maps are accurate even in areas that are rarely traveled, since they are compiled primarily from a complicated process of aerial photography. They are generally completely reliable for topographic features, but they should be used with more caution with reference to man-made features and vegetation. The survey date is printed in the lower right-hand corner, and changes subsequent to that date will not appear on the map. The magnetic declination, which will be discussed below, is usually updated more frequently. Another complication in using the survey maps for trails, jeep roads, and the like, is that the policy on which ones should be included seems to vary with area and time. These maps cannot be revised very often, and those who make them up must decide whether a trail should be included, recognizing that it may be allowed to disappear the next year. For this reason, some quadrangles show only very heavily used and well-maintained trails and roads. Others include every track. For trail information it is usually best to consult another map in conjunction with the U.S.G.S. map. If you are traveling without trails, this will not be a problem.

The U.S.G.S. maps are available in several overlays; that is, additional information is printed over the basic map, sometimes in different colors. The most useful overlay for wilderness use is that in the contour edition, which shows height of land by the use of contour lines, includes features like roads and buildings, and often shows forested and clear areas. Contour lines are the most accurate way of showing differences in elevation, though a bit of practice is required to read them. Contour mapping is discussed more fully below.

U.S.G.S. maps are available at local offices, from the central offices listed in Appendix C, and from many backpacking shops. Index maps of individual states are available free; they show the names and locations of all the quadrangle maps. Sheets that explain all the symbols used on the maps are also available free of charge.

There are many other sources of maps, some of which are excellent, and most of which are not. Commercially available maps made for sportsmen are sometimes good for trails, but they are often just badly reproduced and expensive copies of maps made by some government agency that will supply them free of charge. Since your taxes paid for the survey to begin with, you might as well reap the benefits, if any. The quality of the maps of conservation agencies, counties, fish and game departments, and so on, is variable. The Forest Service will provide maps of national forest areas. Those that are of recent date are often very good for trails and access roads, but many are out of date and should be used with caution. They are not terribly good representations of the topography of the area, and they should usually be used in conjunction with U.S.G.S. maps.

Private lands such as those owned by lumber companies have often been mapped by the owner. It is usually wise to get permission before using such areas, anyhow, and you can ask about maps at the same time.

The best sources of information on trails and routes are usually the guidebooks and maps published by outing clubs or by companies aiming specifically at wilderness travelers. Such information is usually much more up to date than that included on maps designed mainly for other purposes, and it often includes descriptions of routes that are very helpful, even though they may be designed for the summer walker. In some cases, such maps may be adequate by themselves, like the excellent series published by the Appalachian Mountain Club. Other maps are more sketchy and should be used to supplement U.S.G.S. maps. Even a guide with no map at all that includes a recent description of a trail will often be enough to tell you that a trail shown on a ten-year-old map still exists, and you may then hope that the brush won't be too thick. In areas like the Sierra Nevada where the small brush is covered over by the first few snows, the winter traveler can steer by the topographic map and compass without concerning himself over trails. In other areas, where cover is thick and snows not so deep, a trail will often greatly increase your speed.

READING THE MAP

Those who have become experienced in the use of topographic maps learn to read them as easily as they do the printed page or road map. All these skills are learned, however, not inbred, and to the novice looking at his first topo map everything except for lakes and roads is likely to be completely unfamiliar. The main difficulty is presented by the *contour lines.* A contour line represents a given height of land. That is, it follows the same route on the map that you would follow if you were to walk along being careful never to move up or down, but stayed at the same altitude. If you were on a hillside and you followed a contour line, you would eventually walk all the way around the hill, ending at the same place you started. Put another way, the contour describes the shoreline that would be formed by an ocean at its altitude. Contour lines are drawn to represent steps in altitude, so that the altitude change between any two contour lines is always the same on a particular map. If the contour interval is twenty feet, for example, you could reach the next contour line on your hill by walking up the hill until you were twenty feet above your earlier track. If the hill is very gentle, this might be a long way; if it is very steep, it will be a short distance. If you now follow your new contour line around the hill, you will be staying inside the contour you traced before. Where the hill is gentle you will be farther away from the lower contour, and where it is steep, the lower contour will be just below you.

The illustrations show a few common patterns on contour maps. One of the best ways to learn to read them is to buy a few contour maps of different kinds of terrain and study them for a while, picturing the features they represent. It may be worthwhile to get a couple of U.S.G.S. maps of the same area, one a contour edition and the other a shaded relief edition. The latter gives a more pictorial version of the landforms and may help you relate them to

A simplified contour map and photograph of the same place. The cross on the map shows the spot where the picture was taken, and the arrow shows the direction. The contours are at 200-foot intervals from 7,600 to 9,000 feet. Note that the rock gendarme on the left does not show as a separate summit on the map, because the contours are too widely spaced. The large cliffs on the peak show as closely spaced contours, and the ridges and gullies are easily discerned.

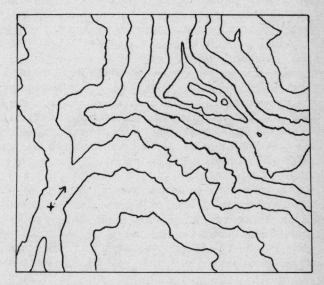

Reading the map

the contours. Pick up the map of an area near your home; then take it out and compare the map with the actual landforms.

You will notice that contour lines do not cross, since they represent different heights of land. In the case of a vertical cliff, a number of contour lines may come together for the length of the cliff. (Technically, the lines cross to show an overhanging cliff, but this would be unlikely on any normal map.) The altitude gain represented by each contour line is listed in the legend of the map and will vary a great deal depending on the scale of the map and the terrain that is being depicted.

Within the limits of the scale of the map, the contours will give you a very good picture of the pattern of the landscape. Even if visibility is limited, by keeping track of where you are located on the map, you can tell a great deal about the terrain around you. If the visibility is fairly good, you will probably be able to establish your position on the map by simply comparing the landforms around you with those shown by the contours. As you go up a valley, for example, this is just a matter of keeping track of the landmarks you pass. In climbing a mountain in clear weather, you can estimate your altitude fairly accurately by checking the altitude of some high point of land that is at the same level you are. Such a check might save you from the mistake of a late afternoon dash for a peak or pass that is still several thousand feet above you.

As you become more skilled at reading maps, you will be able to tell more and more about the landscape by just looking at the map, but there are limitations imposed by both vertical and horizontal scale. If the map has 200-foot contours, for example, which is quite common in mountainous regions, a ridge full of jagged 100-foot cliffs and hills might look quite smooth on the map. Details of terrain other than general forestation, swamps, etc., will not appear on the map. This provides the adventure of discovery, of course, but it is important to remember when you are planning a trip from a map or steering a course in a snowstorm. A map with 100-foot contours will not show the 50-foot cliff you are about to step over.

The easiest way to steer a course with a map is by matching the details of terrain of the map and the country around you, but this is not always possible. In flat country it may be a long way between recognizable features like rivers. You may be in an area that is so heavily forested you cannot see more than a few yards. Some mountainous areas and some lake country include so many features of almost the same kind that it is impossible to tell one hill or lake from another by comparison with the map. Finally, a really bad storm in any country can reduce visibility almost to zero, so that one is lucky to be able to see his footing, never mind any landmarks. In any of these circumstances, it is necessary to keep track of the direction you are traveling if you are not to become lost.

DIRECTION FINDING

The first maxim in determining or maintaining a direction is a negative one: convince yourself that you don't have any sense of direction. You may be an astute observer and have learned all sorts of tricks for finding your way in various kinds of surroundings, but whatever methods you have, they are based on outside clues, not some internal compass. It has been proven a number of times that no one can walk a straight line without some external guide.

Most people who have spent much time in the wilderness have had this fact demonstrated to them at some time or other. One very common experience in storms, dense woods, and similar situations is the feeling that the compass is wrong, that it is broken or being deflected by a metallic deposit. This feeling is almost always incorrect, but it sometimes takes a good deal of self-control to keep oneself from dashing off in circles, following instinct. Men who become seriously lost often do just this. Remember, if your compass is really acting erratically, the last direction finder you should substitute for it is your instinct, which is guaranteed erratic, one hundred per cent of the time.

One method of determining direction, by reference to landmarks, has already been discussed. There are two other means of use to the wilderness sojourner: reference to celestial objects and the use of a magnetic compass. Other reference systems, from moss on trees to prevailing winds are generally unreliable and are, in any case, too local to be of much use in navigating a strange area.

Celestial bodies allow precise position finding, but only through the use of instruments that the snowshoer or ski tourer is unlikely

15°

True North

Magnetic North

Approximate Mean Declination, 1959

How declination is shown on maps. The arrow showing magnetic North shows
the direction a compass needle would point, and the true North arrow shows
the direction of the geographic North Pole.

to carry. Some types of expeditions may need such devices and the
knowledge of their use, and interested readers are referred to the
bibliography. The tourer may want to check his compass by use of
the North Star, but referring to the declination shown on the map
is easier. It is unwise to depend on navigation by the stars in preference to a compass. You may get hungry waiting for the clouds
to break. Using the stars for direction is greatly facilitated by a
good knowledge of the constellations. The pointers and the North
Star are the only accurate way to check declination on a compass,
but if you are using the sky as a rough directional beacon—
perhaps for an early-morning start—it is pleasant to recognize
other constellations and to know where to expect them to be at the
time you are looking.

Many methods have been suggested for establishing bearings
using the sun. At best they are time-consuming and dependent on
a touching faith that the sun will be shining when you want to find
your way home. At worst they are often grossly inaccurate. Those
who are interested can look into some of the books suggested in
the bibliography, but these methods are of little use to the traveler
on trips of a few days or weeks in the wilderness. Get a good
compass and a good map of the area to which you are going, learn

FINDING YOUR WAY   206 to use them, and take them. If you can't remember to take your compass, you are unlikely to remember the exact direction of the sunrise on a particular day. The wilderness traveler should never travel without a compass, unless he is in an area where terrain alone will guide him out, even in blizzard conditions.

COMPASSES

A pocket compass is the standard direction-finding device for general use in the wilderness. It will not enable you to find your position, unless you have some additional information. It will, however, give you an essentially constant directional reference, which can be used to keep you going in a straight line, to keep track of changes you make in direction, and to establish the relation between directions on the ground and those shown on a map.

A compass is simply a magnet mounted on a pivot so that it is free to turn. The case is supposed to protect the moving parts and to help you to relate the position of the magnet to the land around you and to your map. The magnet itself may be in the form of a needle or it may be glued to a round dial, so that the whole dial turns. In either case, the magnet will turn until it is oriented along the lines of the earth's magnetic field (providing there is nothing else around to deflect it).

WHERE THE COMPASS POINTS

The directions marked on a compass tend to lead to misconceptions, and it is important for anyone who travels much in the wilderness to understand that the compass needle or face rarely points toward the North Pole. It lines up with the earth's magnetic field, which is rather irregular, and which wanders around enough to confuse anyone. The earth's magnetic North Pole is in northern Canada over a thousand miles from the geographic North Pole. If you think of your compass needle as pointing at the magnetic North Pole you will begin to understand that in many parts of the country the error between magnetic North and true North is quite large. The situation is even more confusing, however, since the actual field is deflected by many factors.

The difference between the direction the compass shows and true North is called the *magnetic declination*. The average declination in a particular area will be shown on the border of the U.S.G.S. map of the area. This declination figure is updated frequently, since the earth's magnetic field fluctuates. In the eastern United States and Canada the compass will point west of true North; in the western parts of those countries it will point to the east of true North.

If you are using your compass to take bearings as you travel, effectively making your own map, you can simply use magnetic bearings. Except on very long trips you would be able to ignore declination altogether, since you are not likely to travel far enough for the declination to change significantly. In this case you are simply using the compass for a constant direction finder, and you are not concerned about the relation between your directions and true North. If you are referring to a map of the area, however, you must convert your bearings to true bearings by adding or subtracting the declination. Except in a few areas, the declination is great enough to throw you completely off course if you assume that magnetic and true North are essentially the same. Around Mount Washington in New Hampshire, for example, you would be a mile and a half off course in five miles if you followed a magnetic instead of a true bearing. Methods of correcting for declination will be discussed more fully, but you are unlikely to get into trouble if you remember where your compass is actually pointing whenever you use it.

WHAT GOOD IS DIRECTION?

The compass gives you a directional reference that has some relation (declination) to the direction of the North Pole, but so what? You will rarely be interested in going to the North Pole. If you find that you are lost in the woods in a blinding snowstorm and you pull out your trusty pocket compass, it will tell you the direction of the earth's magnetic field at the spot on which you are standing, but you may have difficulty working up an interest in this piece of information. The direction of the earth's magnetic field will not tell you where your car is parked unless you know some other things as well.

Even in the situation just described, where you have neglected to keep track of the other information you need to steer back to your car, the compass will do you some good. It will enable you to steer in a relatively straight line, rather than walking in aimless circles, which is what you will do if you follow your nose. In this case you should sit down and think about what you know of the area you are in, and decide which direction you should go to get out. Then you steer a straight line in that direction.

You will not be able to steer a very straight line by simply holding the compass in front of you and trying to head southeast; you have to walk around obstacles, push on your ski poles, blow your nose, and try to keep the compass needle steady. Probably you will end up by tripping over a log while looking at your compass and the losing it in the snow. The normal way to cope with all this is to take bearings. Taking a bearing is simply sighting an object in the direction you want to go, preferably one at some distance. You can sight over your compass, determining that a prominent dead tree is southwest of you. You put the compass in your pocket and walk to the dead tree by the easiest route. Then you take another bearing.

Bearings can be used to solve quite a few other problems. Let's suppose you have been more prudent. You have brought a map and kept track of your position on it during a mountain trip. The terrain may have been sufficiently distinctive so that there was no need for the compass. You simply followed your topo map and camped in a large round valley, and during the night a storm came up. If the visibility is poor it may be impossible to steer up out of the valley and hit the right pass; you might end up climbing a mountain, instead. In this case you can look at your map and determine which direction you should go to hit the pass. You can then correct for declination and take a bearing in the direction of the pass. In this way, you can steer yourself to the pass.

The compass can, of course, be used to orient your map with respect to the land around you, and this will often enable you to identify landmarks, since you will be able to relate their general direction to the map, as well as their shapes. If you can identify two or more landmarks in this way, you can use bearings to find

What good is direction?   209

your exact position by reversing the procedure mentioned above. Bearings are taken on the two landmarks and the directions transferred to the map. Where the directional lines cross is your position.

Finally, bearings may be used to keep track of your position, either in conjunction with a map or without one. You may draw your own map as you go along, keeping track of the distances traveled, and determining precise directions by taking bearings. All these uses of the compass will be described in more detail below, but since the exact procedure varies with different kinds of compasses, it will be necessary to discuss them first.

TYPES OF COMPASSES

Any compass intended for wilderness use should have a large enough face and sufficiently detailed markings to enable you to take bearings that are accurate within a couple of degrees. The more accurate they are, of course, the better. The tiny compasses divided into eight or sixteen directions are not really adequate for most purposes. Obviously, the compass should be sturdy. At a minimum, it must have a line or marks on opposite sides of the compass, which will enable you to sight landmarks for bearings. Sights attached to the compass are better, and they allow more precision with less effort.

The compass dial should be marked with azimuth readings, as well as the points of the compass. Azimuth marks are simply degree marks, the compass face being divided into 360° running clockwise from North, which is 0° and 360°. East is thus 90°, South is 180°, Southwest is 225°, and so on. This may sound a bit complicated, but if you think about adjusting for a 17° East declination from North Northeast by East, you'll see that it's easier to add or subtract from a numerical direction. For precise bearings the 360-degree system is much simpler to use than points of the compass. The actual markings may run either clockwise or counter-clockwise for reasons explained below. The markings may either be on the case or on a face that turns with the magnet, called the compass card.

The most common type of compass has a rotating needle with

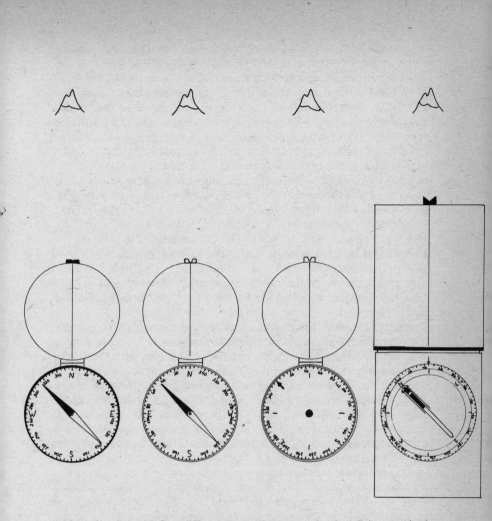

Taking a bearing with four different types of compass. On the left is a standard compass; next is a cruiser type, with reversed directions; in the third, a card type, the entire face rotates; and on the right is a Silva type, which features both a rotating needle and dial mounted on a transparent plastic base.

Types of compasses   211 directional and azimuth markings running clockwise on a face that is fixed solidly to the case. The case will include some sort of sighting device or line that corresponds to the marking for North (0°, 360°). We'll refer to this type as the standard compass in the discussions that follow. A detailed description of the method of taking a bearing with the standard compass will clarify the design of the other types to be described. These designs have arisen because of certain problems with the standard pocket compass.

The illustration shows the process of taking a bearing with four different types of compass. (The bearings shown here are magnetic bearings and still need to be corrected for declination if they are to be used with reference to a standard map.) With the standard compass the sighting line is aimed at the landmark which is 45° from magnetic North, or simply 45°, magnetic. There is no way to read this bearing directly, however. We must obtain it by noting that the north end of the needle points to 315° and that this is the same number of degrees counterclockwise from magnetic North (360°) as our landmark is clockwise. Thus, the bearing is 360° − 315° = 45°.

This correction becomes natural to make after some practice, but there are other types of compass that are designed to remove this complication from the start. The simplest, but also the strangest when one first looks at it, is the cruiser compass, which is the same as the standard except that the markings on the case are reversed; instead of running clockwise, they run counterclockwise. Thus, at right angles to North (0°, 360°) and to the right, we find not East (90°) but West (270°). The advantage to this system is obvious from the illustration. To find a magnetic bearing you simply orient the sighting line and read the bearing where the north end of the needle points.

A second method of solving this problem is to use a compass card attached to the top of the needle on which the directions and azimuth markings are printed. This whole card rotates, so that each directional marking is oriented towards that magnetic direction. The markings are made in the usual clockwise fashion. With this type of compass, taking a magnetic bearing is again simplified. The sighting line is pointed toward the landmark and the bearing is read where this line intersects the compass card.

A fourth method of correcting this problem is used on the Silva-type compasses, which also include several other useful innovations to be discussed below. The Silva arrangement uses a three-part system instead of a two-part one. The sighting line is on a case or a plastic base on which is mounted a compass housing that is free to rotate on the base. The directional markings are on this housing. Inside the housing is the compass needle. The sighting line is aimed at the landmark, and the housing is then turned until North corresponds with the needle. The bearing is read at the intersection of the sighting line and the housing dial.

This basic method of taking a bearing is used whether one is recording the bearing for future reference, finding a landmark guide for a line of progress that has been determined from a map, or using landmarks to locate his position. Any reasonably accurate compass can be used, but the advantages of the three modified systems should be obvious. Before going into any more detail about special procedures, we'll discuss the standard methods of finding your way.

SYSTEMS FOR KNOWING YOUR LOCATION

There are many ways to guide yourself around the wilderness, and the one you choose will depend very much on individual circumstances. An afternoon jaunt along a narrow valley will not require any special thought about the return trip; you will just follow the valley back without even thinking about it. This ability to follow some routes without thought is the most common reason that people become lost, however. While they are following such a valley it is obvious to them that they can follow it back, and when they cross a path into another much larger valley they do not stop to think and realize that the return route is no longer obvious. By the time they suddenly become aware of that fact they no longer know where they are.

It was stated earlier in this chapter that the art of finding one's way in wilderness areas consists largely of maintaining an awareness of one's position in a way appropriate to the terrain and the objective of the trip. In many areas that are fairly open and that have distinctive features, this is done simply by an occasional glance at the map. In the high mountains of California, for example, a compass may sometimes be carried for years without being used, since a combination of map and terrain will serve to guide the wanderer. As long as he maintains an awareness of his location on the map, no bearings are needed. In case of a bad storm, he need merely check his map to find the bearing he should follow, and then he can follow this bearing out with the compass, even though he has taken no bearings on the way in.

Since this method of route finding is a pleasant one to use, it is unfortunate that there are many kinds of terrain where it will not work. Some areas have a few prominent landmarks, yet include no distinctive features in the surrounding terrain. It would hardly be prudent to wander around in the tundra south of the Alaska range without taking bearings occasionally, since there is enough country "generally south of McKinley" for a man to wander for the rest of his life, and one square mile often looks just like hundreds of others around it.

Base lines. One very convenient system for many situations uses any long base line that may be available. The most common would be a road on which your car is parked, but a river, the shore of a large lake, a railroad line, a power-line cut, or many other such lines may be used. In using the base-line system, one simply keeps track of the direction and distance of the baseline and the approximate distance and direction along it of the car, camp, or supply dump. With the base-line system, much less precision is needed in this information than with most other methods. The idea is that you need only find your way back to the reference line and follow it to your objective.

An example of this method is shown in the illustration. The degree of accuracy that is needed depends on the length of the available base line and the distance you are traveling. It is important to be sure that your error is not so great as to cause you to miss the line. Make sure that you know the character of a base line from a map or from examination. The twists and turns of roads and rivers can be very confusing, and unless you are sure of your location when you hit the base line, you are likely to search back and forth along a section of the line instead of traveling far enough along it to reach your objective. Unless the scenery along the line is familiar to you, it is important to aim to one side or the other of your objective. Otherwise, you will not know which way to turn when you reach the line. By deliberately missing the point to which you want to go, by aiming to one side, you will know which way to turn when you reach the base line.

FINDING YOUR WAY

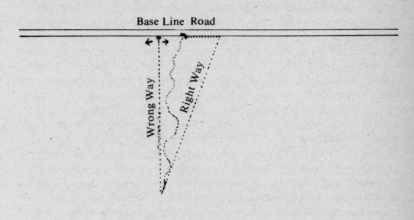

Using a road as a base line. Here the party has proceeded generally south from the base line. When they wish to return, they should not attempt to head directly north to the car, since if they miss it, they will not know which way to turn. Rather, they should bear either east or west of north, and when they reach the road they will know which way the car is. Many other types of base lines are used the same way.

Base-line methods can be used in many sorts of area and on many scales. In forested areas with little visibility ʹand no landmarks, it is possible to set up your own base line by marking out a path in either direction from your camp by the methods discussed below for marking trails. In flat country that has good visibility and at least one landmark, a serviceable base line can be simply a bearing on a landmark that can be seen from a long distance. Where considerable distances are involved, a subsidiary marked line can be set up perpendicular to this bearing line, running far enough on each side of it to compensate for compass error.

Systems for knowing your location

Steering by compass bearings. In many areas it is simply not feasible to use the map alone or to navigate roughly from a line of position. Under storm conditions, this becomes the case in almost any sort of terrain, unless one is following a very well-defined geographical feature. In such a situation it is necessary to find one's way by using compass bearings. There are several ways of relating the map and the compass, depending on what you know and what you need to know. These are discussed below, but first we may as well cover the actual method of taking and following a bearing.

Walking on a bearing is the method used when it is necessary to actually guide yourself with the compass. This is done in a number of situations. If you know where you are on a map, but there is no way for you to guide yourself by landmarks alone, you can mark your desired line of progress on the map. Then the angle between your lines of progress and North is measured, either with a protractor or with the compass used as a protractor. This angle, measured clockwise from North, is the azimuth bearing for the direction you want to travel.

Another situation in which it is necessary to travel on a bearing occurs when you are guiding yourself by a large landmark, though you are not actually traveling to it. You might be heading for a lake ten miles northeast of a particular mountain, and the easiest way to find the lake might be by maintaining a bearing on the mountain behind you. Even if you were going to the mountain, in some kinds of country it might be impossible to see it for miles at a time. In this case you would maintain your direction in between views of the mountain by taking intermediate bearings.

Finally, in many kinds of flat country, in mountains that all look the same, and in bad storms, it is often necessary to base your whole knowledge of your position on bearings you follow. This is often true whether a map is available or whether you are drawing your own along the way. In such cases your knowledge of your position is only as good as the bearings themselves.

Let's suppose you are traveling to a mile-long lake five miles distant through fairly thick and featureless woods. Five miles farther on the other side of the lake is a large mountain that can be seen most of the time. Taking a bearing on the mountain, you check your map and determine that the lake is on a line between you and the mountain. You reason that by heading for the mountain you will hit the lake. If you just travel toward the mountain, though, there is a good chance that by nightfall you will find your-

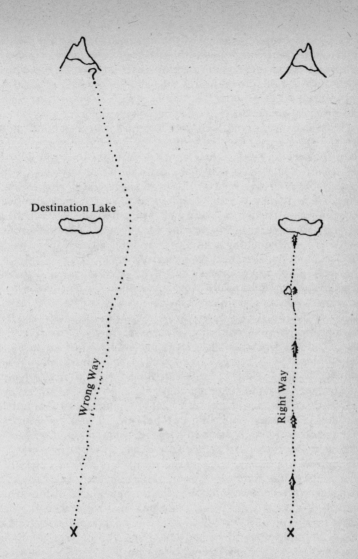

Destination Lake

Wrong Way

Right Way

When using a distant point for a bearing, be sure to pick intermediate points. In the left-hand diagram a snowshoer intended to go to a lake on the same bearing as a distant peak, and he simply headed for the peak, but natural deviations made him miss the lake altogether. On the right, he kept picking intermediate landmarks along the same line, and this enabled him to follow a straight course.

Systems for knowing your location

self within a couple of miles of the mountain but with no lake in sight. The reason is that your course through the dense woods will wander here and there, with a good chance of missing the lake altogether in the middle. If you want to follow a fairly straight line to be sure of hitting your lake, you need two points along your bearing that you can keep lined up as you go along.

To do this, when you take your original bearing on the mountain you should pick a prominent tree as far along the line as possible. By keeping the tree and the mountain lined up you will stay on a straight line. You will make detours, but always having two points to line up will enable you to keep correcting for errors as you go. When you are about half way to your tree, pick another in the same line. It is not necessary to take a new bearing each time, but you should recheck the bearing occasionally. The farther away the trees are, the more accurate your line will be, and the less often you will have to check your bearing.

In very dense forest or very bad weather, you may have to take bearings very frequently to keep from getting off course. On the other hand, if you can line up two distant hills you may be able to travel all day on a very accurate bearing without ever rechecking the compass. In poor conditions, when bearings are taken on trees just a short distance ahead, a large accumulation of error will be inevitable unless bearings are rechecked constantly. In any case, however, it is always best to try to line up two objects if at all possible, rather than using only one.

Where no landmarks are available, the members of the party itself should be used to keep your bearing. If you are alone, of course, you will simply have to keep your compass out and follow it as best you can. If there are several in the party, however, the last man should carry the compass, with the party stretched out as far as safety and audibility permit. The rear man lines up on the others and shouts directions. With two people ahead of him he can keep the party on a fairly accurate bearing, even when the landscape is completely blotted out. This method is clearly more time-consuming than others, however, and will only be used when it is essential, as it is in whiteout conditions.

In following a bearing or a series of bearings over a long distance it will almost always be necessary to make detours. When the bearing line is taken on a pair of distant points this may cause no problem. You might be able to work up a river to a good crossing and then diagonal back to your bearing simply by lining

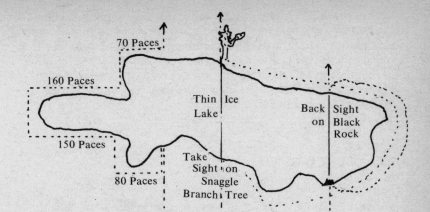

70 Paces

160 Paces

150 Paces

80 Paces

Thin Ice Lake

Back on

Sight Black Rock

Take Sight on Snaggle Branch Tree

1   2   3

Three ways of going around obstacles while following a compass bearing. On the left is the only method that can be used when visibility is bad and the most practical one at some other times. The party paces off their deviation from their course, and deviates at known angles, right angles being the easiest. Then, when the obstacle is cleared, they pace back to their original course. The party in the center sighted a prominent landmark on the other side of the obstacle, walked around to it, and then resumed their course. The right-hand group could see no landmark on the other side, but found one where they were (or could have left a mark). They proceeded around the obstacle and took a back-sighting with their compass to get back on their bearing.

Systems for knowing your location   219

up the two distant points again. When you are steering by compass alone or using trees and rocks only a short distance away this is not possible. In this case you must keep track of your deviations, reversing them as soon as possible. This is generally best done by pacing off each leg of the detour. Any angles may be used, but a series of right angles is often easiest, simply because it requires little thought to execute.

MAP AND COMPASS

Walking a compass bearing is used in many situations, but the bearing itself must be determined from the map or marked on some kind of map for later reference if it is to be of use. The simplest use of compass bearings is simply to steer a course between recognizable points on the map. This is an obvious technique, almost as simple to follow as that of using the map alone, and the only complication is the necessity of allowing for compass declination.

Correcting for declination. The main difficulty to be surmounted in correcting for declination is simply that of developing a system that eliminates the possibility of time-consuming confusion or serious mistakes. If the compass is being used without reference to any map except your own rough sketch, there is no need to convert from magnetic to true bearings, and the problem can be ignored. If, however, you are using map and compass in conjunction there will be a need to convert back and forth.

The particular system you develop for converting will depend on the type of compass you use. In taking notes it is best to distinguish between magnetic and true bearings. I use *m* or *t* following the azimuth in my notes to indicate this distinction, so that I won't have to ask myself later whether or not I made a particular conversion. For example, after crossing a broad, flat saddle before starting down a ravine, I might take a bearing back across the route just used in case of a storm on the return trip. The note might read, "top of ravine, rtn. from big birch 136° m," meaning that the return route lies along magnetic azimuth 136°, sighted from the prominent birch tree at the top of the ravine.

Wrong Way

Direction
of Car

Right Way

Hitting trails, roads, or streams endwise requires deliberate deviation, like that used in hitting a base line. If you try to head straight for the line and miss it, you won't know which way to go. Deviate deliberately, turn to cut the line, and then backtrack if necessary.

To hit a point like a camp without a base line, continue until you know you are past the point. Then turn at right angles, again continue past the camp, repeat this, crossing your original trail, and continuing until you are sure you have passed the possible location in that direction. Now cross back into your rough square, which has become a search perimeter. Keep going around inside the square, closing it as much as possible each time, until you hit the camp.

X

More commonly, the compass is used in direct conjunction with the map, and the correction must be made at the time. The most convenient compasses have a declination-offsetting device that is set to make the correction automatically. If you have one of the more common types of compass, you must simply make the correction each time you use the compass. For example, you might be laying out a line on the map and then following the bearing.

The illustration shows that you are on the shore of a large lake. Your car is parked at the end of a road five miles away. You decide on a line of progress that will take you somewhat south of the road. Then, when you are sure you have gone more than five

Map and compass

miles, you will be able to head due north and cut the road. If you were to aim straight for the end of the road, you would not know which way to turn after traveling this distance.

Having decided the line you wish to follow, you draw it on the map, extending it to the border, which runs north and south. Using a protractor or the markings on your compass, you measure the angle from North, and this is the true azimuth that you wish to follow. Marked on the map, usually in the graphic way shown, is the average magnetic declination in the area. It might be "declination 16° East." This would mean that your compass will indicate a "North" that is 16° east of true North, which is the same as to say that 0° on your compass is at true azimuth 16°. If the bearing you measured for your line of progress was 96°, the compass or magnetic bearing you want to follow would be 96° − 16° = 80°m. If you were in the eastern part of the country the declination would be West instead of East, and you would then have to add the declination instead of subtracting it.

Orienting the map and determining positions. In the example just given and in many other possible situations, the exact location on the map of both the party and its objective were known. In this case it is possible to calculate a compass bearing directly and then to follow it. In many other circumstances, however, it may be necessary to determine one's position on the map before this procedure can be followed. This may not always be possible, and in cases where such a difficulty is anticipated the party maintains its own map of compass bearings, landmarks, and distances, a method discussed below. As long as landmarks are visible occasionally, however, positions can usually be found using the map and compass.

As a first step, the map should be placed on something flat and stable and oriented to the ground. This may be possible without use of the compass; for example, if you are going up a long, narrow valley, you may not know where you are in the valley, but directions may still be clear. If this is not the case, the map is oriented by simply lining up magnetic North as shown by your compass and that shown in the declination diagram of the map.

Once the map is oriented, it may be possible to relate the terrain shown on the map to the land surrounding it. If at least two landmarks are recognizable, it is possible to establish one's position exactly, though at least three landmarks are preferred. Even one landmark will serve to establish a line of position, which may then serve to help identify a second point of reference.

The easiest way to find your position on the map once your landmarks have been identified is by sighting directly. (You may also sight with the compass and then transfer the bearings, but this is usually both more complicated and less accurate.) Make sure your map is accurately oriented, and be careful not to rotate it while you make your sightings. Now take two small, straight objects to serve as sights; pine needles, matches, or pins would do. Stand one of them on the map point that represents your landmark. Then sight across the tip to the actual landmark. Place the second sighting point on the map somewhere along your sighting line. Now draw a line between the two sights, an operation that can be performed by your companion or by you once you have figured the proper sequence to let you get by with only two hands. The line you have just drawn is a line of position, and your location lies somewhere along it. Another line to a different landmark will give a second line of position, and your location will be determined by the intersection of the lines. The method's accuracy is increased if at least one more landmark is used. It is also best to use landmarks that are approximately 90° from one another, since the error is increased by using points more nearly in line with one another.

There are obviously many applications of this method of determining your position. For example, it can be used with the baseline method; one line from a landmark intersecting a base line will determine your position on it. The procedure can be reversed to help identify an unknown landmark. Once some practice in the basic techniques of using the map and compass has been acquired, common sense will suggest other uses when the need arises.

KEEPING TRACK OF WHERE YOU'VE BEEN

The most important route-finding problem in the wilderness is finding your way out. It's not usually a very serious matter if you miss your objective on the way in, since you can always try again another day—providing you know how to get back to your starting point! Of course, the situation is different if you are traveling

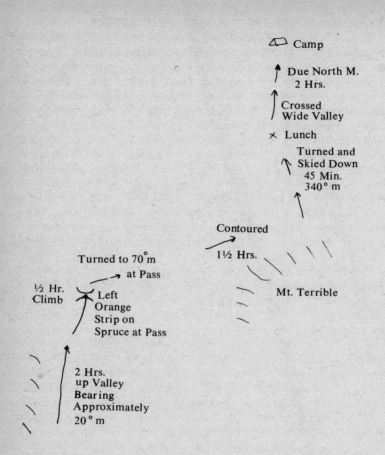

An example of a hand-drawn map kept during a trip. Enough information is included for a return trip even in a storm.

between food caches, since you then have a more compelling reason to get to your destination than the reputed view. When you are carrying your food and shelter, though, it's knowing the way back that keeps your trip from turning into a survival test instead of a pleasure tour.

The most common and useful ways of finding the way back to your car or cabin have already been discussed: keeping an eye on your back trail, knowing your location on a good topo map, following some continuous landmark like a river, using a base-line system of route finding, or some combination of these.

There are two other important methods that are frequently used to keep track of the return route. The first has already been mentioned incidentally; it entails maintaining a continuous record of landmarks and bearings that can be followed back out. This method is useful if you don't have an adequate topo map, and it may sometimes be called for in featureless terrain or bad weather. A record of bearings and landmarks must be kept, often right on the topo map if one is carried. If no standard map has been taken, the best way to keep a record is usually to draw a rough map as you go along. A sample map is shown in the illustration, but the methods are for the most part self-evident.

One useful point to remember is to use bearings over short distances when possible. A long route is thus broken into a number of shorter legs. Small base-line systems can be used to cover sections of the route. The track followed can be planned so that landmarks that are easily relocated are encountered frequently. Each time such a landmark is encountered, it should be marked on the map, distances (in units of length or time) ought to be recorded, and new bearings should be taken. For example, instead of passing near the end of a lake while walking a bearing, you should use the shore of the lake as a new base line and take a new bearing from some easily recognizable point on the shore. In this way the errors that are inherent in walking a bearing can be frequently reduced to zero before they accumulate into large distances.

Blazing a trail. The time-honored method for finding a way back to camp is to blaze a trail, either one that you can follow all the way back or one that you can intersect. In some situations this principle is still useful, though the method of gouging trees is now justified only for trails that will be maintained with some permanence. If the weekend traveler can't find his way without hacking live trees, he has no business in the woods.

Keeping track of where you've been

If you anticipate a possible need to blaze a trail, the easiest way is to carry a packet of brightly colored strips of plastic. These are light and compact, and they are practically indestructible except by fire. They can be quickly tied to branches along your route. Reach as high as you comfortably can, so that subsequent snowfall will not bury your trail. Look back occasionally to make sure that the markers are visible from the direction from which you will be returning. Anticipate bad weather in judging the distance you will be able to see.

If you should have occasion to use plastic strips as markers, take them *all* down on your return. They will probably look beautiful to you if you are coming back in a bad storm, but to anyone else they are just unsightly trash, falling into roughly the same category as aluminum beer cans. They stay bright and conspicuous for years. If some emergency makes it really impossible for you to clean your route when you leave, then have the grace to come back the next time you can to clean your trail. We go to the wilderness for a bit of adventure, but finding it is no excuse to litter the woods with junk.

Above timberline and in other treeless areas, there may be nothing to tie your plastic strips to. If no natural projections are available, the best method of blazing a trail is with wands—sticks three or four feet long. The light bamboo sticks sold for gardens make good wands, especially if a bit of bright plastic is tied to the top for visibility. The longer the wand, the better chance it will have of staying above the level of newly fallen snow. Try to pick windblown spots for the wands, where they will be less likely to be covered by drifts. This is an easy matter, since such spots are also often the most visible places available. Wands should be picked up on the return trip and carried home.

Either streamers or wands can be used in conjunction with another system. Bearings can be taken to and from them, and a line of markers can be used to form a base line in the woods. A marker can be left on one side of an obstacle to give a quick back bearing from the other side. For example, suppose you walk on a bearing to a river, but cannot cross at the point you reach. A marker can be tied at that point, and you can then find a crossing without pacing off distances or worrying about direction. When the other side is reached, you can walk along the shore until you are back on your original line as shown by the marker. On the return trip it serves as a blaze. The reader will have no difficulty thinking of other uses.

FINDING YOUR WAY

ERRATIC COMPASS?

The vagaries of the earth's magnetic field have been mentioned, as has the fact that the compass cannot be trusted to point toward any particular spot. The compass declination in both the Northwest and the Northeast is greater than it would be if the needle pointed directly to the magnetic pole. Within a particular area, however, the declination is fairly constant from one mile to the next, and the foot traveler rarely needs to concern himself about the small variations that do exist. Surveyors and mechanized travelers are not so lucky, but their problems will be left for others to explore.

It is common knowledge that a compass will be deflected by the proximity of any magnetic material such as iron or steel. Obviously, one should not take compass readings near knives, on top of cooksets, or next to steel belt buckles.

There remains the problem of local magnetic disturbance, which occasionally occurs when large ore deposits and the like are near by. Such spots are rare, and the likelihood of your actually coming upon one while using your compass is small. Areas of magnetic disturbance stir the imagination like the hungry wolf packs of the North. People who have got themselves turned around commonly panic and immediately blame the attack of a wandering magnetic field for the fact that their compass does not point where they instinctively feel it should. Chances are overwhelming that the compass is pointing in just the direction shown by the declination diagram on the map. If you are really in doubt, take a series of careful bearings as you move along a straight line. If the bearings don't vary within a mile or so, there is no problem with the compass.

Incidentally, with a compass having a needle, make sure you know which end is which. If the ends are colored or marked in some other way that might be ambiguous, mark the compass "white = N," or something similar. Confusion in an emergency might raise doubts in your mind that wouldn't occur on a warm afternoon.

MORE ON COMPASS FEATURES

Some of the basic types of compass have already been discussed, along with the essentials for wilderness use. Though any compass with provisions for sighting and reading bearings with fair accuracy is adequate, there are a number of other features that are convenient. Three ways of facilitating the reading of azimuths have already been mentioned: reversing the direction of the numbers on the dial, using a compass card, and using a dial enclosing the needle, which also rotates on the base plate.

The convenience of the sighting device is worth studying if you are buying a compass. The best models will usually allow you to sight in a number of different ways to meet different circumstances. Mirrors are included on many compasses, but they are of two types. One merely enables you to read the dial while you are sighting, without moving your eye from the sight. This is a convenience, but is not to be compared to the true sighting mirror. The latter can also be used to read a bearing, but it is intended primarily to allow you to sight through the mirror, using the compass in many positions that would be inconvenient or impossible without the mirror. The sights are even usable with the compass on the ground. A sighting mirror combined with a fairly large and clear dial makes for a very accurate compass.

The best sighting method for wilderness use is one with an optical system which allows sighting and reading a bearing without the usual eye movement and refocusing. The Wilkie Bearing compass and the Suunto KB14 are the only two I know that meet this requirement very well.

Declination-offsetting devices have been mentioned as a convenience. They usually operate by having the scale rotate with respect to the sight, though the exact method varies with the type of compass. The declination is set at the beginning of a short trip and left alone, though occasional changes may be necessary on a longer trip. In any case, the declination offset is not changed constantly and doesn't have to be as convenient to change as other settings. It may even be an advantage if a screw is used which doesn't permit accidental changing.

A field compass is much more convenient to use if the needle is damped so that it comes quickly to rest. This is especially true when a compass bearing is being walked in poor weather, so that constant reference to the compass is necessary. The best damping is achieved in liquid-filled compasses. An alternative method is induction damping, which uses an electromagnetic force generated by the needle's motion to damp that motion. The induction method is satisfactory, but does not work so well as a good liquid-filled compass with no bubbles.

Several features make the use of a compass in conjunction with the map much easier. A straight edge attached to the compass case or frame in line with the sights makes it much simpler to orient the map and to transfer bearings back and forth between map and compass. An arrangement on the compass that can be used as a protractor is very helpful. Finally, the use of transparent base plates on compasses, so that the map can be seen through the compass, is extremely helpful. Many operations such as orienting the map are more convenient with this type of compass.

A few accessories are helpful in map work. If the compass cannot be used as a protractor, a light, flexible one should be carried for measuring bearings. A straight edge is often needed, though some item like a saw blade usually will serve. A small pencil should be available to draw lines and make notes. (Ink will run if it gets wet.) A couple of folded sheets of tracing paper serve for notes, and in a pinch they can be used for triangulation if you're doubtful about landmarks. Sightings can be made on as many landmarks as possible across a center point on the paper and lines drawn along the sighting. Then the tracing paper is tried out in various positions over the map, in hopes of finding the combination of landmarks that line up.

Paper, map, and pencil are usually carried in a transparent plastic map case, which may be tied to the pack or clothing. Frequent reference can then be made to the map without getting it wet and worn. The professional method is to cut the map in sections and mount it on cloth. Spaces are left between the cuts to allow folding without damaging the map. I have used this method, and it is the best way to preserve the map, but I confess that I generally just put the map in plastic folded so that the section in which I am immediately interested faces out. As I move along I refold the map or switch maps. Enough trips to the same area require the purchase of a new map because of wear, but with this technique, sloppy as it is, my location is usually in the middle of a visible section of the map instead of right along a fold somewhere. If the route lies along the intersection of two quadrangles, I fold the map in the case so that the edges come together.

If you mark your proposed route on the map beforehand it will be easy to find, and keeping track of your actual progress can be done with the pencil. Don't forget to note information you may need to know later. For laying out a route at home an inexpensive map measurer is convenient. This has a little wheel on the bottom that you roll along your proposed route. The scale above shows the length of all the twists and turns. Don't forget to watch the contours. Two miles won't go so quickly if you have to climb 3,000 feet.

There is an extra challenge to finding your way around the hills and the woods in winter. The use of the compass and map take a little time to master if you are not used to them, but they are not very complicated once the knack is acquired. Once the art of finding your way is achieved in winter you are unlikely to have trouble in any other season, and your freedom to travel where you are inclined to will be greatly enhanced.

X

Steep Snow: An Introduction

For many of us, the very essence of the wilderness is conveyed by the sight of a steep snow slope sweeping up the side of a mountain. The way this white ramp contrasts with darker rock and blue sky awakens a special exhilaration. It seems almost free from the law of gravity. This chapter attempts to survey some of the skills often needed by the skier, snowshoer, and backpacker who likes to travel in steep-snow country and who would like to extend the limits of the terrain he can travel safely.

The regions where steep snow abounds are a special province

In spring and summer the snow enthusiast can follow the snowline to higher altitudes. Mount Shasta, once a volcano.

for the tourist of the white wilderness, since the snows linger in the mountains long after they have disappeared from the lowlands. In the high ranges, snow can be found at any time of year, though it takes on a somewhat different character during the summer months. As spring marches in, the devotee of snow country can simply travel higher, providing he lives in an area convenient to the high mountains. Spring often provides some of the finest touring and camping weather, with long days and sometimes with fewer storms.

Steep snow may provide highways to areas that are hard to reach at other times of the year. An easy snow slope can cover a ramp that in summer is nothing but a tortuous and shifting pile of small stones. Where the snow does not cover scree, it may cover thick brush or treacherous dirt slopes. In addition to an easy climb up, the same slope may provide a thrilling run down on skis. Even the mountain traveler who has no interest in climbing the mountains themselves is likely to encounter occasional spots where the crossing or climbing of a short, steep section is necessary if he is not to turn back.

Despite all its attractions, steep snow is dangerous to the ill-equipped, the inexperienced, and the overbold. The same slope that

Steep snow: an introduction

Steep snow slopes like this may provide easy avenues to the peaks, but they can also be dangerous. In the Palisades.

provides a safe and easy staircase in one condition may within a few hours turn into a thousand-foot sliding board or an avalanche waiting for the unwary traveler to trigger its collapse. If such a change occurs while you are above the slope, you may find yourself in a very uncomfortable situation when you get back down to it. The hazards of avalanches to those passing below steep-snow slopes are discussed in the next chapter, and they demand the constant attention of anyone traveling in steep-snow country.

HOW STEEP IS STEEP?

The arts of dealing with steep snow are the proper province of mountaineering, and they comprise the most difficult and the longest apprenticeship of a notoriously demanding craft. Snow that would be considered steep by the experienced mountaineer is a subject that will not be touched on here. A really steep snow slope is a fine subject for contemplation by the general traveler in snow

STEEP SNOW: AN INTRODUCTION 232

country, as well as a source to be studied for possible avalanche hazards. Negotiating such angles requires equipment and techniques that deserve a book of their own, and trying to cover them here would be impossible.

"Steep snow," as used in this chapter, means simply snow that is difficult, impossible, or dangerous to negotiate with normal walking, snowshoeing, and skiing techniques and equipment. This definition, like the mountaineer's, has as much to do with equipment and snow conditions as it does with the actual angle of the slope. The snowshoer will often have trouble with slopes that don't really trouble the experienced mountain skier. Hard snow at a rather low angle will give the hiker trouble, while snow that is twice as steep might not bother him if it is soft enough to allow step-kicking.

CLIMBING AIDS AND SAFETY MEASURES

The equipment and techniques that are used to deal with steep snow fall into two categories: those designed to help climb up the slope in the first place, and those intended to prevent a slip or a fall from having serious consequences. The technical climber is likely to have a rather large arsenal of tools and techniques in each of those categories, but the backpacker's inventory is very small. Crampons, which are rigid frames with spikes protruding at the bottoms, can be attached to boots or snowshoes to keep the feet from slipping, and a similar device is sometimes used on skis. An ice ax provides a means of arresting a fall on snow slopes and makes many passages quite safe that would be exceedingly dangerous without the ax. The ax may also be used as a climbing aid, though for the backpacker it is more important as a safety device.

The safety devices are clearly the more important of the two sorts of equipment, but they are quite useless without practice in their use. Acquiring this experience is the prerequisite to any attempts to cross or climb slopes where a fall would be dangerous. Before delving into the lore of such slopes, however, we should consider the techniques that can be used to handle the many steep sections one sometimes encounters that present obstacles but not hazards.

Climbing aids and safety measures   233

SNOWSHOE TOOLS AND TECHNIQUES

Snowshoes tend to be particularly awkward when the going is steep, because it is usually impossible to dig the edges into the snow, as can be done with skis or boots alone. Still, snowshoes may be absolutely necessary for the non-skier in soft snow or in snow that has a crust that will hold up a snowshoer but not a walker without skis or snowshoes. In steep-snow country some kind of short, tail-less snowshoe is nearly always the choice, and there is a great advantage in having the foot well forward on the snowshoe, at least going uphill. The standard bearpaw is the usual choice to provide these features, though some mountain snowshoers prefer to modify one of the longer and narrower shoes by either moving the toe hole forward, cutting off a section of the rising toe, eliminating the tail, or a combination of these modifications. The presumed advantage to these modifications over the standard bearpaw is that traverses are somewhat easier because of the narrower shoes. I haven't noticed that they provide a really significant advantage over the standard bearpaw, however, since on steep slopes one usually has to climb straight up anyway.

With any snowshoe design, steep snow calls for the addition of some sort of snowshoe crampon or traction device. In general, any cleat- or spike-like projection will do the job. The more spikes, and the longer they are, the better job they will do in difficult situations like slick crust, but the most effective arrangements with more than a couple of spikes over an inch long will have to be removable or they will cause trouble in normal woods walking. Whatever arrangement you use, remember that it will do the most good under the ball of the foot, where your weight will rest. If you don't want to go to a lot of trouble improvising snowshoe crampons, buy a pair of instep crampons, which are discussed below, and devise some strapping arrangement that will allow you to fasten them securely to the snowshoe under the ball of the foot. It is often necessary to saw off the side lugs to do this, but some types of instep crampons will fit without this being necessary, and this type can double as instep and snowshoe crampon.

In soft, steep snow, the usual method of ascent with snowshoes is to kick the toe of the snowshoe directly into the snow. Then you put your weight on it as gingerly as possible, in hopes that the step won't break, causing you to slide back twenty feet. When you do break loose, it's usually better to try a new track the second time, since the first one gets harder and harder with successive attempts, gradually developing a vertical headwall at the top. Where rocks underlie the soft snow by a few feet, you can sometimes get purchase with the toe of your boot sticking through the snowshoe toe hole. This is a rather delicate maneuver, and is advisable only when there is a soft landing below.

When the snow becomes a little harder, the step-kicking usually becomes quite effective, and no difficulties are experienced. As it gets too hard for step-kicking, the snowshoe is stamped flat, with traction coming from the crampons and from the toe of the boot protruding through the toe hole. With either of these methods, the climber should be careful not to move the foot around once it is placed, since this is likely to break loose his support. Step gingerly.

Naturally, when the snow becomes hard enough to support your weight without snowshoes, they are taken off and tied to the pack, and climbing, crossing, or descent proceeds on foot. The most difficult conditions occur on breakable crust that is too weak to climb without snowshoes but too slippery with them; snowshoe crampons usually solve this problem. An equivalent situation occurs when steep snow changes from hard crust to powder every few feet.

On any kind of steep snow a fairly long ski pole is a tremendous help as a prop, and many climbers prefer a pair of them. If an ice ax is carried it may be of some help on difficult steps if the shaft is plunged into the snow and the head used as a handhold.

SKIS ON STEEP SNOW

The merits and limitations of various types of skis in steep snow have already been discussed at some length, and there seems no reason to repeat them. Skis that are designed to handle steep snow are generally much easier to use in difficult situations than snowshoes, providing the snow is deep enough and the skier is competent. It is usually easier for the skier to climb a steep slope using climbers than to remove his skis and resort to step-kicking. By the time the slope becomes hard enough to make skiing dangerous, crampons are often required to progress easily without the skis.

The limits of the skis can be extended somewhat for high-mountain skiing with the use of ski crampons called Harscheisen. These are serated edges that attach to each side of each ski and protrude about an inch below the bottoms. They can be used on hard windpack and icy crust to make short steep sections safe that would otherwise require normal crampons.

STEP-KICKING

As snow becomes hard and steep enough to prevent the hiker from gaining purchase by just stepping in it, it becomes necessary to kick steps into the slopes. There is nothing very difficult about this in principle, though someone doing it for the first time will probably find it rather tiring. One simply stands on one foot, raises the other to a comfortable height, and kicks the upper foot into the slope. Harder snow may require more than one kick. The procedure is continued until the top of the hill is reached. In coming downhill, the leg is usually straightened and the heel plunged down into the snow. This works on snow that is quite steep as long as it is soft enough, and the necessity of facing into the slope and kicking steps down is not likely to be encountered by the conservative backpacker. If it is, the procedure is to bend the upper knee as much as possible and then to kick a step with the lower foot.

The practice of carrying an ice ax and its use for self-arrest are discussed below, but it should certainly be carried on any slope requiring more than the simplest step-kicking. If an ax is not available, the slope should not be attempted. When it is carried, the shaft is usually plunged into the snow as an anchor whenever extra stability is needed during step-kicking.

In most climbing it is easiest to proceed up with traverses and switchbacks. Occasionally, because of the extra effort needed to make the steps, it may require less total effort to climb straight up. It is usually easiest to follow a straight line going downhill. There is normally no danger in going straight up or down in the sort of climbing being discussed here, since the possibility of a slip should not present great hazard. If such a danger does exist, because a slip might not be controlled, a straight line should not be followed, since it puts the whole party in a line, and if one person slips, everyone below him will also be knocked off. However, no one should be on hazardous terrain without a climbing rope and the skills to use it. Crampons have not yet been discussed, but if they are being worn the climbers should not be in line, since the danger is always present that the crampons of a slipping climber will mutilate the man below even in an otherwise harmless fall.

THE SAFETY FACTOR

Avalanches aside, the greatest danger presented by steep snow is that of an uncontrolled slip. Once a slide is started on a snow slope, it may be very difficult to stop without some special methods. Unless there is a positive means of stopping available, it is foolish to try to cross or climb any slope other than a very short one. As a general rule, you should never attempt any maneuvers on a snow slope unless you are absolutely sure that a slip would not be dangerous, either because the slope is short with no danger at the bottom or because you have the means of stopping.

The means of stopping a fall on steep snow is provided by the ice ax, and this is its main function for the general snow traveler. Stopping a slip with an ice ax is accomplished through the technique of self-arrest. Learning self-arrest will enable the backpacker and winter tourist to extend his horizons considerably and with safety. Learning in this case requires practice, however. It is not enough to know how the arrest is performed intellectually; it must be practiced until it has become instinctive and until the traveler has become a competent judge of its limitations.

The best way to learn the technique of self-arrest is to have an experienced climber teach you, perhaps at one of the beginning snow-climbing seminars sponsored by many climbing clubs in this country. Barring this, you can teach yourself. You'll have to find a fairly steep snow slope with a good smooth runout and no rocks around that you might hit if you lose control. Take some friends along who are interested in learning; spending the day sliding in the snow is a lot more fun with company. It's also a good idea to

Easy summer snow. Quite safe with only an ice ax—and perhaps crampons early in the morning. No rope is needed, but plenty of previous practice in self-arrest is essential. In the Minarets.

STEEP SNOW: AN INTRODUCTION

carry spare clothes, since you'll get wet in the course of a day's falling in the snow. If your slope is a bowl that gets progressively steeper the higher you go, you will be able to practice your technique on more and more difficult terrain, and you will be able to learn enough about self-arrest to handle easy slopes with confidence. The ability to handle and judge more difficult situations only comes after a lot more practice. Pick a day when the snow is fairly well-consolidated. Loose snow requires wading to climb or stop, and when it gets steep enough to require arrests it presents an avalanche danger.

The ice ax is the indispensable tool of anyone who wants to venture on slopes where an unchecked slip would be dangerous. Without it even the experienced mountaineer will slide helplessly down easy snow slopes. For self-arrest and other such uses, the length of the ax should be about the same as the distance from your palm to the ground. Lengths a few inches longer or shorter than this are perfectly all right, but don't buy one of the very short axes that are now becoming common. Such axes are very practical for the technical climber on severe ice walls, but for the beginner on easy snow they are useless and dangerous.

Position of the strong hand on the ax head. A strong grip is needed to control the ax. The pick is pushed into the snow while held under the shoulder. Mittens or gloves must be worn in practice.

The safety factor

Ready to go into arrest position. Pick under the strong shoulder and the weak hand controlling the cane end to keep the point from catching and pulling the ax away. Wrist loop is not used in arrest, except in special circumstances. It is used to prevent loss of the ax where this would be hazardous.

Other features are not important in occasional use by the wilderness traveler. The ax should have a wrist strap attached to a glide ring, but it will make no difference to you whether there is a carabiner hole or where the teeth are placed on the pick. You will probably be happiest with a fairly light ax, since it will travel most of the time on the pack, and the extra weight of a heavier ax is of use only in step-cutting or belaying by climbers on high-angle slopes.

Practicing self-arrest should be begun with the novice simply falling into the basic arrest position on a gentle slope. Dress warmly, with all your clothing zipped up and tucked in, and be sure to wear gloves. To arrest a fall the ax is held diagonally across the front of the body. One hand holds the head of the ax as shown in the illustration, the fingers curling around the top of the head and the thumb underneath the adze. The pick is held just under the shoulder, and the other hand grips the opposite end of the shaft, next to the spike, holding it firmly down by the hip. The whole weight of the body can then be forced down on the ax, pressing the pick into the snow. With the pick forced into the snow, the back is arched slightly, putting the body's weight on the pick and the toes, which are also dug into the snow.

After you have the feel of the arrest position, climb up the hill to a spot that is steep enough so that you will slide a bit if you slip, and practice going into the arrest position. If the snow is relatively soft, dig everything in immediately. If the snow is harder, dig the pick and your toes in a bit more smoothly and gradually, so that the pick will not be wrenched from your hands as you dig it into hard windboard or crust. As you begin to get the knack, work onto slightly steeper slopes, and simulate real slips. Try to get into the positions you would be in if a slip occurred while you were not expecting it. It should be clear by now that where a slip is possible you should always hold the head of the ax in your hand in the position you would use for self-arrest, with your hand around the head, the pick sticking out from the little finger side of the hand.

After you are completely confident about self-arrests that involve falling forward into the position, you are ready to start practicing with more awkward falls—backwards. The problem in falling backwards is that you end up sliding downhill head-first on your back. As with all slips on steep snow, it is necessary to gain control very quickly, before a lot of speed is picked up. A very short delay will have you bouncing every which way, sometimes in the air, with no idea which way is up or down. The most important thing to remember in all slips is to apply the arrest immediately; in hard snow it must be applied smoothly, not by jamming the pick or toes into the snow, which would cause you to somersault or lose the ax, but by beginning a steady application immediately. With the backwards fall, the ax is grasped in the arrest position while you are on your back. Then you roll over onto the pick side of your body—not the side where the spike is protruding and might be ripped from your hand. As the pick begins to drag, your feet will rotate around it, and by the time you have turned over onto your stomach, your feet should be headed downhill, and you are back in the normal arrest position. It goes without saying that this maneuver should be practiced on easy ground first; things happen very quickly on steep terrain.

As the beginner acquires experience with the techniques of self-arrest, his confidence will develop, but he should take great care that all practice is carried out on slopes with a run-out and with no protruding rocks or other objects. Loss of control above hard objects can lead to very serious injuries. Snow is always unpredictable, and a wide margin must be allowed for error, even by

The safety factor 241

experienced snow mountaineers. An unexpected patch of ice may lie below you that will greatly affect your stopping distance, even if you don't lose your ax to it.

The cardinal rule in all situations where an arrest is being performed or may be called for is to *hang on to your ice ax*. You can't perform an arrest without it, except on very easy snow. On hard snow, the pick must not be jammed into the ice too quickly, or you will not be able to hold onto it; it is pressed in quickly with a steady pressure, but not jammed. If you start to lose your hold, pressure on the pick is reduced. *Maintain control of the ax.* Losing hold of the spike end makes the ax almost as useless as losing it altogether. In addition to this, the ax is sharp, and if your wrist strap is being worn, the flailing ax can injure you or one of your companions as you speed by.

The beginner practicing arrest will presumably be on a slope that does not require crampons, and so will not be wearing them. If he should buy or carry crampons later on, he should practice arrests while wearing them. Great care is needed if the toes are dug in not to catch the points of the crampons in hard snow and cause a backward somersault. While wearing crampons, it is safer to rely on the pick and the knees for arrest, if possible.

THE LIMITS OF SELF-ARREST

Having learned the techniques of self-arrest, you will be able to undertake a lot of easy climbs and traverses on steep snow with confidence. More than in any other area discussed in this book, however, a very conservative approach is called for in making safety judgments. Going up a snow slope is often easier than coming down (in a controlled manner, at least), even when the consistency of the snow remains the same. In addition to this fact, it is a rare day in the mountains when snow conditions on a steep slope do not change. If the snow that is just right for step-kicking at noon goes into shadow soon after, you may find it board-hard in the afternoon, and it may be quite impossible for you to descend with your skills and equipment. In this case you may have to bivouac until the next day.

Any serious climbing requires the use of rope techniques for safety, at least as a reserve in case of difficulty. The discussion of these techniques is well beyond the scope of this book and requires carrying many extra pounds of equipment as well. For this reason, before you venture onto steep snow, ask yourself the following questions, and answer them carefully:

1. Is there any avalanche danger, or is any likely to develop, that might present a problem on the way back?

2. Can each person in the party easily stop a slip on this terrain with the equipment he has? Is the safety margin wide enough to take into account possible ice patches and changing conditions on the return trip?

3. Are there any dangers below on the slope that negate the value of an arrest as a safety factor—rocks, trees, cliffs, steeper sections, ice—or that might negate it on the return trip? You might be able to arrest before sliding over the cliff below now, but what about this afternoon? What if someone slips and arrests—he has to climb back up—has he also room for a second arrest?

4. Have you thought about the problem of handling this section with an injured man? When you are tired? In a storm? If you misjudge, can you go around another way or will this be the only way out?

CRAMPONS

Crusty or windpacked snow is often so hard that kicking steps in it is difficult or impossible. Such conditions require either cutting steps with the ice ax, the use of crampons to give the feet purchase on the snow, or both. Step-cutting will not be discussed here, since a slope that is steep and slippery enough to require it is also one where a climber, at least an inexperienced one, should be protected with a rope. Crampons may be useful to the general mountain traveler, however, if they are used carefully.

The most common crampons for occasional use on easy terrain are instep crampons, which are small frames with from four to six spikes each. They strap on the insteps of the climbing boots. This type of crampon is relatively light and useful for negotiating occasional stretches of hard snow that may be encountered. It is per-

Crampons 243

fect for the skier, snowshoer, or early spring backpacker to carry for a few short steep stretches.

More serious climbing requires a crampon that runs the full length of the boot and is generally hinged in the middle to allow some flexing. This type comes in several designs, but the novice should choose a set with ten points on each crampon. The points should be about one and a half to one and three-quarter inches long; crampons with fewer and shorter points are designed for ice and are not as useful for the beginner. Crampons must be fitted to your boots. They must fit tightly, and the strapping arrangement should be absolutely secure. The boots should not be able to shift on the crampons when they are pulled in different directions. All the points of the crampons should be vertical; horizontal or angled front points are intended for technical climbing on steep ice and are both useless and dangerous for any moderate climbing. The front set of points should be flush with the toe of the boot, neither forward nor back of it.

Use of crampons requires practice on progressively steeper slopes. All the cautions that have already been mentioned apply all the more if crampons are being used, since they make it possible for the climber to get into more difficult situations and present additional hazards as well. In principle, the technique is simple; the crampon is stamped or planted flat against the slope and left there until it is lifted for the next step. The ankles must be flexed to the angle of the slope, so that the crampon will be flush with it. If the crampon is planted straight down so that it forms an angle with the slope it will tend to break out. In practice, the use of crampons on all but the gentlest slopes requires strength and flexibility of the ankles, which can only be developed with time. A few attempts on practice slopes will show the beginner the limits of his craft.

Several special dangers inhere in the use of crampons. They must be kept sharp. Dull crampons tend to break out unexpectedly and require much more force to set. In any case, they make the wearer less secure. Since crampons are sharp, they are also dangerous. The hazards of falling on one's companions have been mentioned. When learning to walk with crampons, take care to avoid snagging your pants legs, which can cause falls or leg injuries. When the crampons are not strapped on your boots they should be in the pack or made safe with some kind of secure shield. They should not be tied loose on the outside of the pack; if you fall they may gouge you, and if you turn around suddenly when one of your companions is nearby, you might make him a customer for the plastic surgeon.

Wet snow tends to pack in between the points of crampons. This is an extremely dangerous situation, since the effect is that the crampon does not bite at all. This is likely to happen at an unexpected moment. If snow conditions make sticking and packing snow a problem, a piece of plastic bag or plastic sheeting can be used to cover the bottom of the boot and crampon. The points of the crampons are poked through, but the plastic is tied on so that the rest of the soles are covered. The snow will adhere much less to the plastic, and packing will be less of a problem.

A FEW NOTES ON SNOW CLIMBING

This chapter has not been written as an introduction to mountaineering or technical climbing. Ascent of steep snow with more advanced techniques than those mentioned here requires the availability of a rope or at least the application of experience that must be acquired with the protection of a rope. The reader interested in pursuing the art of mountaineering is best advised to find an experienced person to teach him. Many climbing clubs have instruction programs for beginners. Several books on the subject are listed in the bibliography.

Use of the climbing tools discussed in this chapter is perfectly safe for the general traveler in snow country, providing he is conservative in keeping his aims within his experience. The ice ax is used by the climber to cut steps, to help belay the rope when it is used for protection, and to provide holds, but for the unroped novice it is carried for self-arrest. In soft snow, whether climbing or descending, the beginner may wish to plunge the shaft into the snow so that the head can be used as a hold, or he may use either head or spike as a balance point. He must remember, however, that the primary use of the ax in this sort of climbing is as safety factor, and whenever this safety factor is needed, the ax must be in a position that will enable the climber to go into arrest in case of a slip. Use the ax as a hold if you like, but only providing you don't have to sacrifice the arrest position to do it.

The safety strap should be used where you might drop the ax. Don't carry the ax carelessly at the top of a steep section after you no longer need to hold it in preparation for an arrest; if you drop it, you are likely to be stuck with no safe way to get down. The strap is intended to prevent accidents like this.

Glissading is discussed in many books. It simply means to slide down a snow slope on your feet or the seat of your pants, using the ice ax as a rudder and brake. The ax is held in the arrest position, except that the slider reaches around enough to drag the spike in the snow behind, so that the hand on the shaft can press it into the snow. Glissading upright is rather like skiing. Sitting down is easier and wetter. Glissading is good fun on the rare occasions when the conditions are right: the snow fast enough, but not so fast that you might lose control; no rocks, cliffs, or other hazards below that might be dangerous in case you do lose control; visibility good enough to be *sure* that glissading is safe. Don't glissade if there is danger of getting cold. Even standing glissades often end in face-down arrests, and if you're getting chilled the last thing you need is a good wallow in the snow. Glissading is great fun, but it has caused far too many accidents. You must be absolutely sure that the slope is safe before you deliberately start a slide, and you should go into arrest at the slightest hint that you are losing control. Glissading down an unknown slope when the entire length is not clearly visible is asking for trouble.

This chapter has deliberately emphasized caution, since there are a number of hazards in steep snow that are not immediately apparent to the beginner. If you are careful to watch for these dangers, however, there is little to fear in crossing and climbing moderate snow slopes. Snow slopes nearly always look steeper than they actually are, and once you are on them they usually instill even more caution than necessary, with no additional advice needed. By remaining aware of less obvious dangers like avalanches and the possibility of later freezing or snowfall, the snow traveler will be able to climb and cross reasonably steep snow with safety and confidence.

XI

Storms and Avalanches

Daily life in our usual surroundings tends to dull our sensitivity to the operation of the world in which people are only a small part. We move from heated or air-conditioned cars to buildings of the same temperature, almost unaware of the progress of the seasons or the day-to-day weather. One of the salutary effects of winter camping is that one becomes rapidly and keenly aware of our size and power in larger schemes of things. It is difficult to spend very much time outdoors in the winter and to still remain oblivious to the cycles of weather and snow and their effects on life.

The winter traveler or camper must learn to adapt himself to certain forces that are acting around him and to avoid the operations of others. Some weather is bad enough to require the hardiest of men to hole up and wait until the storms abate; to become wise in the ways of avalanches it is necessary to make one's observations from a safe distance. Storms and avalanches can be viewed as sublime visitations, enthralling spectaculars, or powerful and wily adversaries. But whatever his mood, the prudent winter traveler will always treat these phenomena with respect.

WEATHER IN WINTER

Watching the weather is a fascinating occupation at any time of the year, and the winter months hold a special interest in regions where snow is present. Rain may vary only in intensity, temperature, and the size of the drops, but snow falls in an infinite variety of forms. Besides this, it stays on all sorts of ground, and it continues to change from the time it falls until it melts. It can form a light insulating blanket over the body of a hibernating chipmunk, or it can stick to a tree in huge loads, until the tons of weight bow and break the trunk. It can form a sound and stable slope or a huge and unstable sheet, ready to slide off with the slightest unbalancing influence. It may slide in harmless sluffs or in huge masses possessed of enough energy to flatten a town without slowing down. Finally, after it has fallen, the snow layer itself has profound effects on the weather that originally produced it.

Nor is weather in winter just a colder version of the patterns of summer. The large-scale air movements that are ultimately the source of much of our weather are quite different in summer and winter, so that most areas have quite different weather configurations from one season to the next. The Sierra Nevada mountains of California, for example, have almost continuous good weather in the summer months, but in winter a stormless week is rare. Other regions have more stable weather in winter than in milder seasons. The afternoon thunderstorms that occur in many mountains in the summer, quite independent of large storm systems, are not present in winter, when a blanket of snow prevents the local heating of the air that causes these thunderheads to form.

In the great variety of winter weather it is the storms that most attract our attention. Esthetically and intellectually we may delight in the differences between balmy afternoons and crisp, cold ones, but inevitably, thoughts of storms sweep milder contrasts aside. Our plans hinge on the presence or absence of signs of storm. We may revise routes or clothing depending on whether it is overcast and snowing, icy cold and clear, or lazily sunny. When signs of a real storm loom, however, choices are reduced to the alternatives of digging in or running. If we are forced onto the trail in a violent storm, the prospect is automatically seen as gloomy. With all this emphasis on bad weather, it is not surprising that most of our observations of the weather are concerned with detection of coming storms.

WATCHING THE WEATHER

The more you learn of the science of meteorology, the more easily you will be able to fit those signs into a coherent pattern. Still, many weather signs are dependent on local conditions, and the best meteorologist will be hard-put to go into a strange area and compete with the weather eye of an observant native whose knowledge of weather is completely unscientific. Stripped of instruments and bulletins from a network of far-flung observers, the professional is on much the same footing as the amateur. If you want to learn to predict storms in your own skiing and snowshoeing country, you'll have to get out and watch. A weather-wise old-timer will often be able to get you off to a strong start.

On the opposite end of the technological scale from the local sage, the first trick in weather watching for the weekend traveler is to watch or listen to the weather forecasts before he leaves. The TV charts of weather systems will tell you a great deal that you could never find out by observation, since they are based on information gathered at observation posts thousands of miles away. The pattern of weather in a particular region also becomes apparent on these charts if you watch them often. Books on weather rarely have a regional point of view. A combination of the knowledge of a few of the general principles of weather, a familiarity with normal regional storm tracks, and a check on the major systems on the map the night before the trip will equip the weekend sojourner with some excellent material on which to base his guesses.

At best, of course, television forecasts give the skier or snow-shoer a rough idea of what to expect and a foundation for his later speculations. Perhaps this is just as well, since the fascination of weather watching comes in large measure from the uncertainty of the best forecasts. Whether you consider it a challenge or a nuisance, the weather bureau is rarely interested in the same areas that winter travelers concern themselves with, and you may have to extrapolate whatever data you obtain over hundreds of miles horizontally and thousands of feet vertically. Finally, on longer trips you will be on your own after a few days. Once you have obtained some knowledge of the general weather patterns of the areas you frequent, you may prefer to ignore the professional prognosticators altogether, finding your own guesses more interesting, if slightly less accurate.

A rough idea of local and regional patterns is probably the most essential weather-forecasting information wilderness travelers can have, whether for weekends or longer trips. Wind direction

Watching the weather   249

will mean different things in different regions. A storm coming through an area near the sea may bring cold rain or snow, depending on whether the low-pressure area at the center of the storm is nearer the sea than the camper, or farther away: thus, whether it is sucking cold, dry, inland air or warm, moist, sea air over him. Patterns in one area are often relatively consistent, but they will differ widely from the norms of another region, even one a few miles away.

In the Northeast, for example, the exact path taken by the storm center very often determines whether a particular mountain will be subjected to cold, dry snow or to rain and sleet. The snow camper may know from watching a Friday weather forecast that a storm is on the way, but he will have to depend on his own observations to guide him in his decisions on the trail. Observations of cloud formations and wind direction can tell him a good deal about where the storm center lies, and this is useful not only in predicting the duration of the storm, but in predicting short-term trends in temperatures and precipitation. In the mountains of New Hampshire approaching storm clouds combined with winds from the east and tending southeast imply that the storm track is inland and that the relatively warm, wet air sucked in from the Atlantic will drop rain or wet snow, unless temperatures are quite cold. Storm clouds with winds from the northwest are more likely to bring in drier and colder air with a tendency to snow and colder temperatures. Each area has many patterns of this sort, and the first step in forecasting is to spend some time learning them.

In observing the weather in an area, the sequence of events is even more important than most individual signs. This is one reason why many who travel some distance to their wilderness rely on the weather bureau; on a short trip you cannot begin to piece a pattern together until it's about time to go home. If you live near your camping spot or go on longer trips, understanding the sequence of events from your own observations is easier.

The most obvious example of such a sequence is a set of barometric readings. Large-scale storms center around areas of the atmosphere where the pressure is relatively low. Air from the surrounding region is under *relatively* higher pressure and is pushed by this pressure into the low-pressure area. Because of the earth's rotation, the air rushing towards the low-pressure area is deflected towards the right (left in the Southern Hemisphere) and the net effect is a whirlpool of air around the low. This whirlpool may be fairly small or hundreds and hundreds of miles wide, and it tends to move generally from west to east. As it moves over a particular spot, a barometer will measure a generally falling pressure as the low center comes closer, and after the low has passed, the barometer will show a rising pressure. Thus, the rise or fall of the barometer is significant, but one individual reading is not likely to mean much; it is the progression of readings that tells the observer something of what is to come.

Clouds and winds also tell the observer much more if he knows what came before. Many fluffy, white clouds at the same level with gray, flat bottoms (stratocumulus) may herald bad weather if they follow a few days of clear, cold weather and are preceded first by high, wispy clouds gradually thickening into a veil. On the other hand, if these same flocks of gray-bottomed piles of cotton follow a storm, they are more likely to indicate a couple of days of good weather.

Types of snow, likelihood of rain or sleet, and special oddities like warm, dry winds are also very much characteristic of particular areas. Most regions have their prevailing winds, characteristic types of snow, and special deceptive conditions. In some regions it is safe to plan on never having precipitation in winter except in the form of snow, so that waterproof gear does not have to be carried. In other areas, like New England, the most dangerous storms are those whipping cold rain along on high winds and following with very cold temperatures, freezing rain, sleet, ice, and finally snow.

Some patterns are generally dependable: cold, clear weather following a storm is more likely to persist than relatively warmer pleasant weather. With an observant eye and a bit of reading on the subject, the outdoorsman can become sage about the succession of sun, clouds, wind, and snow. The more weather-wise he becomes, however, the more inclined he is likely to be to explain the weather after its arrival instead of before. Even professional meteorologists, with reams of data before them and banks of computers to analyze it, do well to predict the course of a storm a couple of days in advance. The more important questions to the winter foot tourist—how bad a storm, snow or rain, wet or dry snow, duration, and so on—are usually either obvious or very hard to predict. The amateur may be reduced to pronouncing wisely, "There is a sixty percent chance that there will be weather tomorrow."

Watching the weather

All this being the case, anyone who spends much time in the winter wilderness is going to be caught by quite a few storms, whether by accident or choice, and he had best be prepared for them. If adequate preparations have been made, he can sit cozily in a shelter with his friends, while the winds howl about, telling them of the many signs that he observed of the coming storm, and carefully dodging questions that attempt to pin him down on the expected duration.

WEATHERING A STORM

Storm is a relative term, and it will mean different things to different people, depending on their location, equipment, and experience. The mere presence of falling snow, for example, need not stop anyone who is equipped with snowshoes or skis; the skiing is often better and the weather warmer when it is snowing. As the amount of precipitation and especially the wind velocity increase, however, it eventually becomes necessary to seek shelter. The traveler should do his best to anticipate the need and to allow plenty of time for setting up camp or an emergency bivouac. Many factors should influence the decision on when to stop, and these must be balanced against each other in the best judgment of the members of the party, but there are several points that must be given particular weight.

The condition of the individual or party is one of the trickiest matters, but one that must be watched constantly. People who are cold and tired do not exercise their best judgment. An individual who is beginning to suffer from hypothermia (exposure) is likely to make irrational decisions, and this is the origin of many tragedies in the back country. The subject of hypothermia is discussed more extensively in the chapter on emergencies, and it will suffice to say here that the more severe the conditions, the more careful winter travelers must be to watch themselves and each other. Waiting too long to stop is likely to make setting up camp a difficult or impossible task. Even if the camp or bivouac is made successfully, a party that has stretched its endurance to the limit may not have the energy left to keep warm.

One of the most common errors in storm conditions is for a

party to keep going too long in hopes of reaching a car, camp, or cabin. The decision of when to stop and dig in is always a difficult one. Perhaps the best way to avoid real difficulties is to stop briefly at the first sign of storm or the first suspicion that darkness may come before the party reaches its destination. The party can discuss the problems at this point, while everyone is still reasonably calm and clear-headed and make a decision on a stopping time based on a reasonable assessment of the situation. For example, if no tent is available and a snow cave must be dug, they might decide that at least two hours before dark would have to be allowed. In storm conditions, there would be almost complete darkness around sunset, so they would have to stop two hours before sunset at the latest. Thus, unless they found themselves unquestionably less than two hours from their destination at the agreed stopping time, without possibility of being lost, they would definitely stop then. A person traveling alone should adhere to this same plan of deciding on a stopping time early, rather than continuing to the last minute in hopes of reaching camp.

Many complications arise in such situations. A party high in the mountains may decide to take certain risks in order to reach timberline, where shelter is easier to make and firewood is available. They should balance the difficulties and energies required to reach timberline against the possibilities of making a snow shelter where they are. A party that is lost in severe conditions would rarely be wise to continue, since they are likely to be in the same position a few hours later, but with their energies and hopes depleted by fighting against the storm to no advantage. On the other hand, a group with one person suffering from hypothermia but only an hour above timberline might well decide that continuing to a spot where a fire could be built would be more sensible than leaving the injured man out in the full blast of the weather for an hour or two while a cave was being made.

CAMPS AND BIVOUACS IN STORMS

When all the party's equipment is being carried, setting up camp in a storm is not much different from the same task at any other time, except that more care is required in anchoring tents and building walls for windbreaks. Parties in wooded areas should not have too much difficulty, since the forest breaks up the wind quite a bit and provides ready-made anchors for guy lines. If you are using a floorless tent in the woods, build up low walls of snow around the sides to keep the wind out. You will also have to build walls to shelter a fire if you intend to build one, and these can be arranged in such a way as to reflect the heat into the tent or shelter. Look around for dead trees and branches that might be broken by high winds, and make sure your tent is not pitched in their path.

Tents pitched in the open are likely to encounter much stronger winds. Mountain tents are designed with low profiles so that they will be stable in high winds. Those with a higher end for entrance should have this end pitched into the wind. Pitching with the high end away from the wind causes much more flapping. Open-front tents and other high tents designed for use in the forest are not very stable in high winds, and if you are caught out in the open with this kind of tent, you may have to build a snow shelter, instead. The tent may serve if it is pitched very well and protected by low snow walls. It may also be possible to lower the tent by weighting the lower parts of the tent walls down with snow and pitching the whole tent a foot or two lower than normal. This will only be possible if heavy snow is available. Another way to accomplish the same end can sometimes be improvised. Rocks or other objects are placed along the tent wall at the height that is to serve as the lowered bottom. These can be tied off with cord which can then be anchored to the ground in the usual fashion.

Drifting snow tends to bury tents in stormy weather, and to prevent their collapse it may be necessary for someone to go outside periodically to clear the snow from the tent. This is especially true when the falling snow is wet and heavy, since large snow loads can build up much more quickly than with light powder. The problem of drifting should also be considered in choosing a tent site during a storm. Large drifts tend to build up on the lee sides of objects during a storm. When you choose a spot that is sheltered from the wind, be sure that it will not also be the site of a large drift, unless you think you might enjoy moving your tent in the middle of the night. A drifted-in tent can ice up and become airtight, posing the possibility of suffocation if it is not cleared.

Much more difficult situations are encountered when a party is caught by a storm away from their camp or base. If possible, of course, one gets back to camp, but once it becomes clear that this may not be possible, the time and energy that remain should be spent on establishing a bivouac that is as comfortable as possible. Anyone traveling very far from his camp or car should give some thought beforehand to the equipment he will need to bivouac, equipment that will vary somewhat with the terrain and weather conditions.

The basic types of shelters which are used in bivouacs have been discussed in an earlier chapter. Anyone caught in a storm is likely to be short on insulation, since the body needs much more protection against the cold when it is at rest than when it is active. Since anyone caught away from camp probably has a deficit in insulation, it is important to use the excellent insulating properties of snow in any survival situation. A snow hole or igloo will provide nearly perfect shelter from the wind and will also usually warm up to around the freezing point or higher in a fairly short time. In forested areas where firewood is readily available a lean-to shelter with an all-night fire in front may be easier to build and more comfortable. In either case, advance preparation in the form of a few tools and some specialized clothing is important. Building a snow hole or igloo is a relatively simple affair if the proper tools are available, but it can be a rather desperate matter if they are not. Proper clothing will not make a bivouac in winter comfortable, but it will make the difference between emerging a bit cold and stiff in the morning and being in really serious condition.

Anyone traveling in a situation that may require a bivouac should carry emergency food. Obviously, it should contain lots of calories and should be edible without cooking or the addition of water; heat and liquid water may be short supply in a bivouac. Any emergency fuel available should be used for preparing drinks rather than cooking food, unless large quantities of fuel are obtainable. Dehydration is dangerous in itself and contributes to many other physical problems. Amounts of food that need be carried depend greatly on the circumstances of your trip. They may range from a few candy bars to a couple of weeks' emergency rations. On most trips of several days to a week I carry a little more than an extra day's food; this can be stretched out for several days in a really bad storm.

Clothing and special gear that are intended to serve for a possible bivouac also vary widely with locale and time of year. In very

Camps and bivouacs in storms   255

cold regions where wet conditions are not encountered in winter, all layers of clothing and insulation should be permeable, and any outside protection should be windproof but not waterproof (except for parts that will rest on the ground). On the other hand, where cold, freezing rain *might* occur, it is essential to have some kind of completely waterproof cover, even at the expense of condensation, to keep insulating layers from becoming completely soaked. If you are bivouacking in some kind of bag or parka, waterproofing is much more critical than in trail clothing or tents, because the fabric will tend to form water-catching pockets so that moisture will soak through that would flow off a standing figure or a tightly stretched tent.

Basic clothing for possible bivouacs should begin with a couple of layers of wool, because of its quality of retaining some warmth when wet. Over these go sweaters or down clothing, depending on your budget and the temperatures you may encounter, and these are followed by all the shell clothing you may be carrying. Finally, there is special bivouac covering, which may be a very large anorak into which you can tuck your legs or may be a large sack into which you can crawl. Unless you are sure that natural ground insulation will be available (and that you will be justified in cutting it), you should carry some sort of ground insulation.

Particular attention should be paid to protection of the head and the feet. The head must be well-protected because it can radiate so much of the body's heat production to your surroundings. The feet need special attention because they become cold easily and are hard to protect. Hats and hoods with drawstrings pulled tight take care of the head. If no special protection is carried for the feet, you should at least change into dry socks and loosen the laces of your boots. Overboots should be put on if they are carried, and any extra insulation available can be wrapped around. If boots are removed, try to keep them near the body where they won't get frozen: frozen boots and swollen feet in the morning are no joke. Special footwear for a bivouac may include down booties or foam inserts for overboots. Special, cheap emergency overboots made of woven polyethylene are available.

Large plastic bags are lightweight, compact to carry, and are invaluable both in planned and emergency bivouacs. They can be used as waterproof sacks for the legs, and they should be used in snow shelters to store any down equipment when it is not in use, to keep it from picking up moisture in the humid atmosphere of the igloo or snow hole. Many large bivouac parkas and sacks are available for outer protection, or you can make your own. Plans for two types are included in Appendix A.

For planned bivouacs a good but expensive alternative for insulation is a combination of a half sleeping bag and an expedition down parka. Some down pants have a zipper combination that makes it possible to convert them to half bags. Such alternatives are satisfactory for planned bivouacs in relatively mild winter conditions. Severe weather, however, is not to be toyed with, and these methods should be used mainly for emergencies. If you *plan* to bivouac or camp in winter, you should normally have a good winter sleeping bag with you.

Special tools for tentless shelters also depend on conditions and plans. Igloos are only practical when snow conditions are good, so a snow knife is not of much use in powdery midwinter snow. Igloos also generally take too long to build to be useful for a one-night shelter, except when snow conditions are ideal. Generally, snow holes are the most practical emergency shelters, and if they are anticipated, a snow shovel should be carried. With one, a snow hole can be dug out quite quickly, but without, the process is likely to be an ordeal.

When snow depth is not sufficient for a snow hole, an igloo may still be built. At worst, walls of snow may be heaped around, and some sort of a roof may be possible to improvise. The walls will at least serve as a windbreak. Shelters are discussed more completely in Chapter IV. The important thing to remember in bivouac conditions, when inadequate insulation is available, is that snow shelters can be raised to tolerable temperatures with body heat, and they usually require less effort with a more readily available material (snow) than lean-tos with all-night fires. The last thing the average outdoorsman caught in a winter storm thinks of is digging himself into the snow, but this is usually just what he should do.

STORMS AND AVALANCHES

The camper on the great plains or in the north woods has the same difficulties with howling winds and deep new snow that his

After a heavy storm, steep open slopes like these can be a deathtrap for a careless tourer. Castle Peak.

counterpart in the mountains does. After the end of the storm, however, he has only to dig out and plow his way along the trail. The mountaineer has another problem after and during the storm: many of those falling tons of snow are going to come sliding down off the sides of the mountains, and it is important that he be somewhere else when they do. The next section of this chapter will deal with this problem of the high country. It may be ignored by those who never travel to high altitude, but is important to those who do.

AVALANCHES

The winter traveler of flat or rolling country never needs to concern himself with avalanches, but for anyone spending much time in the high mountains they represent the most serious danger he is likely to encounter. Like many other powerful natural phenomena, a big avalanche is spectacular, and it is an event best observed from a safe distance. Many of the big Western ski areas have crews of specialists who spend a great deal of time, skill, and money controlling the avalanche paths in the relatively small amount of territory covered by the ski areas themselves. The reason is simple: the danger to recreational skiers would be intolerably high without adequate methods of prediction and control of avalanche slopes.

In the high mountains of the western United States and Canada and on some Eastern mountains the dangers presented by avalanches to those who ignore their threat is very real. It is especially so to the cross-country traveler, who will have no avalanche teams to protect him with signs or artillery, and who is likely to pick avalanche slopes as choice routes of travel, particularly for the skier. Anyone spending much time in back-country avalanche terrain should learn as much as possible about avalanche conditions, unless he is playing some sort of mountaineer's Russian roulettte.

Avalanches are a complex subject—one that is not completely understood even by experts who have spent their lives studying it —involving the mechanics of the always-changing internal structure of the snow, detailed long-term weather observations, and a great deal of knowledge of particular slopes that cannot be obtained by casual inspection. Despite these complications, however, the basic reasons for the occurrence of avalances are fairly simple, as are many of the safety rules that follow from them.

WHAT CAUSES AVALANCHES?

When snow falls on the ground, the force of gravity continues to act on it. On flat terrain, this force will cause settlement, but since there is no longer anywhere for the snow to fall, there are no other important effects. If, on the other hand, the snow comes to rest on a slope, the force of gravity is always trying to pull the snow down the slope. Our concern here is the situation that occurs when a large mass of snow accedes to the constant downward pull suddenly and at a rapid rate. Experience has taught mountaineers that it is unhealthy to be perched on a large quantity of snow at the time that it decides to make its downward trip.

Of course, there are very few truly flat areas of any size, and it

Even generally safe mountains like this one can present avalanche hazard under the right conditions. If there are any grounds for suspicion, stay out of those prominent gullies and keep to the trees.

is clear that snow will not avalanche on slight inclines. Avalanches will only occur as slopes become steeper and the pull of gravity along the slope increases. On the other hand, snow will not cling to vertical faces in large quantities; the snow falls off these precipices almost as fast as it comes down. It is on the intermediate slopes that avalanches form, where the incline is gentle enough to permit large quantities of snow to build up, but where the pressure on the snow to flow down the slope is still compelling.

Many things besides the angle of the slope are important in determining avalanche formation, however, the next most obvious one being the nature of the slope itself. Snow will not slide down in large masses where it is well anchored to the slope at many closely spaced points. Heavily forested slopes rarely avalanche. Irregular, rough, boulder-strewn slopes will not avalanche until enough snow has fallen to fill in the irregularities of the potential avalanche path and form a smooth sliding surface. Smooth rock slabs or grass slopes form a fine sliding surface, however, and may avalanche with much smaller amounts of snow.

We begin to reach more complicated ground in considering the conditions of the snow cover itself. Snow falls in an almost infinite variety of forms and mixtures. It begins to change the instant it is

STORMS AND AVALANCHES

formed in the atmosphere, is continuously modified by temperature, wind, and humidity as it falls to earth and goes on changing after it becomes a part of the snow cover, under the influence of a bewildering variety of conditions. Still, despite all the factors that influence its course, the basic cause of an avalanche is this: when the forces holding the snow—be it one snowflake or huge slab— are exceeded by the force of gravity pulling it down along the slope, the snow will slide. In sliding, it will exert pressure on other masses of snow, and if this pressure and the pull of gravity exceed the strength of their anchoring forces, they, too, will begin to slide down the mountain.

This unbalancing action that starts the avalanche may occur because of an increase in the forces pulling downward, as when more weight is added to a layer of snow during a storm, or it may result from a decrease in the strength of the anchors holding the snow, or it may be the result of the combination of both. In practice, the consideration of this balance is complicated by the variable nature of the snow cover. When the snow is loose with little cohesion between individual snow crystals, the problem is difficult enough, but as the snow layer becomes more coherent, forces are transmitted through it. Thus, an unstable part of a snow slab may be supported by being anchored at its edges to the rest of the cover. Alternatively, a stable portion of the cover may be pulled from its anchors by the weight of neighboring areas of unstable snow. Many different types of avalanche are recognized, and since some of them are very different in character it is convenient to break down the discussion of avalanche danger according to some broad classifications.

TYPES OF AVALANCHES

The first and most important division of avalanches is between *loose-snow avalanches* and *slab avalanches*. A loose-snow avalanche starts at a point when a small amount of snow is set in motion, perhaps by a clump falling off a tree or by a snowshoer disturbing the slope. This moving mass disturbs and carries off more and more snow as it slides, until the avalanche has run its course, leaving a V-shaped path with the point at the top. Slab avalanches

Types of avalanches 261

begin with a large mass of snow that begins to move at the same time, forming a long, wall-like break at the top where the slab separated from the rest of the snow cover.

Slab avalanches are subdivided into *hard slabs* and *soft slabs*. The hard slabs tend to hold a skier or walker with little, if any, sinking before avalanching. The debris of a hard-slab avalanche contains chunks and blocks of various sizes. Soft slabs are formed of softer snow that allows the traveler to sink in his tracks, sometimes half an inch, and sometimes to his hips. When it avalanches the soft slab tends to break up and proceed like a loose-snow avalanche.

Avalanches may be *dry, damp,* or *wet*. Dry avalanches contain no free water and are usually at temperatures below 32°F. Damp and wet snow avalanches are at 32°; the former will pack and contains some moisture, while the latter has considerable free water. Dry-snow avalanches contain a good bit of air in the snow, damp ones much less, and wet avalanches have little air mixed in the snow. Wet avalanches tend to form large snow balls that make a channeled track. They move more slowly than dry avalanches and weigh much more.

Avalanches usually begin by traveling on the ground. They may be temporarily airborne in falling over cliffs, and even while they are sliding down slopes a great deal of snow may roil into the air. A large, fast-moving avalanche will also produce a shock wave in the air. Distinctions among these phenomena need not concern us much, but there is one type of avalanche that departs in character from these in a major way. Apparently, when a dry-powder avalanche reaches a certain speed, it becomes an *airborne powder avalanche*. Presumably, what happens is that the shock wave in the air and the associated turbulence become the main propagating vehicle of the avalanche. The cloud of powder and shock wave from this type of avalanche move at tremendous speeds, on the order of two hundred miles per hour, and they proceed with much less friction than a normal avalanche, so that they can travel much farther beyond the steep slopes where they begin.

Large avalanches are quite likely to be mixtures of the types mentioned above. A loose-snow avalanche may trigger the release of a slab. Dry snow from high slopes will carry along the wet snow it encounters lower down. The main purpose of classification here is to help the winter traveler to recognize dangerous conditions. Any kind of avalanche danger carries with it the possibility that large masses of snow may be released once sliding starts.

THE STABILITY OF THE SNOW COVER

The fact of the continuous metamorphism of the snow cover has already been mentioned. This characteristic and several others are very important in the formation of avalanches. Snow is a plastic material: it will deform under stress and will gradually change its shape in order to eliminate the stresses caused by the deformation. This plasticity will cause snow that is lying on a slope to creep gradually down the slope. Many of the stresses within the snow layer are caused by different rates of creep from one spot to another.

Metamorphism usually results in the snow layer becoming stronger and more coherent. Settling takes place and bonding occurs between the grains of snow. This process is hastened whenever the snow is moved around and disturbed so that the crystals tend to interlock and fall together. Metamorphism is speeded up by higher temperatures, and mechanical disturbance may be accomplished by avalanching or by wind. The hardening produced by these processes generally contributes to the stability of a slope and decreases the possibility of avalanches. However, when they increase the coherence within one layer of the snow cover that is poorly bonded to the layers below, a slab is created, and it is such slabs that avalanche when the anchors around their edges are no longer strong enough to hold their weight. Stresses generated by creep may serve to snap a bond at one edge of a slab. The release of this anchor often puts undue strain on another, which then snaps in turn. The propagation of the fracture lines around a slab proceeds with incredible rapidity. At this point the slab may either avalanche, perhaps releasing other slabs as well, or it may slump to a new and more stable position.

Unstable slabs are most often created by windblown snow. The crystals of the snow are broken up and stirred together by the turbulence of the wind and are thus given great cohesion. The layer formed by such wind-driven snow is called windslab. Great quantities of snow can be deposited in such a formation, often with poor bonding to the surface of the base below. These slabs formed by wind-blown snow are the most common source of avalanche danger, especially in the Sierra Nevada and Cascade ranges. Most such slabs are formed on leeward slopes (those facing away from the wind), but in heavy snowstorms they may be deposited on slopes facing in any direction. Slopes facing into the wind are more likely to accumulate wind-packed snow that is well bonded to the layers below.

Metamorphism generally tends to produce more rounded, compact, and larger grains of snow and to improve the bonding between layers. This process, erasing the original character of the snow crystals, is known as destructive metamorphism. Sometimes, however, a change known as constructive metamorphism occurs, which produces more complex crystals. These crystals are cup- or scroll-shaped and are known as depth hoar. They have very little cohesion and form a very weak layer that often forms a sliding base for very dangerous slab avalanches. Depth hoar is particularly hazardous because it undercuts what may previously have been a very stable snow cover. Depth hoar is most common in the Rocky Mountains, but under the right conditions it may occur elsewhere. Once formed, the depth-hoar layer may gradually disappear under the influence of constructive metamorphism, or it may remain like a cocked trap well into late winter and spring.

AVALANCHE SLOPES

Avalanches can occur on a very wide range of slope gradients. Wet snow avalanches in spring with enough water to lubricate themselves will sometimes occur on slopes of less than 15°. Such avalanches may endanger property, but they are not usually much problem to the winter traveler, because they move so slowly. As the gradient of the slope becomes steeper, dangerous avalanches are more likely to occur; then, as it becomes steeper still, they become less likely again, because the snow slides off before significant amounts accumulate. The most likely angle of a slope on which dangerous avalanches may start is around 30–45°, but danger may begin on gentler slopes if a particularly good sliding surface is present or on much steeper ones if snow can accumulate. Such angles are difficult to judge accurately, anyhow, without actual measurement, and they are given as a rough indication of danger. With enough experience, the snow mountaineer will learn to judge the angle at which appreciable danger begins.

These considerations apply to the slope where the avalanche begins. An avalanche already in motion will continue onto much gentler slopes, so that the traveler must remain aware of the slopes above. This information is important, nonetheless. Most avalanche victims trigger the avalanches themselves, so the conditions where avalanches may start are a subject of considerable interest. It is dangerous to pass under an avalanche slope, but the chances of being caught are not nearly so great as those encountered by someone who crosses through the breakaway zone and thus risks triggering the avalanche himself. Avalanches rarely start on heavily forested slopes, but scattered trees yield no protection and should not be taken as an indication of safety. Small clumps of trees are present on many slopes that avalanche with every major storm. Brush and rockfields also keep slopes from avalanching, but only until the drifting snow has filled in the anchoring irregularities; once a smooth snowfield is present they provide no protection against avalanching of the upper layers of snow. Grass and rock slabs form good sliding surfaces for avalanches extending right to the ground.

Gullies and *couloirs* are natural avalanche paths; that is why they are there in the first place. They are the drainspouts of a mountain and are exceedingly dangerous if any of the slopes above are likely to avalanche. Ridges, high knolls, and similar barriers are the natural safe spots on a mountain.

Because of their tendency to place extra tension on the surface of the snow, convex slopes of a given angle are more likely to avalanche than concave ones. This should not be taken to imply that concave slopes are safe from avalanches, but examining the contour of the slope may enable you to guess the most likely point of fracture of a slope, so that you can keep well above it. Avalanche swaths are often recognizable where they have been cut through timber in a fan-shaped path, usually with the wide end at the bottom.

The orientation of the slope is likely to have a good deal of influence on the likelihood of its avalanching. In the discussion below of particular types of avalanches, it is pointed out that some

Avalanche slopes 265

are far more likely on slopes facing in a particular direction. Slabs caused by wind drifting are much more likely on leeward slopes, for example; these same slopes are the ones most likely to be overhung by cornices whose fall may provide a trigger.

LOOSE-SNOW AVALANCHES

In general, loose-snow avalanches are less likely to be dangerous than slabs. This is true because the conditions that precede them are much easier to detect, because the danger of their occurrence is less likely to persist, because they are likely to be smaller, and because one is more likely to be able to get out of their way or escape alive if caught.

When temperatures are low, loose-snow avalanches often come down during or shortly after a storm. They tend to develop when dry snow falls in calm conditions. When much wind is present, the snow is more likely to be wind-packed or to be deposited in slab formations. Dry, unstable snow is very shifty, providing little flotation for skis or snowshoes, and tending to flow back into your tracks behind you. True powder snow, which is something like bread flour in its lack of cohesion, may often form loose-snow avalanches. Powder results from the metamorphosis of dry snow that has not been subjected to much wind-drifting. Metamorphosis removes the feathery arms that have caused the interlocking of the snow crystals so that they can flow more easily. Such powder-snow avalanches may occur days after a storm if conditions remain well below freezing.

The danger of dry loose-snow avalanches can only persist when temperatures are very cold. Most of them come down during heavy snowfalls and in the few hours afterwards. Some come down after metamorphosis has produced true powder conditions. If temperatures warm up to around freezing, the danger is likely to disappear in a few hours, though it will be very high when temperatures first rise. Instability of such powder is easily tested on small slopes with the same exposure and gradient as larger and more dangerous mountainsides. If the snow is unstable on the small slopes, it is likely to be unstable on the large ones. (Remember that different conditions will prevail at the top of a slope with a vertical drop of a few thousand feet.) Avalanche debris at the bottom of the slopes gives an indication of danger. If you are traveling along a valley and note that several possible avalanche paths have been active recently, you should be very wary of one that has not yet slid.

Completely different kinds of loose-snow avalanches occur in warm, thawing conditions, especially in spring. A snowpack that may have been quite stable loses its coherence in thawing and is lubricated by percolating meltwater. Very large and heavy avalanches may occur in these conditions, which, like those preceding dry loose-snow avalanches, are usually fairly easy to detect. The snow may become wet as a result of being warmed by radiation, by generally warm temperatures, by warm wind, or by percolating rain water. The surface layers may become unstable, or the whole slope may become rotten because of the soaking of a layer of depth hoar deep in the snow pack.

Probably the most common avalanches of this type are those that come down in spring in the later morning and early afternoon after the top layers of snow have been softened by the sun. Such avalanches usually occur on sunny days, but the snow may also melt by absorbing radiation from high, warm clouds, even when no sun appears and when air temperatures at ground level are below freezing. Signs of instability can usually be seen from some distance: sunballs roll down the slopes, small slides may be observed or a large one heard, and small slopes of similar exposure to large ones show signs of surface instability. Damp snow in the top strata will slide off in layers, giving poor footing and even sliding out from under skis. This instability is in marked contrast to the afternoon mushiness that may occur on top of stable spring snow. In the latter case only the top few inches are soft, and there is a firm base underneath.

With really wet snow that has been completely soaked and undercut by rain or meltwater, instability is usually marked by soft snow that will not bear much weight. Even the skier is likely to go in up to his knees or hips. Wet snow is very heavy, and if it is also this soft, it is quite dangerous. Such conditions often indicate that a lower layer of depth hoar has become soaked and has collapsed, and subsequent avalanches are quite likely. If these conditions predominate in the main snow layer, a frozen layer on the top should not be regarded as indicating much stability.

Any of these types of wet-snow avalanche may be produced

even in midwinter if a very warm wind should begin blowing. Such winds occur occasionally in many mountain ranges, but they are most common in North America on the eastern side of the Rocky Mountains, where they are known as chinooks. A chinook can raise temperatures eighty degrees in a couple of hours. A chinook is formed when a wet air mass loses its moisture in condensed snow or rain as it goes over the top of the mountain range. The precipitation of the moisture causes the air to be warmed, since the water gives up its heat of vaporization. As the air descends to lower elevations on the far side of the mountain range, it is warmed further by higher pressures. The warm, dry wind that is produced can melt a great deal of snow in a short time, far more than either sun or rain, and the beginning of a chinook will usually presage a torrent of avalanches within a few hours.

SLAB AVALANCHES

The greatest danger from slab avalanches lies in the difficulty in predicting them. The slab may lie dormant on a slope for months before a heavy snowfall adds too much weight too rapidly and brings half the mountainside down. Still more difficult for the transient tourer to predict is the slab avalanche resulting from the undercutting effects of depth hoar. Even an expert working in one area for the whole winter cannot predict when or whether a slab will come down. He gets an answer by taking a 75 mm. recoiless rifle and lobbing a few shells at it. The best for which the back-country traveler can hope is to be able to recognize a situation of potential danger and to stay clear of it. Pressing the limits of avalanche hazard is risky even where a rescue party is standing by; in wilderness situations it is foolhardy.

Slab formation is generally associated with wind-blown snow, and while slabs are usually produced during storms, wind-drifted snow may form them with no new precipitation at all. Virtually any type of snow can form slabs, though the characteristics of the slabs themselves will depend on the type of snow. The softer slabs that usually result from snow falling at moderate temperatures will usually slide during or shortly after a storm, and will stabilize fairly quickly, either by avalanching or settling in place. The hard-

STORMS AND AVALANCHES

er slabs that are most frequently formed by high winds at sub-zero temperatures may persist in a dangerous state for weeks.

Slabs usually form on lee slopes, though during a snowstorm with moderate winds they may form on any slope. With moderate temperatures, stability usually follows not too long after the storm, unless some particularly poor base, such as an ice layer or depth hoar, underlies the structure. Under very cold conditions, any slope prone to slides that has not actually avalanched is suspect. A hard slab can persist for weeks after the last storm and be triggered by a crossing skier.

Conditions of extreme danger from slabs will show in the instability of small slopes as well as large ones. Such instability may reveal itself when cracks shoot out from a traveler's feet, skis, or snowshoes. Small cracks that extend only a few feet may indicate a harmless crust, but if the cracks begin to extend ten feet or more and cut deep into the snow layer, severe avalanche danger is certain to be present. The absence of such signs should not be interpreted as a sign of safety; they may not appear except when it is too late. A hard slab, especially, may be buried under quite a bit of new snow, so that the observation of surface conditions will tell nothing.

JUDGING HAZARDOUS CONDITIONS

Despite the difficulties of avalanche forecasting, the careful mountaineer can usually avoid too much risk to life and limb by watching for danger signs, finding out as much as he can about the condition of the snow pack, and practicing a general conservatism of judgment where avalanches may slide. For the weekend traveler, the first step should be to check with a local expert when that is possible. If you visit an area only a few times a year, you are unlikely to spend your time digging pits in the snow to find out whether a layer of depth hoar has formed or whether a thick glaze of ice was produced early in a particular year. Such an ice layer may bring down avalanches with every storm in places that never slide in normal years, so that even if you take a particular tour every season it is worthwhile to check with a local snow ranger or ski-area avalanche-control expert. If you find a few such people in the areas you frequent, you can always call them up the night before you leave. They can tell you if there is some particular hazard you ought to know about and what kind of slopes you might need to avoid. Besides enabling to you steer clear of dangerous slopes, this information may enable you to cross others with a confidence you could not have otherwise.

Watch for avalanche slopes. Any slope over about 25° should be considered suspect unless it is heavily forested. As a rough guide, if you are wearing snowshoes and cannot climb straight up the fall line in normal snow without kicking steps or wearing crampons, the slope is probably steep enough to avalanche. If you are a skier using well-applied touring waxes and you have to angle your skis more than 45° from the fall line to climb, the slope is probably steep enough to avalanche. A skier using climbers and going straight up the fall line is on a potential avalanche slope when the slope starts feeling steep, but well before most climbers stop biting.

Remember that once the steepest part of the slope begins to avalanche, the slide will carry onto gentler slopes and may run over flat land and even up the opposite side of a narrow valley. You must pay nearly as much attention to slopes above and below you as to the angle of the slope on which you are traveling. Be particularly wary of slopes overhung by cornices. These are lee slopes —those most subject to slab formation—and they are topped by potential avalanche triggers. Gullies and slopes that have avalanche tracks cut through trees are particularly dangerous and should be avoided.

In avoiding an avalanche slope, it is safest to go above the area of potential danger. Next safest is traveling below the slope, preferably beyond the potential run-out. Most people caught by avalanches have triggered the slides themselves, either by adding extra weight or by cutting away some of the supporting snow of the slab. Even the slight weight of a person can overstrain a small section that is helping to hold up a large slab. By releasing one section, a man can start a redistribution of forces that will cause half the mountainside to start sliding. For this reason, unless slides are coming down every few minutes, it is usually safer to pass under a potential avalanche zone than through it: you take a chance of an avalanche coming down but not the much greater chance of releasing one yourself. If at all possible, however, one should stay completely out of both the potential slide area and the

STORMS AND AVALANCHES 270

A small cornice on the skyline. This tells you the direction of the prevailing winds and the likely spots for slab formation in storms. A falling cornice is a common avalanche trigger. This one was fairly safe at the time the picture was taken, but it could be hidden by storm when the slope was most dangerous.

run-out zone. It is worth going a long way around to avoid serious avalanche hazard. After a big storm, a party may have to take a different return route, for example, if the original approach came up a narrow ravine below two steep, open slopes. A slope that has already avalanched is generally safe, providing that there are not more possible slide areas above that might have been undercut by the first avalanche. Remember, though, that the next slope along the trail, if it has similar exposure to the first, is certainly hazardous if it has not been released. If numerous small slides have come down on a loose slope, or if cracks are visible where slabs have released but not avalanched, the underlying slopes are probably stabilized.

Danger signs. Most avalanches come down during or shortly after storms. The snow falling in the storm may avalanche itself, or the added weight of the new snow may release old unstable layers below. The more rapidly the snow falls and the denser the flakes, the more likely it is to cause avalanches. Two feet of snow falling in a single night are far more likely to cause major instability than two feet in two days. If temperatures are near freezing at the be-

Judging hazardous conditions

ginning of a storm and get colder as it goes on, the new snow is much more likely to bond well to the old layer than if temperatures start cold and warm as the storm continues. A great deal of wind-drifting snow will cause slabs to form on lee slopes even if snowfall is not heavy.

After a major storm has passed, if temperatures are near freezing, the main avalanche danger may be avoided by delaying travel a few hours. If temperatures are very cold, danger will persist for much longer. Testing small slopes may give some indication of the condition of larger and more dangerous ones. If the main danger seems to be from windslab, the wind-beaten slopes may be quite safe. Such wind-packed slopes tend to be crusted with a wavy surface, and they are often very stable while their neighbors across the valley are shedding tons of snow.

On sunny days in spring the dangerous period for thawing avalanches is in late morning and in afternoon. If you need to cross avalanche slopes in this weather, get an early start and be across before the sun gets to the snow. Slopes with a northern exposure get less sun and are safe for a longer part of the day. In winter any sudden rise in temperature may release avalanches. Rain, warm winds, or thawing temperatures that remain above freezing for more than a day may produce deep thawing and great danger of thawing avalanches.

CROSSING AVALANCHE TERRAIN

When at all possible, dangerous slopes should be avoided altogether, even if this requires long waits or detours. Occasionally, however, it may be necessary for a party to cross a hazardous zone, and some precautions may save lives if anyone is caught. If there is any possibility of crossing such terrain, each member of the party should carry an *avalanche cord* and use it. An avalanche cord is a bright colored length of nylon parachute cord 50–100 feet long. One end is tied to its owner and the other end is allowed to trail. Chances are good that if the wearer is caught in an avalanche, at least some of the cord will be on the surface, and it can then be followed to the victim. The best cords have metal markers every two meters. Each one gives the distance from the end and has an arrow pointing towards the end tied to the victim. If there are a couple of short sections of line showing, the markers can save rescuers time in deciding where to dig first. Minutes are crucial in avalanche rescue and avalanche debris is often very hard, so this is important.

For parties planning on taking risks, several other items of special equipment should be carried, and other groups should consider carrying them. Each member of the party should have a sectional avalanche probe, which is far more effective than reversed ski poles in searching for a victim, and the party should have at least two aluminum shovels.

Aside from special equipment, a person about to cross an avalanche slope should dress warmly, donning mittens, hat, and so on, zipping up his jacket, and pulling up his hood. All equipment should be adjusted so that it can be jettisoned quickly in case of trouble. Packs, ice axes, ski poles and the like may help to show the victim's path if they come off in an avalanche. If they remain attached to his body, they will tend to drag him under and to twist his limbs in most uncomfortable ways. The pack may be carried on one shoulder, and the waist strap should be removed. Straps of ski poles and ice axes should be removed from the wrists. Snowshoe bindings should be loosened so that they can be kicked off in case of trouble. Skis are the only possible exception to this rule. The skier may leave his bindings as they are, maintaining some chance of skiing out of the way of an avalanche, or he may loosen them so that the bindings will release easily, taking the chance that this may trip him if he tries to ski out a slide. In any case, Arlberg straps should be released so that the ski will be freed if the safety bindings do come off.

The most important safety precaution of all is to cross any dangerous area one by one. The rest of the party must stay in a protected spot—perhaps a rock outcropping or heavily forested zone—until the first person is all the way across the danger zone. This procedure should be followed for each man. The first crossing does *not* prove that the slope is safe. Avalanche literature is replete with instances of later members of a group being caught after several have crossed safely. Only one person at a time should be in a danger zone. All the others should watch that person carefully and be ready to make note of his location if he should be caught by a slide.

If you are caught in an avalanche you may be able to get out by

Crossing avalanche terrain 273

quick action if you are on the edge of the slide. This happens quite often because the cutting action of the victim's feet or skis is what precipitates the avalanche in the first place. If this first desperate attempt is unsuccessful, you should jettison your equipment and then try to making swimming motions to stay on top of the avalanche—a gesture unlikely to have very much effect except in a very small slide. Keep your mouth shut, and don't get it full of snow. As you come to rest you should try to get your hands in front of your face to make a breathing space. Once the sliding snow stops it generally becomes quite hard, and you are not likely to be able to move much at all. Experts generally recommend one hard push after you come to rest to try to push out. If that doesn't work, relax and don't panic (easy to say). Many avalanche victims apparently quite literally die of fright. With your companions nearby you have a pretty good chance if you stay calm and don't use up your limited oxygen supply on the luxury of fear. Don't waste much energy shouting. You may hear your companions, but they are very unlikely to hear you.

For survivors of an accident the first step is also to keep calm. Speed is vital, but it is useless if it is also misdirected. The first step when you see the avalanche is to watch the victim and make a careful note of where you last see him. Try to note the relation of this spot to visible landmarks. When the avalanche is over, *mark* the spot where the victim was last seen before you rush off and lose it. Mark it with something that will stay put and stay visible. Don't just drop something on the ground if it's snowing.

The victim will be somewhere down the fall line from where he was last seen. Make a quick search for objects like packs, gloves, etc., that may show his path. Kick up the snow around the place where he was seen to uncover clues. Is there a section of avalanche cord or a hand or foot showing? There are quite a few cases of survivors of accidents taking off for help twenty miles away when the victim's boot was sticking up like a signpost. A cursory examination may very well save the victim, especially if an avalanche cord was worn. Mark all spots where any objects belonging to the victim were found. Probe around these spots with an avalanche probe if you have one, or with an inverted ski pole, the tail of a ski, or a tent pole. Also probe around any trees or other obstacles in the path the victim would have taken. These are the most likely spots for him to be, together with the bottom and side debris.

Once a quick cursory examination has been made, several decisions have to be taken regarding the next steps, decisions that will depend on the size of the party and its location. Victims of avalanches who are not killed right away by traumatic injuries usually die by suffocation. An ice mask forms around the face and prevents the victim from getting air. For this reason and other more complicated ones, the length of time a victim may survive varies a good deal. If he is fortunate enough to have an air space, he may survive for some time, or various factors may limit this time to minutes, depending on the air available, fear, consciousness, cold, and so on. In general, avalanche-rescue groups assume that chances are still fairly good for the first two hours, and that they drop off very rapidly after that time. It follows that unless you have many more people available than can be used in the search, going for help is only sensible if help can return in less than two hours. This is not usually the case in wilderness situations.

Most wilderness travelers will be on their own and will have to conduct the best search they can without additional help. After the cursory search, the area of the fall line below the last seen point should be searched thoroughly. The most likely spots for the victim to have lodged should then be probed as carefully as possible. Have the searchers stand in line and probe every foot of the suspected areas systematically. Keep them in a line, so that effort is not wasted nor sections missed. Keep careful track of those areas that have been searched.

Throughout the search, the rescuers should make some attempt to sound calm as well as act that way. The victim can very often hear what they are saying, since sound carries well into the snow but not out of it, and his morale is not likely to be improved by tactless comments or apparent panic.

If anyone is sent for help, it is important that he not let his haste involve him in another accident. Two people should be sent if possible, but everyone else should be used in the search. Those going for help must be extremely careful not to be caught in a second avalanche. They should not go so fast as to become completely exhausted, since one of them will probably have to guide the rescue party back to the scene of the accident, unless they can be directed with no possibility of mistake. This caution is especially applicable if you are the only survivor. Your friends' lives depend on your getting back.

Whoever takes charge of the search must also take responsibility for the safety of the searchers. Providing no further danger threatens, the search should not be abandoned for 24 hours, but if the storm that brought down the first avalanche is continuing, there can be no purpose served in risking the lives of the survivors of the first slide, especially after the first two hours are over. Neither is there any justification in having accidents sustained by exhausted men after the first few hours. Searching an avalanche is very tiring, and once exhaustion sets in, the would-be rescuers are not likely to do any good and are quite likely to get hurt, a prospect that would greatly complicate the situation and could only harm the chances of the avalanche victim, since energies then have to be diverted to care for the new casualty.

GADGETS FOR PROSPECTIVE VICTIMS

Many methods have been tried to make searching for avalanche victims faster and require less manpower. In the past, probing has usually been the only method available, and the problems it involves are the reason it has not been thoroughly discussed here. It requires probes and a great deal of manpower to thoroughly search an avalanche track, even one of moderate size. The best that a small party can usually do is to search the likely spots near the surface.

If you plan trips that involve serious and unavoidable avalanche risk for other reasons than a suicidal drive, it would be worth investigating a recent device consisting of a small radio transceiver, one of which is carried by each member of the party. When traveling in hazardous areas all members switch the radios to transmit a signal. Then if someone is caught in an avalanche, the remaining members switch their radios to receive and follow the signals to the victim. If you use one of these devices, don't forget to turn it on, and put it in a secure pocket on your body. Otherwise, your friends will happily dig out your beeping rucksack.

For most purposes, the best way to stay out of trouble in the wilderness is not to get into it in the first place, and this holds particularly true of avalanches. Even a small avalanche is no joke. I have never been caught in one, but those people I know who have had the experience have not emerged with any desire to repeat it.

Freak avalanches can catch the most experienced mountaineer, but the chances of this are quite remote. Most avalanche accidents occur in situations where the hazard was quite predictable, and they could have been avoided.

XII

Emergencies and Accidents

Storms and avalanches are natural phenomena that occur whether there are people around or not. In a wilderness situation there is nothing one can do to prevent them; he has either to arrange to be somewhere else when they happen or to be prepared for them. Emergencies and accidents are something else: they happen to people. An avalanche or tree only becomes part of an accident if someone manages to be buried or knock his head on a branch. Most accidents and emergencies can be prevented, and the unpleasant consequences of those that occur can be minimized by adequate preparation.

There is nothing inherently dangerous about wilderness travel in the winter, providing the traveler is able and equipped to deal with the various problems that he may encounter. It is true, however, that there are a number of characteristics of the snow country beyond the roadhead that can turn a difficult situation into a dangerous one rather quickly. There is much less room for error. In summer an ill-clad fool can wander off into the woods in many areas of North America, and if he doesn't manage to do himself in by falling off a cliff, he has a good chance of still being in fairly good shape when the search party finds him a few days later. Mistakes like this are not so likely to end well when snow is on the ground.

The conditions of winter are likely to exacerbate all sorts of problems, especially since many difficulties are most likely to

Emergencies and accidents 277

occur when the special characteristics of the cold months are most in evidence. You are more apt to break your leg or to become lost in a storm at the end of the short winter day than at the beginning, and when snow conditions make travel most arduous rather than when they make it easy. All sorts of complications reinforce one another: a man who is suffering from the cold or fatigue is both more liable to injury and less able to cope with one that occurs; his mind is less keen and more apt to lapses of judgment in route finding and in decisions about stopping, splitting the party, and so on.

STAYING OUT OF TROUBLE

Part of the satisfaction of winter travel inheres in meeting the challenge of a difficult environment, and anyone who spends very much time in the wilderness, especially in winter, will encounter some trying situations. There is a difference, however, between losing one's bearings and being totally lost, between being storm-bound and being in a desperate survival situation, between being injured and being in danger of death. The difference usually depends on the foresight a party has shown in preparing for difficulties. Winter storms, especially in the mountains, are sometimes of such severity that a man cannot expect to survive in the open. With a few extra rations and bivouac gear one can take shelter and sit out the storm—uncomfortably, perhaps, but without having ever been in an emergency. In this same situation an individual or party that tries to bull through for a few extra hours before stopping may become badly chilled and be in very real danger.

Most of the common sorts of trouble can be completely avoided. Proper route finding will keep you from losing your bearings, and if you do lose them you should still have a good enough idea of your location to find your way out. Adequate clothing, food, and calmly applied common sense will keep a difficulty from turning into a disaster.

The main rules for staying out of trouble are fairly simple. The first is to keep your goals well within the capacity of the party. One experienced person cannot safely make the same trip with six beginners as he can with only one. A group that is lightly supplied with extra clothing and food will not be able to safely undertake as long a trip as the same party could with more supplies. A large, experienced, and well-supplied group can plan on being capable of evacuating an injured member of the party, while a group lacking any one of these attributes cannot. Judgment of the party's capacity must be made on many levels, but the obvious method is to look for weaknesses and to ask yourself how far they can be safely tested or how they can be eliminated. A three-man ski party may be perfectly safe where help is available, but the same size party would undertake much higher risk in a really remote region. The risk may be well worth taking, but it should be recognized for what it is, and appropriate allowances should be made.

The second rule is one of adequate preparation, and this is again a matter of judgment. Many examples have been mentioned elsewhere, such as the fact that if a party is planning to split, extra items like maps and emergency kits must be carried for each group. Adequate food and clothing in case of difficulty are obviously needed, though quantities vary; you need not carry so much on a weekend ski tour as on one planned to last several weeks. Less obvious matters for preparation involve the supplies and knowledge necessary to deal with emergency medical problems, which again vary with the type, length, and remoteness of the trip. Each member of the party should have adequate knowledge of first aid and medical care, since if an injury occurs, it may be sustained by the person on which everyone relied for aid. Again, preparations required where aid can easily be summoned are different from those needed deep in wild areas.

Despite the best-laid plans of mice and skiers, difficulties will sometimes occur. Emergencies frequently arise from such situations, not because of the nature of the circumstances themselves, but due to the badly thought-out actions of the party in trouble. Care and thought are most needed just when people are most inclined to act hastily on impulse or panic. Parties do not normally split up in a storm because of a misguided but carefully thought-out plan; they just thrash madly off in different directions and realize too late that they have lost both the trail and the other half of the group. The need for calm and deliberate action is obvious from an armchair view, but it is important to keep reminding oneself and one's party of this need in real situations of stress.

Though every difficulty is somewhat different and some are impossible to anticipate, there are many problems that can be simulated at home so that one can learn to deal with them there. For example, it is obviously advantageous to learn how to build fires in the wet and to lay out a compass bearing before these skills are actually needed. Instruction programs on first aid and emergency medicine can and should include practice with mock-up injuries in difficult situations, enabling the students to make their errors and get over their squeamishness without serious consequences. Even emergencies that cannot be physically simulated will be easier to deal with if they have been mentally pictured and thought out, not just skimmed over in a book. The more a wilderness traveler can prepare himself in advance for problems he may encounter, the wider his safety margin will be.

GETTING LOST

There is a particular instinctive panic that takes over when people realize that they have lost their bearings. The common reaction is to *do* something about it, to rush off in one direction or another in the desperate hope of becoming oriented again by a familiar landmark. The usual result is, of course, that the lost person becomes more and more disoriented, with the pitch of fear and expenditure of wasted energy increasing until he is exhausted. Obviously, this is not the best way to go about things, and providing there is no immediate danger threatening, like that posed by an avalanche slope above, it is time to stop and think things over as soon as it is discovered that one is off course or confused about direction.

Until the border of hysteria is crossed, no one is ever *completely* lost, since he is bound to know something about his location. If you should lose your bearings, sit down and make yourself comfortable. Get out your map and compass if you have them, and consult with your companions, if any, about what you *do* know. You must certainly know what continent you are on and a good deal more, besides. You probably know your location within a few miles. If you have a compass, you know which direction is which, and if you also have a map, you can orient it with the compass. Even if you have neither map nor compass, you probably know something about the area you are in. The essence of dealing with your situation is applying what you do know to the problem of finding your way, and this demands a careful and realistic evaluation. Even if your camp is only a mile away, it may be more sensible to head for a road five miles away that is impossible to miss, if there is no systematic way of finding the camp.

If you are lost in a storm, the best course of action is usually to build a shelter and wait for the weather to clear, rather than courting exhaustion by continuing father along a course that may be in the wrong direction. It should go without saying that a person who is really lost and who expects a search party ought to stay in one place and concentrate his energy on making himself comfortable and visible.

Even without a compass, it is possible to follow a straight line in terrain with some landmarks like trees. Simply line up two distant objects and keep them in line, choosing a third object in the same line before either of the first two is reached. Traveling in an arbitrary straight line is better than circling but still leaves a good deal to be desired. Try to remember everything you know about an area before heading off in a random direction. If it is bordered within reasonable traveling distance by roads or other unmistakable landmarks, moving in a straight line is a good idea, but if you are on the edge of a large wilderness area, it would be better to stay put until you have a directional reference. All this is simply meant to suggest by example that it is necessary to apply common sense and good judgment in emergencies, rather than blindly following half-remembered and often fallacious rules of thumb. There is, for instance, the rule that following a watershed down will lead eventually to civilization. This may apply in the area where you are lost. On the other hand, the watershed might lead through a couple of thousand miles of wilderness before emptying into the Arctic Ocean, or just a few miles to a lake that drains by underground streams. Furthermore, blindly following a watershed is not always the *easiest* way out, even if it does eventually lead where you want to go.

If you make sure to have a compass and map with you whenever you travel in any extensive roadless area, you will not have to worry about this sort of problem. Even if you are lost, there will usually be an obvious route to some kind of landmark, which can then be used to locate your position. The most featureless terrain is luckily also the most likely to have long, straight roads, which can be intersected by simply traveling in the right general direction.

Getting lost 281

STORMS

Storms are generally a real problem only when they combine with other difficulties. If shelter and adequate food and clothing are available, one can simply wait until the weather lets up. Unfortunately, injuries often occur while a party is traveling in bad weather. Chilling and exhaustion are also more likely to beset a party under these circumstances. It is precisely such pyramiding of difficulties that must be prevented to avoid disastrous consequences.

Preparations are obvious and have been mentioned in the form of adequate clothing and extra food. Parties traveling some distance from camp over difficult terrain should carry bivouac equipment. An injury can slow such a party to a crawl, and a night out without bivouac gear can be fatal.

When a party is caught in a storm, it is important to pitch camp early, especially if the weather is beginning to take its toll on some members. Continuing on until dark in a desperate attempt to reach a road or car is foolish. Setting up camp will take much more time and effort in the dark, fuel will be hard to gather, mittens and other equipment are likely to be lost in the scramble. In a really bad storm—rare except in high mountains—one has no choice but to take shelter for the duration. When the weather is bad enough, there is simply no longer a question of what to do.

Even a party that is short of food will be better off stopping when a storm becomes difficult. Going hungry for a few days is a bad idea, especially in cold weather, but it is not really serious if one does not allow severe chill or exhaustion to occur. If one does, the hungry body's reduced blood sugar will hamper its ability to cope with fatigue and cold.

The great majority of injuries in the wilderness occur when a person is tired. A cold party, stumbling along through a storm at twilight, is asking for trouble. Stop before you find it. Watch for signs of fatigue and chilling in your party, both because they are important in themselves and because these signs may well precede a broken leg. Continuing in a storm calls for greater care than in fine weather.

Never split the party in a storm. It is amazing how easily a person can become separated from the rest of the group in bad weather. People may travel in different directions without even noticing.

Someone may stop to clean his glasses or answer a call of nature, without his absence being noticed. He may then be prevented from rejoining the party because its tracks are already filled in, or simply because he is too tired to catch up. A positive effort is required to keep the party together in bad storm conditions, but it is essential that this effort be made. The extra problems of finding a lost member of the party are hardly needed to add to the other difficulties presented by a storm. Even if the party gets together quickly, it will have lost time and may have gotten off course as well.

INJURIES AND MEDICAL EMERGENCIES

If reasonable care is exercised, the wilderness traveler may never have to deal with a serious injury, but it is obvious that anyone who goes very far from the beaten track must be prepared in case he is not so lucky. Any party traveling in wilderness areas should be capable of taking care of the common types of injuries and medical emergencies. This often involves a good deal more than conventional first aid, which concerns itself with handling a patient for a short time, until a doctor or ambulance can reach him. If you break a leg ten miles from the nearest road, you will have to depend on your companions to take care of the injury for a few days, and perhaps they will have to haul you out as well.

Anyone who spends very much time in the wilderness should get as much training in first aid and emergency medicine as possible. The Red Cross beginning and advanced first aid courses should be standard preparation, but additional instruction is desirable. A mountaineering club in your area may have a special course in emergency medicine. If not, you might be able to organize one with some friends, finding a doctor who is interested, perhaps one who spends time in the woods and mountains himself. Such a course should include as much practice as possible, preferably in circumstances that simulate genuine accident situations. Practicing examination for injuries outdoors on a snowy night with a flashlight will give you a better background and a longer memory than the same practice conducted in an overheated room. The bibliography lists some useful books.

In addition to proper first-aid training, you should have a regular physical checkup, and so should the friends you go with. Anyone who has special medical problems should talk with his doctor about consequences that might be important in emergency situations in the wilderness and should carry any special medicine he might need. It is important that his companions know about these special problems, so that if he should be injured they will know what to do. A diabetic coma would be recognized quickly by a companion who was aware of the possibility, but anyone who is not a doctor could hardly be expected to make a correct diagnosis if he was not aware that his compaion had diabetes.

Finally, a first-aid kit must be carried at all times in wilderness travel. The possibility of carrying one large kit and a number of smaller ones has already been mentioned as a useful approach for larger groups. It may also be worth considering the desirability of carrying supplies that go well beyond the range of "first aid" if you plan many extensive trips in remote regions. The importance of certain prescription drugs in proper care for the injured over a period of days or weeks makes the discussion of this problem with a doctor worthwhile. The use of such drugs falls into the province of medicine rather than first aid, but so does any care that aims at preserving or recovering the health of a patient far from doctors and hospitals. In extensive wilderness travel such tools can mean the difference between life and death for an injured person. Prescriptions and instructions for proper use of pain killers, antibiotics, and the like must be obtained from a doctor, so no attempt will be made to discuss them here. Anyone interested in the subject would be well advised to read *Medicine for Mountaineering,* as a basis for discussion with his physician. It is *the* book on emergency medicine for wilderness use, and is worth many careful readings by anyone who wants to prepare himself for emergencies in the back country.

Providing all members of the party are healthy to begin with and have not greatly exceeded their capacities, the most likely medical emergencies to be encountered are those resulting from accidents or cold. By far the most common sort of accident is a sprain or fracture of an extremity due to a short fall, and this is fortunately not a dangerous injury under normal circumstances. Most accidents in the woods, even when they occur, can be handled without great danger to anyone's life, providing they are dealt with in a calm and sensible manner.

INJURIES WHERE SECONDS COUNT

Fortunately, there are not many types of medical problems that require extremely quick action on the part of the person who is rendering aid. Undue delay is bad, of course, but there are only a very few cases where the first aider or rescuer does not have time to think things out and to act carefully and deliberately. In most cases, much more damage is done by hurrying than by working slowly and thoroughly.

There are two main exceptions to this rule that are likely to be encountered in accidents occurring in the winter woods—injuries involving a victim who has stopped breathing or who is bleeding severely. In such cases seconds count, and action must be prompt if it is to do any good at all. For this reason, the first things a would-be rescuer should check when arriving at the scene of a serious accident are the victim's breathing and the possibility of serious external bleeding.

Common reasons for the victim to have stopped breathing, other than his already being dead, are drowning, electrical shock, and poisoning. None of these are nearly so likely in snow-covered wilderness areas as in other locations, but they are all possible. Avalanche victims are also sometimes recovered alive but not breathing. Artificial respiration should begin immediately on any victim who is not breathing but not obviously dead. If a second rescuer is available, he should examine the victim for bleeding, check the victim's pulse, check for other injuries, and insulate the victim from the snow, while the first person continues artificial respiration. If only one rescuer is present, he will have to perform these tasks as best he can without interrupting resuscitation. If a pulse is not present, external heart massage must also be started immediately. Either artificial respiration or heart massage alone is useless without the other, if both breathing and the heart have stopped.

Artificial respiration. Mouth-to-mouth resuscitation is much more effective than any other method available outside a hospital, and it is less tiring and more foolproof than other types of artificial respiration. The victim's mouth and upper throat should be cleared of any foreign matter—snow, water, vomitus, etc.—a task that may be more easily accomplished if he is lying on his side with his head downhill, but which must be gotten out of the way quickly. The victim is then moved onto his back—carefully—and the head is tilted back as far as possible. The jaw is pulled or pushed forward, either with your thumb hooking under the teeth, or by pushing from both sides of the back of the jawbone. The combination of the backward-tilting head and the jutting jaw will keep the victim's tongue clear of the back of his throat, so that the airway to the lungs is open.

With all this accomplished, pinch the victim's nostrils closed with the hand that is not holding his jaw, take a deep breath, cover his mouth with yours, and blow into his lungs until you see his chest rise. Release your mouth from the victim's, and listen for the air escaping his lungs while you are exhaling and taking another breath. Then blow into his lungs again. The cycle should be repeated every four or five seconds. When you blow into the victim's lungs, the air should go in easily. If there is resistance, then the airway is not clear, either because you have not got the tongue away from the back of the throat or because there is foreign matter lodged in the airway. Check the jaw first. If it is well forward, turn the victim on his side, head downward if possible, and give him a few good whacks between the shoulder blades. Situations like this may cause conflicts in cases of a possible spine injury, but the airway must be cleared quickly, regardless of other troubles. Once a person has stopped breathing for five minutes, his chances of recovery dwindle rapidly. Usually, one does not know how long respiration has been stopped when the victim is found, so artificial respiration should be tried, but if you have not started resuscitation within ten or fifteen minutes of the time the victim stopped breathing, you are wasting your efforts.

Resuscitation should be continued as long as the victim's heart is beating, and the rhythm should be coordinated with any attempts to breathe that he makes. The victim's stomach may become bloated with air and expand to prevent the lungs from filling completely. This should be checked every few minutes. Pressure with your hand during exhalation will usually empty the stomach of air, but be alert for vomiting when this is done. If the victim vomits, turn him quickly on his side and clear the vomit before resuming artificial respiration.

External heart massage. There is no point attempting artificial respiration if the victim's heart is not beating, unless some measures are taken to pump the oxygenated blood through his system.

Check for a pulse at the carotid artery, rather than at the extremities, since a weak pulse may not be easy to find at spots like the wrist. To find the carotid artery, simply press a forefinger gently into the soft area of the neck immediately adjoining the larynx. This is easy to find on yourself; the pulse can be found on either side, but don't press on both sides at once, lest you knock yourself or your subject out.

If no pulse is felt, a sharp blow to the center of the rib cage may start the heart. The blow must be hard to do any good. If the first one does not work, try about four more in fairly quick succession. If no pulse is felt, external heart massage must be used, and two rescuers will almost certainly be necessary, since it is doubtful whether one could give a massage and artificial respiration at the same time with any effect.

The idea of external heart massage is to pump blood by squeezing the heart between the breastbone and the spine. The back must be resting on a fairly firm surface for this to be accomplished, but there should be no sharp projections that might gouge the victim when pressure is applied. Kneel beside the victim, and with elbows locked put both your hands on his chest, one on top of the other. The heel of your lower hand should rest in the center of the subject's breastbone, just above the lowest point. To pump the victim's heart, lean forward, putting pressure on the breastbone and pushing it down an inch or two. Pressure is then released, and the cycle is repeated once every second. An assistant can check for a pulse at the carotid artery.

The combination of artificial respiration and cardiac massage are a last desperate effort, and they will probably fail to revive the victim. Since there is a chance that they will work, they should, of course, be tried, but the poor prognosis should be considered if there are conflicting interests. An obviously living accident victim should not be allowed to bleed to death while efforts are being made to revive someone who is probably dead. If the pupils of the victim are dilated and fail to respond to bright light, the situation is probably hopeless, and the would-be rescuers should not continue efforts if avalanche danger or some other threat to their lives is present.

Fortunately, injuries of the nature just described are less common in the snowy wilderness than on the highways leading to its edge, and the wilderness traveler is more likely to get an opportunity to put his first aid to the test on the drive to the mountains than on the ski slope.

Injuries where seconds count 287

MAJOR BLEEDING

The second possible rush emergency that might occur on a winter tour is the occurrence of massive hemorrhaging. Arterial blood is under quite a bit of pressure, and the total amount of blood in the body is only around ten quarts. Major bleeding has to be stopped right away or it will be fatal. *The proper treatment for bleeding is pressure directly on the wound.* If you have some sterile dressings handy, press those onto the wound. Probably you will have to start with a handkerchief or just the palm of your hand. Stop the bleeding first, while someone else looks for the first-aid kit. Sterile dressings are nice but they won't do your patient much good if he is dead. As soon as possible get some large sterile pads on the wound and apply the pressure on those.

Fortunately, most bleeding looks worse than it really is. The sign of arterial bleeding is its vigor—it spurts out hard and rhythmically—and it is harder to stop than venous bleeding. The diagnosis is simple in practical terms, since the treatment of arterial and venous differs only in the amount of pressure and time required to stop the bleeding. Once you get the bleeding stopped, keep the pressure on the wound until you are sure it has clotted. *Don't* look underneath your dressing after a couple of minutes, especially if the bleeding is major. Wait fifteen or twenty minutes. Your patient can't afford the extra blood it will cost him to satisfy your curiosity, and you will lose time because you will have to control the bleeding all over again. If you have anyone to help you, have him maintain the pressure on the dressing while you go on to other things.

Tourniquets should not be used. They are needed so seldom that even doctors in emergency wards, who deal with bleeding every day, often spend years without applying a tourniquet, and the likelihood of needing one on a wilderness trip is very small, indeed. Pressure points are also a poor alternative for actually controlling bleeding, though they may be useful for changing dressings without causing additional bleeding, if you really know them well enough to apply pressure in the right place on the first try. Direct pressure on the wound is, however, the way to control the bleeding most effectively, and it has the additional advantage of simplicity.

EXAMINING AN ACCIDENT VICTIM

If someone becomes injured or sick it is important to make a complete examination as soon as possible. You may have to interrupt the examination to stop bleeding, protect the patient from the cold, and treat him for shock, but the examination should be carried out thoroughly as soon as possible. In an accident situation it is very easy to overlook injuries that may be much more serious than superficial but obvious ones. While you are taking great pains with a superficial face wound, your patient may be bleeding to death from a laceration in the leg.

The most important thing about the examination is that it be thorough, and for this it is necessary to follow a pattern. The order is not particularly important, but it should be practiced so that nothing will be missed. A routine like this can also be very useful in putting everyone in a better state of mind. Talk to your patient. He is your friend, not a bag of potatoes. If he happens to be a stranger, there is even more reason for you to show him that you know what you are doing and that he can trust you. Ask the victim what happened. Ask him how he feels and what hurts. Watch his face during your examination. If it shows pain, find out why. Be careful not to cause any further injury while you are making the examination. By far the most common injuries that are likely to occur on a wilderness trip are fractures, and you will cause additional damage by careless handling of the patient before the broken bones are splinted. Remember that a good "bedside manner" is more than a nicety in an accident situation in the cold. Shock is the most likely cause of death, and fear and pain contribute to shock. It is up to you to calm the person you are trying to help and to alleviate his pain.

If a person is unconscious, these considerations are even more important. It is much easier to injure a person who can't scream at you. He may still indicate pain, which is both a warning and a clue to injuries. You do not know how unconscious he is. Hearing is one of the last senses to be dulled, and your patient may be able to hear you even if he seems quite senseless. Imagine how you would feel if you were badly hurt and some jerk was poking and prodding you and saying things like, "My God, look at all that blood. Do you think he's going to die?" Talk to your friend, even if you don't know whether he can hear you. Try to be calm and tactful and to sound competent, whether or not you feel so. Tell him what you're doing, and tell him it might hurt. Don't tell him everything is all right. He knows everything *isn't* all right!

The nature of an examination will be determined to some extent by what you already know. If a person has become sick while you are stormbound in a tent, you will not be checking for broken bones, but beware of skipping steps because of unwarranted assumptions you may have made. If you have to treat someone you have found somewhere, the examination must be broader than with one of your companions whom you have been observing all along. It is primarily the latter case with which we're concerned. The kinds of problems that are likely to be encountered by a healthy person on a winter trip in the wilderness are fairly limited. They include a few special problems resulting from the cold environment, but consist mainly of traumatic injuries—those resulting from physical violence: cuts, broken bones, or internal injuries.

Circumstances resulting in trauma are obvious: falls, collisions with trees, and so on. When the victim is reached, the would-be rescuer should first check his breathing, a requirement often satisfied by the emanation of colorful language from the subject. After a cursory check for major bleeding, some effort should be made to make the patient comfortable before proceeding. Several sleeping pads may be slipped under him for insulation from the snow, or clothing may be substituted if pads aren't available. Several people should be used to lift the injured man, and everyone should know what motions are to be made beforehand. If there is any danger of spinal or neck injury, particular care must be taken to move the whole spinal column as a unit. The patient should be gotten into a sleeping bag at the same time. All this can be accomplished smoothly and with little movement of the victim, if several people are available and their movements are well coordinated. The patient merely needs to be lifted a few inches from one side while someone slips the pads and sleeping bag into position from the other side. If, as is usually the case, injuries are on one side, this side should be on the zippered side of the sleeping bag, so that you can work on them while keeping the victim warm.

These actions to keep the patient warm need to be started quickly in the winter snow, even before a thorough examination has been made. In more clement surroundings this might be inadvisable, but in the cold and snow the always serious problem of shock is greatly exacerbated. The patient must be kept as warm as possible while further examination and treatment are carried out. If it is convenient when the patient is moved, the legs should rest above the head by six inches or a foot as further treatment for shock.

Examination of the accident victim usually starts at the head and proceeds to the feet. Breathing is checked first, and treatment for impaired breathing should be made immediately. Besides suffocation in water or snow, breathing difficulty could be caused by a head injury, by foreign matter lodged in the mouth and throat, or by a chest injury. Chest injuries and maintaining an airway with an unconscious victim are discussed below. Foreign matter such as snow or vomitus should obviously be removed from the airway. Artificial respiration must be administered immediately if breathing stops.

If the victim is unconscious, he should be examined for signs of a head injury. Bleeding or passage of a straw-colored fluid from the ears or nose may be significant, but bleeding may be due to local injury. Check the eyes. Are the pupils dilated and are they sensitive to light? Feel gently for signs of injury, and take care for a broken neck, movement of which could kill your patient.

If the person is conscious, talk with him. In addition to cheering him and obtaining information from him directly, a head injury may be indicated by confusion. Irrationality is also a symptom of several other problems, including severe and dangerous chilling. Anyone who has had a bump on the head sharp enough to have knocked him unconscious for a few minutes must be watched carefully for at least the next twenty-four hours for signs of brain injury. A blood clot developing under the skull can press on the brain and end in death.

Below the head, the examiner should go over the shoulders, arms, torso, pelvic area, legs, ankles, and feet, feeling gently but firmly to detect any wounds, tender spots, or broken bones. Pressure and twisting action from both ends of the major bones should detect most complete fractures, but it must be applied very carefully and stopped immediately at the first sign of pain. If you have good reason to suspect a fracture, assume that you have one, rather than risking more severe injury by testing the bone further. Sprains can be difficult to distinguish from fractures, especially after muscle spasm has stiffened the area.

The signs of fracture are usually easy to recognize except at the

Examining an accident victim

joints. Fractures and bad sprains of the knee, elbow, ankle, or wrist should be treated in about the same way, anyhow, so there is not much difference for our purposes. Final diagnosis can wait for doctors with X rays. Particular care must be taken of these injuries, since pinching of the nerves in the area of a fracture due to improper handling can cause permanent damage.

Fractures are likely to cause swelling and extreme tenderness in the area around them, and unless there is only partial cracking, the victim probably (not always!) will be unable to put normal weight on the injured member. Deformities are sure signs of fractures, including the sometimes inconspicuous shortening of a limb. Shortening is easily detected by comparison with the uninjured member.

No attempt will be made here to describe an examination of a person who has become seriously ill on a trip without the intervention of an accident. Excellent descriptions of such techniques may be found in *Medicine for Mountaineering,* which has been mentioned before. It is worthwhile, however, to keep a written history of any illness, whether accidental or not. Paper and pencil should be included in the first-aid kit, and a thorough history should be taken as soon as circumstances permit. The history should include all the information you have obtained in your examination, and with a person who has become ill, it should at least include a description of his complaints, a record of his temperature every few hours, any symptoms you have noticed, and any medications that have been administered. The history should go with the patient. It may greatly simplify the work of the doctor. It will also enable you to think systematically and will thus give you a better chance of acting intelligently.

FRACTURES

Broken bones are the most common injury likely to be encountered on any wilderness trip, particularly one undertaken on skis. Most fractures are closed: there is no break in the skin. Treatment is simple in principle if not in practice. The fracture must be immobilized so that no further damage will be done by movement of the sharp ends of the bone. Unless imminent danger requires moving the victim immediately, the fracture should always be immobilized before he is transported.

Immobilization is usually accomplished by splinting, which consists of fastening the injured part to something that will restrain it from moving. As a general rule, proper splinting requires immobilizing both the joint below the fracture and the one above. In a break of the lower leg, for example, the foot and the knee must both be restrained.

Usually, the person giving aid should not attempt to straighten deformities, since this entails the danger of doing further damage to blood vessels or nerves, as well as general tissue. There may be exceptions to this rule, however, which will have to be decided in the best judgment of the person giving aid. If circulation to an extremity beyond the fracture seems to be impaired, this may be caused either by pressure on an artery, which may be relieved by straightening (or may be worsened), or it may be due to bleeding from an artery that has already been ripped by the bone ends, in which case straightening will bring about no improvement. Straightening may also be necessary in some cases to make the patient comfortable or to make splinting possible. If it *must* be done, straightening should be accomplished with tension on both ends of the break, with very slow, careful manipulation and attention to any pain experienced by the victim. Severe pain is a warning, and it should be heeded. Straightening a bone that has been partially immobilized by spasm in large muscles like those of the thigh is next to impossible, so if any manipulation is necessary, it should be done as soon as possible.

The fracture of any large bone damages a good deal of tissue, and thus causes quite a bit of blood loss. This may not be apparent to the person giving first aid, because the blood is not pouring out messily the way it does with a bad cut. It spreads out into the surrounding tissues instead, but in the conditions of the outdoors in winter there can be enough blood lost as a result of the fracture of any of the major bones to pose a grave threat of shock. The fracture of the thighbone, the pelvis, or a combination of smaller bones should alert the person giving aid to anticipate shock and to institute treatment for it, especially in cold conditions.

The difficulties of splinting are also greatly increased in the situations likely to be encountered by those touring in the snow country. Materials for making splints are likely to be scarce. Particular care must be taken both to keep the injured part of the body and the victim himself warm, and the danger that a splint may restrict circulation must be very carefully avoided. If any of these problems are ignored in a cold environment, the injured extremity is likely to become frostbitten in addition to the initial injury. Boots should be removed and replaced with soft, non-constricting insulation, except when the boots are an essential part of the splint.

Finding materials for splints requires quite a bit of ingenuity in wilderness situations. Many injuries can be splinted in whole or in part by using other parts of the victim's body. Arms can be bound to the body. A leg can be splinted partly by tying it to the other leg. A finger can be taped to its neighbor. These methods have the advantage of conserving warmth. Padding should be placed near all bony projections like knees, or the patient will be uncomfortable in a short length of time. Some cloth should separate any skin surface from another to prevent maceration. Air mattresses, sleeping pads and pack frames can all be used to help improvise splints, but ski poles, skis, ice axes, and snowshoes should be used as a last resort, since they may be needed for other purposes. Available branches and sticks are obvious sources of rigidity when properly padded.

In your enthusiasm for engineering splints, try to remember your patient. Besides watching him for shock and cold, you need his advice to make a good splint. *He is the expert; he knows what hurts and what is relatively comfortable,* and this is the best guide to proper position in splinting. If you can make the patient comfortable, then you have found a good position for splinting him. The patient's comfort and immobilization of the injured area are the two main considerations. Don't assume that you know better than the injured person what position is best for him; you probably don't.

Any injured extremity must be well-padded and insulated, but it should also be easy to get to. It must be checked frequently for signs of impaired circulation or frostbite, and this will be put off if it is made too difficult to gain access to the limb. Even a healthy person who is inactive is likely to become cold despite his wearing much more clothing than those around him. An injured person has much less heat-producing capacity, and any impairment of circulation to the feet or hands by the injury itself or by splints is likely to cause very rapid chilling and cold injury.

Fractures that are not disabling, such as those of fingers, arms, and so on, should be properly splinted, but unless they cause inordinate pain or there is evidence of nerve damage or impairment of circulation, they need not be considered as emergencies. There is no compelling need for the fracture to be set, and the party should plan a relaxed and organized retreat. Harrowing forced marches are particularly foolish in such cases.

A broken leg or pelvis will probably be disabling, but the major threats lie in possible complications. If shock and cold injury are warded off, there is no great danger in keeping the patient in a tent for a while until an orderly evacuation can be carried out. The poor fellow has suffered enough without his friends bouncing him out through the woods in the middle of the night.

WOUNDS

The major problem resulting from lacerations, cuts and other flesh wounds has already been alluded to—the danger of major bleeding, especially in the event that an artery has been severed. Stopping bleeding is the first job of anyone giving first aid to an injured person. With bleeding under control the rescuer must anticipate the possibility of shock, which should be expected to follow any major injury, and treatment should be started as soon as possible. Shock is discussed below in more detail. Finally, treatment for flesh wounds must include any measures possible to promote healing and to prevent infection of the wound. Since the means of combating infection that are available on a back-country trip are quite limited, the winter tourer is fortunate that his environment is relatively clean and free of bacteria.

Once bleeding has been controlled, the person giving first aid should clean the wound as much as possible, but without risking another incident of major bleeding. The hands should be thoroughly washed before working on the wound. Sterile swabs or pads from the first aid kit should be used for cleaning out any foreign material. Sterile water should be used for washing the wound if possible. Melted new snow may have to be substituted if fuel supplies are inadequate for boiling water. The are around the wound can be washed with a solution of aqueous Zepharin or pHisohex, neither of which will damage the tissues nor dye the surrounding skin red and thus mask developing signs of infection. If the wound was made by a protruding compound fracture, which does not seem to have been significantly contaminated, it is probably best to confine cleansing to the skin around the wound. If there is foreign matter on the bone end, it should be removed, but any contamination of the bone should be avoided with great care, since infection of the bone can be very dangerous. When the wound has been cleaned, it should be covered with a sterile dressing and then with a bandage. The same cautions about insulating injured limbs and taking care not to impede circulation apply to limbs injured by flesh wounds as to fractured limbs.

In cases where severe arterial bleeding has occurred, particular care should be taken not to dislodge blood clots once they have formed. The additional bleeding that will result can probably not be tolerated by a patient who has already sustained considerable blood loss. For this reason, it is advisable to wait a few days before attempting transport of an accident victim with this type of cut, providing other considerations do not make immediate evacuation necessary.

Compound fractures—those that have a surface wound extending to the fracture—usually result from a sharp end of bone poking through the tissues and skin. The dangers, and hence the treatment, are those associated with both fractures and flesh wounds. Bleeding must be stopped first, of course, and the wound should then be dressed. If the bone is still protruding, it should not be withdrawn back into the skin unless this is absolutely imperative, since the possibility of dangerous infection will be greatly increased. The limb must be splinted like any other fracture before the victim is moved.

No attempts should be made to close a wound with sutures or other devices, since infection is far more likely to spread if the wound has been closed. Pus in a closed infected wound is forced into the tissues around the wound instead of draining.

If much time passes before the accident victim is evacuated, the dressing on the wound should be changed periodically, and both the wound and the surrounding area should be examined for signs of infection. An infected wound will become red around the edges and is likely to be swollen and to exude pus. If an infected wound closes over, it should be opened, preferably by dissolving the sealing matter with warm water before forcing the edges open. The wound should be thoroughly cleaned and should be probed with a sterile instrument to open any pockets of pus. A dressing should then be placed on the wound that will allow it to drain and not encourage closing. When possible, soaking infected wounds is helpful. Dressings must be changed after soaking.

All dressings from infected wounds should be handled very carefully to avoid spreading the infection with the tremendous number of bacteria present in the pus. The preferred method is to handle such dressings with forceps to be sterilized afterwards. The dressings should be burned. Such procedures may or may not be possible in your situation, but they should be approximated to the greatest possible degree.

SPECIAL PROBLEMS

Injuries of the head are particularly dangerous, because they threaten the brain, a vital and easily damaged organ. Luckily, this type of injury is rather unlikely in most wilderness situations in winter, with the exception of winter mountaineering. Participants in the latter activity should consider wearing hard hats for warmth and protection in case of falls.

With wounds of the face and scalp, considerable bleeding may be expected, since these areas are well supplied with blood. This bleeding can be readily controlled by pressure. Such wounds are particularly resistant to infection, but additional care should still be taken, since infection would be especially dangerous so near the brain and the eyes. Injuries to the eyes and eyelids themselves are quite uncommon. The affected eye should be carefully bandaged after washing and the unaffected eye should be covered to prevent movement. In washing, foreign particles may be removed, but great care should be taken not to damage any blood clots or tissues of the eye itself. Broken bones in the face do not usually cause much serious trouble. Only the jawbone needs splinting, and this will reduce the victim to a liquid diet.

The most serious injuries to the head are those involving damage to the brain or the skull that protects it. Any blow to the head that is followed by unconsciousness has involved some damage to the brain: that is the reason the victim is unconscious. Usually, no complications follow if the person regains consciousness within fif-

Special problems 297

teen minutes or so, but even someone who has been unconscious for a short time should be watched carefully during the next twenty-four hours. The reason is that after an injury, bruising, bleeding, and swelling can occur in the brain, just as in any other part of the body, but since the brain is enclosed in a rigid case, swelling will produce pressure inside the skull. Too much pressure will cause unconsciousness and finally death.

In examining a person who has received a blow on his head, you should be alert for signs of brain injury, whether he is unconscious or not. A scalp wound, bump, or tender spot may be associated with a skull fracture, but this will be difficult to determine, except in cases so obvious that they kill the victim. Signs of brain injury include: pupils which are of different size or which are dilated and do not react to light; irrationality or confusion greater than would be expected from the circumstances; bleeding or leakage of yellowish, clear fluid from the nose or ears; a slow pulse rate; irregular breathing, nausea.

Depth of unconsciousness may give some indication of the seriousness of a coma. A person who still shows some reaction to stimuli—voices or other noises, touch, or pain—is in a relatively light coma, and there is some chance that he may regain consciousness and be able to walk out. A deeper coma is more likely to last a long time and require the victim to be carried out. In any case, there is no treatment possible for the brain injury outside of a hospital. Treatment must concentrate on care for other injuries and supportive care. It is particularly important that the patient's airway be kept open, since the muscles of a comatose patient may be so relaxed that his tongue will drop back into his throat and suffocate him. If possible, a record of pulse and breathing rates, together with any information of a deepening or lightening coma, will be of help to the physician when the patient reaches him.

A broken back or neck is a particularly dangerous fracture because of the danger to the spinal cord, the central nervous column that carries impulses between the brain and the body. Actual damage to or pressure on the spinal cord may cause lack of feeling and paralysis in those areas below the fractured vertebra. In less severe cases it may cause some loss of sensation in those parts, tingling, pain flowing around from back to front and down the arms and legs. When checking for loss of sensation or power of movement, always check both sides of the body, since only one side may be affected.

A fractured vertebra threatens damage to the spinal cord, but damage may not be sustained at the time of the injury. After any fall that might have broken the spinal column, it should be carefully checked for possible fractures. Any painful, sensitive, or swollen spot along the spine should be assumed to be a fracture, and the victim should be treated accordingly. A spinal fracture must be adequately splinted before the patient is moved at all. The splint should insure that no lateral or twisting movement can take place. Evacuation should normally be postponed until a wire basket stretcher can be brought in, though this may not be practical. Temporary splints are usually best made from packframes, skis and snowshoes. With a fracture of the neck, the head must be padded and strapped so that it cannot move at all from side to side, with a small pad about the size of a fist under the nape of the neck. *A broken neck must not be flexed,* lest the victim be killed. For splinting the spine, a pad should rest under the small of the back.

Injuries of the chest and lungs pose the particular threat of interference with breathing, so they require some special attention. The most common chest injury is a broken rib, normally not a serious injury. Pain in the chest wall following a sharp impact may result from a broken rib or from simple bruising. If the pain becomes more intense when a large breath is taken, it is probably a broken rib. Except in rare cases, the rib will be adequately splinted by the surrounding muscles, and no special treatment is required. If the patient is suffering from too much pain, but he is not having difficulty getting enough air, the rib can be taped to make him more comfortable. Several strips of tape running from the spine to the center of the chest roughly along the line of the injured rib and applied after a breath has been expelled will make the patient more comfortable. Taping should not be attempted if the victim is having trouble getting enough air, since it will partially immobilize one side of the chest and will impair breathing. The tape should be removed after a couple of days.

Occasionally, considerably greater damage is done to the chest, and breathing may be impaired in one of several ways. A rib may be broken in such a fashion that the sharp end penetrates the thick layer of muscle surrounding it and actually perforates the lung. Symptoms are those of a normal broken rib, except that pain is more intense, the patient will have difficulty in breathing, and there will be at least some bleeding into the lung so that blood may be coughed up. This type of injury can be very dangerous, since pressure can build up in the injured side of the chest and interfere with breathing even in the good lung. Such pressure can also be created by bleeding into one side of the chest cavity. The chest should be taped on the injured side, and the patient should lie on the injured side, before and during transport. This serves a combined purpose: lying on the side helps to splint it; not so much air can get into the injured side, where it does no good, anyhow; and blood will pool in the injured side and run out the windpipe, rather than flowing into the good lung and damaging it, too.

Another type of chest injury that will produce great difficulty in breathing is caused by a blow to the chest so massive as to fracture several ribs in a number of different places, destroying the rigidity of a section of the chest wall. When the victim tries to inhale, the injured section of the wall is sucked in, and when he tries to exhale, it puffs out. Thus, instead of moving air in and out of the chest, the diaphragm is merely moving the injured wall of the chest back and forth, and the patient may well be suffocating. This condition is known as flail chest. Immediate first aid is to roll the victim onto the injured side with the injured part of the chest resting on a wadded up jacket or similar object. The flailing section will then be immobilized so that the victim can breathe with his remaining lung capacity. The patient may also be transported in this position.

Finally, there is the possibility that an accident may occur that completely punctures the wall of the chest, creating what is known as a sucking chest wound. If the whole wall of the chest is actually perforated, the lung on that side will immediately collapse, as air rushes into the chest through the wound. Subsequent efforts by the victim to breathe will merely force air into and out of the wound, and since this air only goes into the plural cavity and not into the lungs themselves, the victim gets no usable air and will suffocate in short order. A sucking chest wound demands immediate action on the part of the first aider. The wound must be stopped up without delay with the cleanest thing that can be grabbed quickly, even your bare hand. As soon as sterile dressings can be got out, they should be substituted for your first resort, but the transfer should be made carefully to avoid any air leaking through the wound. The dressing must then be thoroughly taped to prevent leaking, and the victim should be transported on his side as soon as possible. A clean plastic bag is a good emergency dressing for a chest wound of this type.

With any sort of chest injury, there is great danger of pneumonia developing, because the pooled fluids in the injured lung make an ideal medium for the growth of bacteria. Whenever possible the patient should be encouraged to cough in order to clear the lungs, even though it is painful. This is especially important with an injury like a normal broken rib, which does not appear to be incapacitating and may not even force abandonment of the trip. The victim will be likely to favor the injured chest and avoid coughing, so that conscious forcing of a cough is necessary. The more serious injuries will almost certainly develop bacterial infections without antibiotic therapy, so evacuation is essential, but if evacuation must be delayed, coughing should be encouraged as long as the patient seems strong enough and there is no puncture of the chest wall.

Internal injuries and emergencies. Internal injuries are not very likely to result from any accident that would occur on a winter trip, other than a long fall. A severe blow to any part of the trunk can cause one of the internal organs to rupture, and severe pain following such a blow should lead the examiner to suspect the worst. Immediate evacuation is essential. The same rule applies if someone begins to show symptoms of appendicitis—gradually increasing abdominal pain associated after a few hours with nausea and fever. Severe internal injuries produce internal bleeding and shock, as does peritonitis, the infection of the abdominal cavity that may follow internal injuries or rupture of the appendix.

SHOCK

After any severe injury, the rescuer should expect shock, a complicated syndrome resulting mainly from a loss of blood pressure. The most common cause of shock is severe bleeding, which rapidly reduces the amount of blood left in the circulatory system. The first reaction of the body is to contract the blood vessels in surface areas and extremities in order to make more blood available to the vital organs. The heart beats faster, so that the remaining blood is pumped around the body more quickly. As the body functions are depressed, shock begins to set in. The patient is likely to become irritable, confused and then listless. He may be nauseous. The skin becomes pale and clammy, and then sweaty. The pulse is fast but weak, and respiration is shallow and may be irregular, with occasional deep and sighing breaths. The patient is thirsty because he wants to replace the liquid lost. He is likely to feel nauseous.

All these problems are intensified by the difficulties of a cold environment. Dehydration will predispose a person to shock, because his reserve of fluids is already low. Cold speeds up the general depression of the body's functions and increases the demands being made on an overtaxed system. Treatment for shock should be started after any injury outdoors in winter, since therapy is far more likely to be effective if it is begun before severe signs of shock appear. Shock will nearly always follow severe injuries and often fairly minor ones. Unless the patient has suffered a heart attack, a head injury, or breathing difficulty, his feet and legs should be elevated slightly. In cold weather, it is vital to try to keep him warm. It is not enough to wrap him in a sleeping bag, since he will not be able to produce enough heat to warm it up. Someone should get in with him. Heated objects may be used, but only with great care. Since circulation at the surface of the body is impaired during shock, the patient can be severely burned by temperatures that would not harm someone whose blood carries away excessive local heat. Also, because of depressed conditions and possible cold injury, the patient may not be aware he is being burned.

Whenever possible, the fluid losses suffered by the injured person should be replaced. Sips of water will help if he is not too nauseous. Put a pinch of salt in a cup of water. Warm liquids are all right, but they should not be hot, and they should be administered a little at a time.

Psychological factors are very important in the treatment of shock. Fear and pain are likely to greatly increase the patient's difficulties. A calm and helpful manner in giving first aid, together with care in handling the victim to avoid unnecessary pain, will do much to avoid the complications of shock.

COLD INJURIES

In cold weather, of course, the possibility of cold injury is always present, but it practically never bothers the healthy, well-clothed, and well-fed traveler. Even more than with other emergencies, the cure for cold injury is prevention. In fact, most cases of cold injury accompany other emergencies. In mountaineering, for example, frostbite rarely occurs on easily accomplished assaults. It happens on desperate, last-ditch retreats.

When the body becomes chilled, it begins to reduce circulation to the skin and to the extremities in order to maintain the proper temperature in the vital organs. Once circulation to the hands and feet has been reduced or stopped altogether, they will become progressively colder until they finally begin to freeze. No matter how well the extremities are insulated, they will not warm up again until the central core of the body is warmed. The body will sacrifice the hands and feet in order to preserve the organs that are essential to life. Chilling of the central core is known as hypothermia, or exposure, and it results in death if it proceeds too far. Its prevention is central to the prevention of cold injury, since frostbite generally follows hypothermia. The hands and feet will only begin to freeze when circulation to them is reduced. This may occur because of tight-fitting boots or because of an injury, but it is usually the result mainly of chilling of the body as a whole.

To prevent hypothermia, you must prevent your body from losing more heat than it is producing. If you continue to lose heat, your body temperature will continue to drop. Clearly, avoiding this progression involves a balancing operation. If the air gets colder or the wind stronger, you must either increase your insulation or your heat production. Most cases of hypothermia occur when something slightly out of the ordinary throws one of the factors in the heat equation far out of its normal value and there is no compensating reserve available. For example, cold rain soaks a person's clothing, and thus greatly reduces the insulation he has available, leaving him susceptible to temperatures and winds that would not otherwise have been much bother. Exhaustion or injury may greatly reduce the capacity of someone to produce heat, so that clothing that is quite adequate for those in good shape no longer protects him from the effects of the cold.

A person beginning to suffer from hypothermia will generally

Cold injuries 303

be awkward in his movements and judgment. He may be irritable and deny suffering any ill effects from the cold. He may shiver and complain of the cold. His nails and lips will be blue or pale. He will stumble if he is moving, and his speech will become slurred. He will forget things. The terminal stage of hypothermia often includes the pooling of liquid in the lungs, producing a bubbling sound in his breathing, and perhaps causing frothy sputum to be coughed up.

Under difficult circumstances, members of a party should watch each other carefully for signs of hypothermia. Action must be taken quickly to be successful, especially under the circumstances that are likely to prevail on winter trips. In early stages, the person suffering from the cold should be encouraged to increase his heat output. He should be given carbohydrates to eat, should be better protected from the cold, and his companions should help him to warm up. If the party is stopped, he should be encouraged to shiver or do isometric exercises. He should be insulated from the snow or ground. Someone can get into a sleeping bag with him to help him get warm. Hot drinks may help physically and psychologically.

If the victim is farther along, assistance to him in building up his supply of heat must be more vigorous, but exercise on his part is not a particularly good idea (he will probably be past being able to do much anyway). Food given to a patient suffering from severe hypothermia should probably be limited to sweet and salty warm drinks given slowly in small swallows. The blood supply available to the stomach at this stage is limited so that heavier food cannot be digested. General treatment should be similar to that for shock. The person giving aid should expect signs of increased cold at various times during rewarming of the victim. Blood that has been trapped in the cold tissues in the extremities is returned to the heart and may produce sudden cooling of the central core. The victim should be supplied with as much heat as possible during such secondary chills, since these can overburden an already weakened system.

Frostbite is an injury resulting from freezing of the tissues, usually the hands, feet, or the extremities of the face. Frostbite is a serious injury that can be prevented with reasonable care. In addition to maintenance of the general warmth of the body, each person traveling in extremely cold weather must pay careful attention to his extremities, particularly the feet. Tight boots or footwear inadequate for the conditions can result in cold feet. Painfully cold feet must be attended to, not ignored until they become numb. Frostbite usually gives adequate warning: extremely uncomfortable feet that suddenly cease to hurt must be taken care of immediately. It is better to stop and warm them even earlier, since the job is easier then. In conditions of cold wind, the party should pair off, with each person responsible for watching a companion's face. If the skin starts to become pale, a halt must be made for warming before serious freezing takes place.

Minor frostbite, where only the surface of the tissues has begun to freeze, should be rewarmed immediately against warm skin of the victim or of a companion. A vigorous burning sensation and subsequent minor blistering and peeling will be all the difficulties suffered. Deep frostbite with the flesh frozen solid, is another matter altogether, and the decision on how to treat it can be very difficult indeed.

The proper treatment for true frostbite is rapid rewarming in a water bath maintained at a temperature between 108° and 112° F. Temperatures must not be allowed to rise higher lest the rewarming be accomplished by cooking the frozen part. Rapid rewarming results in saving the maximum amount of damaged tissue, and where the choice can be made, it is far better to delay rewarming until it can be done properly, even if the delay lasts many hours.

Rewarming should never be attempted until the patient can be cared for as a litter case. Walking or skiing out on a frozen foot will not do a great deal more damage, but once the extremity has been thawed, such abrasion will kill more tissue. Decisions about treatment of frostbite should be made with these considerations in mind, but many difficulties are likely to arise in applying them. For the small party without the manpower or equipment to evacuate an invalid, the decision would probably be to head back without rewarming, but the victim can obviously not be left out in the cold at night to prevent his foot from thawing. The only satisfactory solution is to avoid frostbite and situations from which it might result.

If rewarming is to be attempted, the frozen part should be suspended in a container so that it does not touch the sides. The larger the vessel the better, since water temperature will be difficult to maintain in a small container. Direct heat should never be applied to the rewarming vessel while the injury is in it, since burning the injured part is hardly likely to promote proper healing. Ideally, water at the proper temperature should be poured in from another container. The temperature must be checked constantly, preferably with a thermometer, but *never* with the injured part. If no vessel large enough for rewarming is available, the injury can be wrapped in cloths and the water poured over. Rapid rewarming is quite painful, by the way, and the victim should be prepared for an unpleasant experience.

After rewarming, the injured area must be propped in such a way that nothing rubs against it. If the patient is still under a first aider's care, the main rule of subsequent treatment is to soak the injury daily to keep it clean, and otherwise to leave it strictly alone. Frosbite injuries have a very unpleasant appearance, and both the victim and those caring for him should expect this, but no tissue should be touched or picked. Eventually, if infection is avoided, any dead tissue will fall off of its own accord, and any interference will merely result in much more damage being done. This is a rule for doctors dealing with frostbite, so it certainly applies to laymen.

It should go without saying that methods like rubbing a frostbitten area with snow belong to chambers of horrors rather than discussions of sensible treatment. No seriously frostbitten area should be rubbed at all, since this can only cause more damage to already injured tissues. Any warming that is done with the hands should be accomplished without rubbing.

RULES FOR AVOIDING COLD INJURY

1. Carry clothing adequate for any weather you may encounter, including enough extra so that you will be able to keep an injured member of the party warm even though he is not exercising. Include *wool* clothes, which will retain some insulating value even when wet. If rain might be expected, a *waterproof* shell layer must be carried. Getting wet in cold weather is not just uncomfortable; it is frequently fatal.

2. If you would be required to bivouac under emergency conditions, carry equipment to fashion a bivouac in the area in which you are traveling—a shovel for a snow hole, saw for fires and lean-to, etc.

3. Carry enough food. Under normal circumstances your body can run on its own fat, but its heat-producing capacity and capacity for exercise are greatly reduced. Don't let your body's available sugar supplies drop. Have a snack or a piece of candy frequently.

4. Don't become dehydrated. Make sure you get adequate supplies of water and salt. Dehydration can contribute to exhaustion, hypothermia, frostbite, shock, and perhaps altitude sickness. Don't drink alcohol in really cold weather, and if there is danger of frostbite don't smoke. Both drugs affect circulation.

5. Don't sweat. Evaporation of perspiration produces chilling; wet and salt-impregnated clothing loses its insulating value, and large quantities of hard-to-get liquid water are needed to prevent dehydration. Open your clothing or remove it when you are working hard to avoid perspiring.

6. Put on clothing as soon as you start becoming chilled. If you wait, your body will have to burn a lot of extra food just to get you warm. It's better to use the heat that is produced as a side product of other muscular activity. As soon as you start to cool down at the top of the hill or lunch stop, start getting out the extra sweater.

7. Don't over-exert in really cold weather. A great deal of body heat is lost in warming the cold air you breathe. If you are panting, you're warming a lot more air, and you may become chilled from the inside no matter how thick your down parka. Panting also increase fluids lost to evaporation, which loses more heat and contributes to dehydration.

8. Take care of your extremities, especially your feet, which may be in snow much colder than the air temperature. Wear footgear adequate for the temperatures you will encounter. Don't lace them too tight or wear so many socks that they are tight. Wear wool socks and change them when they become damp. Stop to warm your feet if they get cold. Don't touch metal objects with bare hands in very cold weather.

9. Watch yourself and your companions for signs of hypothermia and frostbite. Pale or white spots on the face indicate frostbite. Irritability, irrationality, stumbling, clumsiness, heavy speech, bluish lips, breathing difficulties, and dilated pupils warn of hypothermia.

10. *Bivouac early.* A well-prepared bivouac started while you are still in good condition will enable you to survive very difficult

Rules for avoiding cold injury 307

conditions. Going on too long is likely to result in a spiraling chain of difficulties for a party and for your body.

GETTING THE VICTIM OUT

The difficulties of transporting an injured person over snow-covered wilderness terrain are formidable, and they should not be taken lightly. Serious consideration should be given to going out for help, or at least for a sled or toboggan. If you have a large party and the victim's skis are available for the manufacture of an improvised sled, it may be best to try to get the victim out yourself, but the smaller the party, the more advisable it becomes to send someone out at least as far as the nearest rescue toboggan. If skis are not available for the manufacture of a sled, this is even more true.

If you are attempting to transport an injured person, his injuries *must* be adequately splinted to withstand the trip. He must be strapped on the sled, toboggan, or drag so that he is reasonably comfortable and so that he can brace himself against jolting, and he must be kept warm. The vehicle must obviously be arranged with enough safety lines so that any downhill sections of the trip will not result in the loss of the sled.

If someone is being sent for help, two should go whenever possible, in order to provide a reserve for possible additional accidents. When supplies are low, it may be best for all but the injured person and one companion to go out for help and supplies, leaving as much food and clothing as possible with the victim and his nurse.

RISKS, RESCUERS, AND RESPONSIBILITY

Because of the possibility of accidents and other emergencies, every small party in wilderness areas is dependent to some extent on outside help if it gets into trouble. It is a fine tradition in wilderness areas on this continent that help is freely given when it is needed. It is also traditional that this help has been pot luck, and that parties going into the wilderness have been expected to be basically self-reliant. Many thousands of man hours have been given by the U.S. Forest Service, the Park Service, various military services, state and local officials, privately organized rescue groups, and outdoorsmen who happen to be available, to rescue people who have gotten into trouble in the wilderness, generally at no expense to those rescued.

The system that has developed has the important virtue of retaining the freedom for the individual that many of us prize as the most valuable aspect of the wilderness experience. The essential premise has been that anyone has a right to go into the woods and take what chances he chooses, whether he exercises common sense or acts the fool. The risks taken by rescuers to save even fools have been worthwhile because they have preserved a freedom that is valuable to us all.

With increasing numbers of people going into the wilderness every year, many of them inexperienced or willfully careless, it is inevitable that the number of accidents, lost parties, and so on should increase. In many cases, professionals like those of the Park Service and the Forest Service have an obligation to rescue those who get into trouble in their areas of jurisdiction. Rescue operations are expensive and risky, and it is understandable that those charged with the responsibility for wilderness areas want to keep the number of rescues that they have to perform at a minimum. The natural reaction, especially of the bureaucrats, is to attempt to regulate those using wilderness areas, not only for purposes of land management, but by attempting to establish definitions of who is competent, "for his own good."

This tendency for more and more regulations to appear is repugnant to me and to many others, since it limits the freedom of people to enjoy the wilderness on their own terms, a freedom that ought to be considered a right qualified only by the obligation not to spoil the land for others' use. Inevitably, the tendency toward regulation goes hand in hand with "improvement" of the land, with administrative procedures designed to make regulation easier and more practical, and with attempts to define and compartmentalize which sorts of wilderness experience you and I should have.

If the tendency toward regimentation is to be curbed, however, wilderness travelers, new and old, are going to have to take a hard look at themselves and their attitudes. The trend toward heavier

Risks, rescuers, and responsibility   309

use of wilderness areas is bound to continue, and if larger and larger numbers of people act irresponsibly, first getting into situations much more difficult than they are equipped to handle, and then expecting the rangers to come in and bail them out, officials will have plenty of excuses for writing more rule books.

Anyone has a right to risk his own neck if he wants to, but those going into a wilderness area have a responsibility toward those who may be called upon to help them. If you aren't leaving anyone at home who might call for help when you don't get back, and if you're not leaving your car in a place where it might attract attention, then by all means go off and break your leg on the nearest snowy peak if you want to, but if a couple of hundred people are going to have to drop their usual activities to come after you, you have some obligation to make their job as easy as possible.

You should tell some responsible person when you plan to go, when you expect to be back, and how much longer you are equipped to last without being in real trouble. You should leave a note on your car with the same information. Finally, you should follow reasonable safety rules and carry normal emergency equipment. In most cases, this will enable you to stay out of real trouble and to hold down the expense and difficulty of any necessary rescues. If you're adequately equipped and break your leg, you can sit out a storm with your companions. A couple of them can go out and get a toboggan and a couple of extra people and take you out without any great fanfare. On the other hand, if you don't have adequate food, clothing, or presence of mind, your rescue will be a survival ordeal for you and an expensive and risky operation for dozens of other people.

At the same time, it is inevitable that some people will get in trouble, and sometimes it will be their own fault. Getting them out of trouble is the friendly thing to do, a traditional obligation of the outdoorsman in this country, and it is also the price that must be paid if we are to avoid expensive professional rescue groups and the regulation-writing bureaucrats who pay them. We have recently witnessed the attempted rescue by one agency of a couple of rock climbers who didn't want to be rescued, and we may be sure that the expense of the operation will be used as an excuse to further control other wilderness travelers. Outdoorsmen should form their own rescue groups to take on responsibilities for these operations as much as possible, and the users of wilderness areas should accept both the responsibility for their own safety and the limitations of existing rescue facilities. If you call in a helicopter to get you out, you are giving the helicopter owner some claim to need to regulate your right to go in. Wilderness use is best regulated by wilderness lovers and users, not by helicopter owners.

Finally, unless our public lands are simply to become copies of many other regimented and bureaucratic areas of our national life, those who love the outdoors must call a halt to excessive regulation of their activities in state and nationally owned wilderness and semi-wilderness areas. There are many legitimate needs for regulation as a conservation measure, some of which will be discussed in the last chapter. The necessity of this kind of control can only be eliminated by educating users of the land in its proper treatment. Other types of regulation are of a quite different kind, however. Winter travelers will find that many areas are closed to use in the winter, some for conservation reasons, but most "to protect the public." If you feel you are being protected by being barred from any place a ranger cannot conveniently watch you, that is your privilege. I don't.

Outdoorsmen should insist that they be allowed to travel where and when they wish, providing conservation of the land does not require its protection. If a government agency does not feel it can be responsible for the rescue of wilderness travelers, a sign disclaiming responsibility is quite adequate to warn those who insist on passing. At the same time, outdoorsmen should assume responsibility for their own safety.

XIII

The World of Winter

Some of the special attractions of the winter landscape have already been mentioned—the special beauty, sharp contrasts of color, and starkness of both calm and stormy weather. Everything in winter seems sharper than at other times of the year. The beauty is of a harsher and colder kind than at other times, and for most living things winter is a time of retreat, of dormancy, or of a struggle for survival. Gone, for most, are the periods of mating, raising young, or general frivolity. The rigors of simply staying alive are dominant.

The energy that supports life on the earth comes ultimately from the sun. It may be received directly by a particular organism, or it may pass through many intermediate steps before being used by some forms of life. However, regardless of the means of collection, all life depends on the sun for its maintenance. It follows that the amount of life that can be supported on the earth, or on an individual part of it, is intimately related to the amount of sunlight that falls on the land. During winter, less sunlight, and hence less energy, is available for sustaining life, and this generally accounts for the more tenuous state of life in the winter world.

This energy deficit in winter is only temporary, of course, and is not at all detrimental to those species that have adapted well to the annual pattern. The interest for the observer lies in the fact that so much of the pattern of nature in the winter is related to the cycle of cold weather. Living species may be helped or hindered by the mantle of snow, but they are rarely unaffected.

THE INTERRELATIONSHIP OF THINGS

For the beginning tourist in the winter landscape, the combination of vigorous exercise, beautiful scenery, and personal challenge will probably be interesting enough. Unless he is already something of an amateur naturalist, he is likely to take only a casual interest in a fresh set of tracks or a passing bird. He is more apt to develop an early interest in some of the larger natural phenomena like storms and avalanches, if only because they refuse to be ignored. The forms taken by snow crystals may attract his interest at first by their influence on his ski waxes or the depth to which his snowshoes sink, and the fascination with their infinite variety may follow from this pragmatic concern or from the more desperate one of predicting avalanche danger. Stars and trees are likely to be subjects mainly of esthetic interest.

The oneness of things. A snowshoer stands above a lake in front of three muskrat homes.

Eventually, though, most people who have developed a love for the woods and mountains in winter dress also become interested in the inhabitants of that world and in the many interlocking patterns that characterize their lives and that of the landscape around them. Whether this interest begins with a study of avalanches or of birds, the observer is liable to find eventually that each part of the world he is watching is connected to everything else. The avalanche watcher soon sees that a formerly safe slope that has been clear-cut by loggers or devastated by the avalanche of an exceptional year is now subject to sliding after every major storm. The topsoil that accumulated there over thousands of years is washed into the valley in a season, and the animal life supported by the little-forested area will no longer be found there.

Anyone interested in the life of the larger mammals will soon find how much they are affected by the amount and kind of snow that falls. A deep and soft snow cover that falls in a short time is likely to trap deer in small yards, where they quickly consume most of the available food and condemn many members of the herd to starvation. The same deep snowfall will make fine insulation for the chipmunks hibernating below, many of which would die from cold in a year when the snowfall was unusually light.

The interrelationship of things   313

Once one begins to learn about some part of the world surrounding the winter campsite, he is likely to be led step by step from one facet to another. He may find that his favorite bird prefers a certain kind of tree, or that moose are especially fond of some kinds of browse. The dependence of one part of the food chain on another will suddenly explain observations that seemed before to be merely capricious. Some pine trees produce cones only in a particular year, and birds that in other years migrate south to find food will stay to feed on the seeds that year. Nature is recalcitrant in her refusal to be bound by the categories we use to classify her. Each part interlocks with many others, and each relationship always turns out to be more complex than it seemed at first. Each cycle of life and death or building up and breaking down is linked with so many others that one can never know more than a fraction of them. The more one learns, the more questions are posed that remain unanswered. Yet the satisfactions of the small knowledge one wins are not dimmed by awareness of its limitations, because a knowledge of the many interrelationships in the winter world can give one a sense of belonging there oneself —a sense of kinship.

WATCHING IN WINTER

The serious naturalist, whether professional or amateur, must interest himself in all the seasons, since one is as much a part of the various life cycles as another. On a more superficial level, however, each season is likely to present particular attractions and frustrations depending on the short- and long-term interests of the observer. The bird watcher, especially one living along one of the major flyways, will have a particular fondness for spring and fall when the great migrations come through, bringing species that only pass through and never stay long. Those with a special love for wildflowers are likely to be impatient of winter snow, even though they know that it is the watering pot for their favorite blossoms. Winter, too, has its special satisfactions and frustrations for the observer quite aside from its deeper meanings and implications.

The disadvantages of winter as a time for observing nature are fairly obvious. Deciduous plants have shed their leaves, leaving them harder to identify. With the leaves have gone those forms of life that used them for food. The mating season has passed and with it the many bright colors and ostentatious manners that make so many species stand out. Most birds have followed the sun and the food supply south, and most of those that remain are quieter, their colors more nondescript. Insects may migrate, hibernate, or coordinate some dormant stage in their life cycle with the winter months, but in any case they disappear from view. Many mammals spend the winter in hibernation, and others sleep through most of the cold months, even though they may come out for short forays from time to time. There is little resemblance to the humming world of spring, with life going on everywhere at a furious pace.

Winter has its special compensations for the observer, however. In deciduous forests, those birds that remain are often much easier to see. The lack of foliage increases the range of visibility, and birds that are very difficult to pick out among summer leaves stand out readily on the stark branches of winter or on the background of the snow. Many more birds than one might expect stay in northern climes. There is a special advantage for the beginner also in the reduced number of species. He has fewer choices to make in the difficult first stage of identification. Spring may be a paradise for the experienced birder, who delights in picking out the single rare European visitor in a flock of varied spring shorebirds, but the recent convert from modern life who has yet to identify his first chickadee may find comfort in the less complicated catalogue of winter. Even among the migrants, there are species that appear in temperate climes only in winter, when they retreat from their usual homes in the Arctic, or who are blown in from the sea by winter storms.

Despite the fact that many mammals either hibernate or sleep through most of the winter, it is often much easier to observe signs of mammal life in winter than in summer. The reason for this lies in the snow cover itself. Most mammals are nocturnal, so that they are rarely seen even in summer, but they do make tracks on soft surfaces, and the snows of winter provide a frequently renewed recording medium that shows the signs of many passersby. In summer, you may have to travel a long way to find a soft riverbank or sandhill that holds tracks of visitors, but in winter, one needs only to go out on a walk to come upon many stories written

Watching in winter

Signs of many mammals are easiest to find in winter. The characteristic tracks of a cottontail.

in the snow. Visibility of mammals is also sometimes improved by the snow cover, lack of deciduous foliage, and the burying of small plants and other hiding places.

The tenuous nature of the winter food supply can also be a friend to the observer, precisely when it becomes a threat to the observed. The threat of starvation drives many animals out to search for food in spite of a caution that would prevail in the months when the food supply was more plentiful. A few species are unperturbed. Porcupines are as happy to eat your pack straps in winter as in summer, and their other tastes adjust easily to the season. They seem equally satisfied with canoe canvas or snowshoe webbing. Other animals are more easily attracted by an offer of food, however, whether voluntary or not. Chickadees will be happy to pick up your crumbs, and if any raccoons are still awake they will make sure that you are, too, first finishing off any leftovers in your pots and then throwing the pans at each other.

LEARNING WHAT'S WHAT

The field of natural history is so broad and has such a long and honorable past that more is known than any one person could possibly digest in a lifetime. At the same time, it is one of the few areas of science to which amateurs can still make significant contributions. More significantly, any wilderness traveler interested in the world around him can observe many things that are fascinating, quite apart from whether anything like it has been seen before or not.

Regardless of whether your interest lies in scientific study or not, identification remains the starting point for those who begin to try to understand the workings of the natural world. Some people are lucky enough to have acquired a basic repertoire of birds, flowers, trees, and animals painlessly in childhood or through some effort when they were older. They can delve fairly easily into whatever area they choose with no help from this book. Others have had a more urban upbringing or recalcitrant character and will have to start from a point close to that from which I began—I *could* tell a robin from a maple.

The modern beginner has at least one great advantage over

those of a few years ago. He may have a poorer background, but he has some very good, inexpensive, and relatively painless guides to help him get started. Many modern guidebooks make the task of acquiring the initial knowledge of a subject much easier than was possible a few years ago. The first few trees or birds or tracks are always the most difficult. After that, patterns begin falling together, descriptions take on meaning that once seemed obscure, or perhaps deliberately obstructive, and each additional species falls into place more readily than the last. Most older guidebooks were particularly difficult for the beginner to use, but that has been changed by the technology of modern methods of printing, together with the enterprise of a number of men who have made special efforts to produce guidebooks that are made for easy use by the layman. Roger Tory Peterson deserves particular praise both for his writing, drawing, and editorial work and for the inspiration he has provided for other authors and publishers.

By far the easiest way for the complete novice to acquire some of the basic information about any field of nature study is by having someone point things out. One weekend with a knowledgeable friend is worth half a dozen with a guidebook. Unfortunately, guidebooks are generally easier to come by than naturalist friends.

For those who are put off by the systematic and somewhat boring approach involved in the use of guidebooks, a good start can be made by reading the delightful works of a few naturalists. Some of the finest literature ever written in this country was created by lovers and observers of wild things. Though it is a less efficient way of accumulating information than more systematic methods, such reading is an enjoyable way to acquire some of the basic information about the intricacies of the natural world. A few titles are suggested in Appendix B.

CHOOSING GUIDEBOOKS

The guidebooks that are currently available would easily fill a small library, and an attempt to stuff them all into a rucksack would serve no useful purpose. The beginner must be selective in his choice of guides both for the sake of his back and his sanity. At the beginning stage it is more important to become familiar with one guide so that one can find things quickly than it is to have numerous references to consult. Frequently the most convenient and thorough guides are those that cover a particular area or season. Because they need discuss a much more limited number of species, they are more compact and easier to search through, though their usefulness is limited by their self-imposed boundaries. More complete guides require a smaller investment, and they are useful on trips to different areas without requiring the purchase or study of a new key for each region you may visit. Your choice will depend on your preferences and the availability of special guides. These are usually more likely to be available for well-known areas like national parks.

The appendix lists some of the useful general guides. Special guides limited to one area and perhaps one season as well are too numerous to mention, but quite a few are published at nominal prices by concerned government agencies. A booklet covering the trees of a national park or forest will be equally useful in the surrounding country.

WHERE TO BEGIN

The most obvious place to begin is at the place that most interests you, but those with catholic tastes may again end up with a rucksack full of guidebooks. You might also consider your temperament, the opportunities you will have for observation, and the things you might pick up at home. Trees, for example, are considerably easier to identify than birds. They stand still. They can be approached as closely as you like, and you can look at them as long as you please. They will still be there on the following weekend if you wish to return for another look. Birds, despite their other virtues, will do none of these things. The rank beginner with but a few weekends a year to spend in the wilderness might do better to stick to trees for a while and get over his initial birdwatching frustrations closer to home.

Animal tracks can be easier to identify than many trees or far more frustrating than the most difficult birds. Those who must have an answer to every question should stay away from them. Each set of tracks has a story to tell, but it is not always easy to

Where to begin

read. Patterns of hunts and chases, of successful escapes and desperate ends are all traced in the snow, but even years of experience sometimes cannot decipher them. This is a good field for the amateur detective, from the easily recognized track of a rabbit to complex jumbles of trails. The observer of tracks must learn the habits of many animals he has never seen before he can be successful in reading the signs.

The star gazer is likely to be able to achieve satisfying results a bit more quickly and surely. He can learn the major constellations at home, eliminating the need to pack heavy guidebooks into the woods. He need not drive his companions mad with his enthusiastic side trips or persistent stopping. He can observe his field of inquiry from the comfort of a sleeping bag. He can even claim a useful purpose when scoffed at by his unimaginative friends, claiming that his knowledge may one day be needed for navigational purposes.

Of course these are only suggestions, and the possibilities for one interested in the world around him on a winter trip are practically unlimited. Certain practical subjects can occupy the attention for a lifetime. The study of snow and of weather are examples that have been mentioned in earlier chapters. The literature of natural history is tremendous, though that part of it devoted to winter is quite a bit smaller, leaving much room for investigation. With a whole world to observe there are many pleasures to be gained by both the dilettante and the serious student.

GADGETRY

The Englishmen who made the first ascents of the snowy summits of the Alps felt the need to carry many heavy scientific instruments with them, both to satisfy real scientific curiosity and to provide a legitimate justification for the otherwise useless pursuit of climbing mountains. Most of us who venture into wilderness regions now no longer feel the need to pretend a useful purpose, and this has lightened our loads considerably. Instruments are also much more compact these days, however, and those who wish to satisfy their curiosity can carry some of them without noticing much extra burden. I will leave advanced instrumentation to those who are interested in it, but there are a few small items that may be useful to the untutored amateur.

A thermometer with a metal case is very valuable to anyone interested in the study of avalanches in particular or the snow cover in general. It may also be of some use in studying the weather and waxing skis. A small pocket magnifier is necessary for studying snowflakes and useful for looking at details of plants. The serious bird watcher will rarely be caught without his binoculars, and several very light and compact models are now available. These may also be of interest to the star gazer, and their use in studying terrain provides an excuse to palliate weight-conscious companions.

Mountaineers and meteorologists may wish to indulge themselves with the purchase of an altimeter or barometer (the same instrument with different markings) to measure air pressure. Good ones are rather expensive. An avalanche student may want his compass to include a clinometer to enable him to accurately measure slope angles. Either can also be useful in navigation. Finally, a light wind-speed gauge may help to pass the time during storms, though you may be disillusioned to find that the wind isn't gusting to 150 mph, after all.

All things considered, it is pretty easy to get along without any gadgets except perhaps a guidebook and a camera. You may want some of them if you develop specialized interests, but for the generalist, they often tend to be more a nuisance than a convenience. If you take a camera, you can spend almost any amount of money you choose. The literature of photography is so extensive there seems little point in producing more here, but it might be worth mentioning that most heavy cameras end up buried in the pack, and are rarely available when you want to take a picture. There is much to be said in favor of sacrificing some optical quality for light weight and compactness.

Gadgetry

XIV

A Plea for Wild Places

A few years ago it was still possible for lovers of wild places to labor under the illusion that, despite man's previous ravages, some wilderness areas on this continent would remain inviolate, if only because nobody wanted them except for the native animals, Indians, and a few outdoorsmen. By now, that illusion would be too heavy a cross for the most confirmed optimist to bear. Loggers are rapidly finishing off the California redwoods and the forests of southeastern Alaska; oilmen are busy planning vast new Arctic Santa Barbaras; the roar of snowmobiles disturbs the peace of forests once almost inviolate in winter, and those areas that have not interested other exploiters now beckon recreational developers.

In addition to this catalogue of well-known pressures, the sheer force of numbers is threatening many areas. Backwoods campgrounds that used to be visited only a few times a season are now trampled by hundreds each year. Wilderness areas that were once the preserve of a few are now invaded by thousands, and by every indication the numbers will continue to grow. Supplying the growing numbers of people who want to spend time outdoors has become big business. Part of the business has consisted of creating a demand for mechanized gadgets, and once the gadgets have been purchased, the new owners want the space and facilities to use their acquisitions.

Quite aside from those areas that have been bulldozed into housing projects or superhighways, many formerly pristine and still roadless areas are suffering from serious problems of pollution. The majority of still underdeveloped areas have remained undeveloped precisely because they are too precariously balanced to support much exploitation. Plant life in many high mountains resembles that of the Arctic: seemingly meager size may represent years of growth. Alpine meadows take many years to recover from overuse. Many high-altitude lakes are becoming seriously polluted and are no longer safe to drink. Nearly all low-altitude lakes have been undrinkable for years. The time has come for those who love the unspoiled wilderness to band together against people who would "improve" it, and there is also a desperate need to educate the bands of newcomers to the mountains and woods. Before setting out on their crusades, however, many backpackers, ski tourers, snowshoers, and mountaineers need to take a hard look at their own practices.

Wilderness travelers are fond of making unkind comments about many polluters of modern industrial society, but, while most of this derision is merited, the practices of the critics in the wilderness of which they are so fond are often as short-sighted as those of industrial polluters. Chimney Pond on Maine's Katahdin was not polluted by a paper company, and the trash and pollution beginning to appear in some of the high lakes of the Sierra Nevada did not come from oilmen. No one spends time on the glaciers of Mount McKinley except mountaineers, yet some of the favorite glacier camps are littered with trash, and there is so much sewage scattered here and there in the snow that some who camp there are having difficulty finding a safe water supply.

Winter travelers and mountaineers are often the most radical conservationists at home, and yet some of them seem to feel that they have a special dispensation in the woods, just because they deliberately choose to brave the harshest natural environments. Thus, a rock climber who will rant and rail about an ordinary car camper who leaves trash lying about the campground feels no qualm about tossing a sardine can off a ledge when he is climbing.

Snow campers are often particular offenders in this respect. They bury trash in the snow that becomes litter on the ground in the spring. They give little if any thought to the location of their privy, leaving pollution and toilet paper as their contribution to other snow campers and to the spring thaw. Because they choose a harsh season, they often seem to feel that they have some special privilege to cut live trees or leave tin cans.

In fact, winter campers have the obligation to take more pains than their warm-weather brethren, not fewer. Since the snow cover in many areas is too deep to permit digging to the ground, anything that is left behind will be deposited on the surface of the

A plea for wild places   323

ground when the snow melts. You should pick a site for your toilet facilities very carefully, and you should dig to the ground whenever possible. If you can reach dirt, dig a hole and fill it before you leave. Toilet paper ought to be burned if this is at all feasible. In places that receive particularly heavy use, such as ski huts, it may be necessary to build a properly designed outhouse with a winter access door.

Trash must be burned or carried out. If cooking is being done on stoves, this will mean carrying paper and garbage as well as tin cans, plastic, etc. If you burn your trash, make sure it *all* burns; aluminum foil, orange peels, and many other things don't. If it doesn't burn, carry it out. Extra plastic bags will help keep your pack clean. If you can carry a full container into the woods, you can certainly get the empty one out.

If you use the same area repeatedly, one alternative is to use caches not only for storing supplies but for refuse as well. You can walk in to your caches in the spring and pick up the trash. This applies only to legitimate caches, though. Nobody has a right to dump a few bags of garbage next to the trail in a national park, saying to himself that he'll drop by and pick it up in June.

There aren't too many places left where the cutting of live foliage is justifiable except in a dire emergency. You should only depend on building fires where plenty of genuinely dead wood is available. Deciduous trees shed their leaves in winter, which does not make them dead—until someone comes along with his little hatchet. Birch bark is a wonderful fire starter, but stripping a ring of it from a tree will kill the birch. Bark should only be collected from obviously dead trees. Beautiful snags should also be left alone for the next visitor to enjoy. The gnarled and tortured branches of timberline trees often take hundreds of years to grow —a lot more time than it takes to find more suitable fuel.

Of course, in a genuine emergency, some of these rules may have to be disregarded, but if you're having that kind of emergency every other trip, it's a phony and you are abusing the woods. If you make planned bivouacs, they should be the kind that don't wreck the area. Those bough beds and lean-tos shingled with live twigs that fill the imaginations of thousands of old Boy Scouts have no place in the areas that most weekend outdoorsmen can reach.

Notwithstanding the remarks just made on the necessity for wilderness lovers to get their own woods in order, the major threat to the remaining wild places in this country does not come from backpackers or ski tourers. It comes from the many people who feel that there are more worthwhile uses for such lands than leaving them in their wild state. Some see profits to be made in clear-cutting the timber from the slopes or strip-mining ore, while others pretend more compatible uses that would be just as destructive. Finally, there are those who feel that the scenic and recreational "potential" of an area must be developed, lest it lie fallow and not be enjoyed by a sufficient number of people (all of whom require various expensive and profitable services, of course).

The most obvious enemies of the wild places are also the most powerful. Oilmen and lumber companies have a great deal of money to use in conservation fights, and they have many well-placed friends in high places. Still, the issues in this type of battle are fairly clear-cut, despite the attempts at window dressing that have recently become the fashion in the public-relations departments of many large corporations. Protection of an area threatened by a lumber company or housing development may be difficult, but in principle it is simply a matter of putting together enough political muscle from those who want to preserve the area.

Recently, there has also been a growing awareness of the broader issues that will ultimately determine the fate not only of wildernesses and open spaces, but of the environment as a whole, both in this country and in the world. There is not space here for discussion of these issues, but obviously wilderness and open space cannot survive the indefinite expansion of population, perpetually spiraling consumption of energy, or bloated and wasteful squandering of both renewable and non-renewable resources. The wilderness lover has a special interest and obligation in these matters, both because he is likely to be more aware of the issues and because wilderness is bound to be considered an expendable luxury in a real crisis. Despite this special place outdoorsmen may have as conservationists, however, the broader issues raised here affect everyone in this society and the world very directly, and they are complex enough to defy summary here. Instead, I would like to consider a few more specialized problems.

A DEFENSE OF WILDERNESS

The first of these problems is the rapidly diminishing area that can be called wilderness, even in a very loose way. Many outdoorsmen would say that no true wilderness even exists in the United States, except for Alaska, and there is a good deal of truth in the contention. I will not be quite such a purist here, but the distinction must at least be made between wilderness and other open spaces and scenic spots. The distinction operates on many levels, and it is an important one. A carefully tended park may be beautiful, but it is not wild. Ski touring on a golf course can be a fine way to spend a Sunday morning, but one occasionally wants something more stimulating.

Of the wilderness that covered almost all of this continent a few centuries ago, we have little left, and that is concentrated in those areas that were formerly of no interest to exploiters. What is left should be saved as best we can save it. Our increasing need for wilderness is amply demonstrated by the growing pressures on what we have. We simply cannot afford to diminish the supply. That supply is every bit as short as those of other resources, and no plastic substitute will be found.

There are quite a few "practical" reasons to preserve the wilderness areas we have left, but there is little point in cataloguing them here. The economic or environmental absurdity of a particular development project only sometimes prevails against the host of technological sophists willing to argue that it is the last best hope for man and General Motors. The hundreds of ecological disasters of which we have daily evidence have not cooled the ardor of those who automatically see an active bulldozer as a sign of progress, no matter what it's doing. The idea that there is a practical use in maintaining habitats and species that provide the planet's reservoir of adaptable life will never carry any weight on cost-benefit sheets. Like the rights of the Indians, it merits lip service among the bureaucrats and politicians only as long as nobody wants the land for any other use and as long as preservation costs nothing.

The need for proper homework on the practical aspects of particular issues and the preservation of particular areas is obvious, but this is a matter of politics, not philosophy. There is no hope at all of saving the woods or the mountains by convincing the resource-management types that this is the best use of the land. We will only end up with more multiple-use schemes and eight-lane scenic highways on which it is both illegal and suicidal to look at the scenery.

The interests of the lovers of "development" have been pandered to for decades. Billions of dollars and God knows how many lives are sacrificed to the internal-combustion engine every year, while it chokes our cities, paves our countryside, and pollutes our air, yet we are told by the developers that in order to be democratic, we must also build freeways through the national parks so that speeding vacationers can cram Yellowstone, Grand Canyon, and Half Dome into the same week.

The winter months have long provided the saving grace of quiet and privacy by sending the motorized tourists home, covering their trash and roads with snow, and sending their engines back to the commuting routes. All this is changing, too, with the increasing demand for and supply of all-weather roads and the locust plague of the snowmobile. The days of complacency for the skier who wants quiet slopes away from the lift lines are gone, and he will have to join ranks with other embattled wilderness lovers quickly if he wants to save any quiet valleys from the howl of the two-cycle engine.

Before anyone accuses me of being secretly intolerant, let me admit to being very openly intolerant. Though I don't much like snowmobiles anywhere, I don't really care much about the rallies in parking lots and on drag strips or about Farmer John, who likes to whiz around his fields in the winter on his new snow machine. However, I don't believe that the snowmobile has any place in wilderness or semi-wilderness areas, and in many other publicly owned lands it should be confined to established roads when it is permitted at all. Like other motor vehicles—speedboats, jeeps, camper-pickups, trail bikes, dune buggies, and their ilk—snowmobiles are incompatible with either wilderness or with peace and quiet.

The reason for both my statements and my intolerance is fairly simple. Quite aside from the damage it does (and the snowmobile does quite a bit), any motorized vehicle just uses up too much space. In areas that depend for their nature and their appeal on a feeling of space and uncrowded open vistas, motor-vehicle operators use up a lot more than their share of ground. The faster a conveyance goes, the bigger the empty space around it must be to allow it to turn or stop, and this space is no longer available for you and me and the trees. This would be true even if such vehicles were quiet, which they most emphatically are not. The whine of a snowmobile engine carries for miles. The effect of snowmobiles and other motor vehicles is to produce crowding in even sparsely populated areas, a phenomenon that is becoming all too familiar even to many sedentary citizens. In an Alpine valley, several parties of ski tourers and snowshoers may coexist without even being aware of one another, and if they do know of each other's presence, they will still not feel crowded. Thus, thirty people can get away from the pressures of the city in that valley, while producing little or no effect on the country or its permanent inhabitants. One snowmobile driven up the same valley makes an inescapable insistence on its own presence. Anyone else in the valley is stuck with an awareness of that presence, whether he likes it or not, and so is the wildlife.

This phenomenon of crowding is not unique to the snowmobile, of course. Lakes that are peaceful and undisturbed by a couple of dozen canoes shrink to tiny warrens of activity with only three or four speedboats. A stretch of beach that is lonely and vast even when occupied by scores of people and thousands of shorebirds becomes crowded and frenetic with only a couple of dune buggies or Ski-doos. Encounters with a few backpackers on a summer trail tend to be sociable and may even increase the feeling of peace and space that pervade the trail beyond. An encounter with a trail bike is longer, since the noise precedes and follows the vehicle, a good deal less sociable, whether the rider tries to run you down or shout a greeting over the noise of his engine, and tends merely to raise the specter of bile and crowding that one is trying to exorcise by heading for the hills in the first place.

Still another reason for my prejudice against motor vehicles in the back country is likely to seem snobbish, or flavored with sour grapes, though, of course, I think it is neither. It stems from the excessive ease with which the operator of a motor vehicle gets to his destination, or at least tries to get there. I think that one's attitude towards one's environment is always inextricably related to the effort and speed and personal involvement one has in traveling through it. Sticky snow to a ski tourer is likely to be challenging in the way of a friend with difficult idiosyncrasies; to a snowmobiler it is more often a nuisance for which he has no affection. The change in attitude is reflected in the piles of trash that are found in the back-country: they seem to pile up in proportion to the aid that people have getting in. A motorized traveler can often carry no more garbage than one on foot, but he is more willing to leave it at the end of the trail. I don't really think that this is due to the inherent virtue of the man on foot, but rather to the feeling that he acquires about the land by direct contact with it. Felt through engine, treads, and gears, the land is an impersonal antagonist, which may be defiled at will.

Beyond the immediate annoyances and ravages of the motorized tourist, he must also be considered as a representative of a pressure group. Many of the individual operators of snowmobiles, trail bikes, and the like are more to be pitied than condemned. They have discovered only recently that there are pleasures and relaxations to be found in distant campgrounds that cannot be matched at home, but a sharp salesman has conned them into believing that the discovery can only be enjoyed with the aid of a ton of expensive and not very durable equipment. In the end, instead of escaping the world of the machine, though perhaps with the aid of some of its advantages, he ends with merely another expensive mechanized amusement park, for which the passport must be renewed annually with a greater number of horsepower and new sleek design.

As part of its advertising campaign for new converts, the pleasure-machine companies must spend money lobbying for more facilities in which their product may be used, and this sort of campaign has the welcome advantage of being useful for the enlistment of new enthusiasts at the same time. If another hundred thousand snow machines are to be sold, the purchasers must have trails on which to ride, and what better place to create those trails than the national forests and parks, where no land need be paid for, where the scenic virtues are ready-made for the cameras of weekend publicity photographers, and where the actual cutting of the trails and safety of the users can be left to public servants already on the taxpayers' payroll and on a budget that is even supported by conservationists. There is money to be made in this enterprise, and it is being made.

One of the necessary ingredients of the snowmobile-trail-bike-all-terrain-vehicle-dune-buggy business is the lobbying for more facilities for the use of "recreational vehicles." The need for such facilities, and the others that inevitably follow them is dictated both by the nature of the vehicles and the need for advertising that accompanies their promotion and subsequent exploitation. Lobbying for such facilities helps enlist the loyalty and community feeling of the machine owners and would-be owners. The facilities provide a place for them to meet and instill in one another

A defense of wilderness 329

the need to buy bigger and better machines, as well as convincing them of the justification for having bought the old ones.

Hence, once there are enough of the "go-anywhere" vehicles in an area, there must be trails on which they can go anywhere. Then there must be emergency facilities and rescue groups to take care of those who can go anywhere but can't get back again, and so on to the popcorn stands at five-mile intervals. Even when trails are not demanded by the owners of the vehicles themselves, they are soon necessitated by the problems of minimizing damage to trees, refuse disposal, and the "safety of the public." The problem becomes compounded by the dynamics of regulators requiring that snowmobilers stay on trails (partly to protect the countryside and partly to make the rangers' job of finding them easier) and the snowmobilers' demands for protection from a hostile environment. (While they ruin trees, they demand safety and complete freedom at the same time; rangers should be either out cutting trails for Ski-doos or rescuing their stranded owners.) The regulations resulting from this symbiosis carry over to other forms of activity, and soon the ski tourer who knows the region like the back of his hand is told by the brand-new ranger that he must stay on the new track cut for the snowmobiler. On his next visit the ski tourer doesn't bother to stop and see the ranger, thus complicating a rescue on the rare occasions when it is needed. This sort of ridiculous escalation seems common to most of the heavily used public areas these days, though such frictions are an absurd and unnecessary transfer of city problems to the woods.

As a modest contribution, I would like to make a few suggestions for administration of those areas that are still free from large-scale development. I make no pretensions to having definitive answers, but there are some points of emphasis that I think are important for conservationists concerned with wilderness preservation.

SAVING WHAT WE HAVE

Despite the depressing rapidity with which developers are making inroads on the remaining hinterland, there is also a new awareness by the public that there just might be something more worthwhile about a mountain than its possibilities as an ore heap, highway route, or ski development. There are tentative feelings to be found everywhere that the ravaging of natural areas and processes has gone far enough. The feelings are incoherent, but they are there, and therefore there is now a real possibility of tapping some of these feelings and converting them to political power in defense of threatened areas that should be preserved. It is testimony to this possibility that some of the richest and most destructive polluters in the country are spending vast sums of money to convince the public that their major corporate purpose is to preserve our forests and avoid disturbing the fish. At the same time, even the biggest pork-barrelers in Congress, who have never bridled at the destruction of great tracts of land by projects that might result in a few big campaign contributions, now feel it necessary to pay at least lip service to the cause of the environment.

Obviously, there is a possibility that the public will be taken in by the cheap tricks of the public-relations men, just as there is a strong chance that the widespread interest in conservation and reclamation of natural resources will prove to be merely dilettantish and will never develop the seriousness that will be necessary to really accomplish very much. The fact remains, however, that environmentalists of all kinds now have a starting point and a lever that simply did not exist a few years ago. Even in the mid-sixties, it was quite possible for a conservationist group to prove to nearly everyone's satisfaction that a particular development project would wreak tremendous environmental damage, as well as being economically foolish and profitable mainly to one private interest. The proof might then rate a three-inch summary on page sixty of the local paper. The problem was that nobody cared. Politicians, with a few honorable exceptions, felt little need to pay attention to the rumblings of conservationists because they were well aware that the issue was rarely one that would capture the imagination of a very large segment of the public.

Well, triumph of voices in the wilderness, and all that! The environment, from air quality to city parks to billboards to wilderness areas, has *arrived* as an issue. Everyone from President Nixon to the president of Humble Oil is now a conservationist. It is even possible these days to interest congressmen in spending a few of the millions we are putting out to destroy the lands of the Vietnamese and Laotians on conserving resources, instead. What all this means is that if they work hard enough, environmentalists,

Saving what we have   331

including those who have a special interest in wilderness, may be able to save some of the country from being paved over for parking lots, providing they work hard enough and refuse to be satisfied with empty promises and armies of study commissions.

One of the first things that conservationists ought to decide in their own minds is what sort of objectives they believe in, quite aside from those that they believe are politically possible. Since everyone is now a self-proclaimed conservationist, the battle lines are no longer being drawn by the enemy. The current tactic of the logger who wants to wipe out a forest is to churn out reams of elegant tracts purporting to demonstrate that the true conservationist course lies in intelligent forest management and that the lumber company's proposed use would result in much nicer forests than those that would grow if they were left alone.

The point here is that it is in the interest of those who wish to continue to despoil our common heritage to cloud issues, to muddle distinctions, and generally to appeal to the instincts of reasonable men to avoid foolish and precipitate action. It is also in their interest to separate issues as much as possible, to use multiple jurisdictions and the proliferation of government agencies as an advantageous shell game, and to keep conservationists busy with red herrings and multiple fronts.

It is not possible to combat these tactics without a fairly clear idea of one's own objectives. Compromises are obviously unavoidable, but a party to a compromise who has no firm conception of his own goals is always the loser. This is particularly true in the conflicts with which conservationists concern themselves. A superhighway can be built or a redwood cut this year, next year, or ten years from now. It takes a great deal longer to go the other way. Conservationists are always fighting a holding operation, in effect, they can never advance. It takes minutes to cut a thousand-year-old tree, but it still takes a thousand years to grow another if you change your mind about the wisdom of the operation.

For these reasons, environmentalists and conservationists must of necessity be reactionary in their attitude towards many types of development. There is plenty of room for creativity in rebuilding the central cities, setting up intelligent transportation systems, cleaning up our air and water, but those areas that remain in a relatively natural state should.be left that way, with creative management taking a back seat to modest efforts of preservation. The obvious fact that this will not *always* be possible does not change its utility as a general principle. Our attitude in the past has generally been that those areas that need to be preserved from development were the exception, and that special justification was needed to divert the onrushing tide of progress. A change in emphasis is basic to a successful campaign to preserve the remaining wilderness in America. The nation as a whole is more ready to recognize such a goal than it ever has been before, and it is up to conservationists to emphasize the need for the shift in attitude. We must learn that the destruction of a wild area is irrevocable except in terms of geological time and that we can afford to wait before deciding that a particular form of exploitation really justifies the loss.

The change in emphasis—shifting the burden of proof to the developer—is a difficult change to effect, but the need for it is considerable. For one thing, it is a change that would represent a real shift towards a conservationist attitude—one of a decent respect for natural processes and an intelligent reluctance to interfere massively with their operation. Such a shift is also a strategic necessity in view of the money and power possessed by those who profit from destructive exploitation of the land. As long as conservationists are always compelled to present overwhelming cases for preservation on short notice to forestall the destruction of vast areas, they can expect to be in a continuous state of tactical retreat. The problem is always one of hundreds of fine areas being threatened at the same time, with the necessity of apportioning limited funds and energy. We have been faced again and again with decisions such as whether the Grand Canyon or the North Cascades is more important to save. We need to turn the tables so that instead of the saving of either requiring a major and desperate effort, the diminution of either will require a long-term, public, and exhaustive study.

An example may be of some use. The Alaska pipeline was probably held up at an early stage only by the grace of the native Alaskans—Indians and Eskimos. Except for the native land-claim dispute and some other pieces of good luck, the pipeline, which will probably do great harm to the only vast wilderness area left in the domain of the United States, would have been built with relatively little public notice and only minor bureaucratic red tape. No pressing national need, aside from certain political and bookkeeping conveniences for the oil companies, requires rapid exploitation of the North Slope oil fields. A rational policy would require very circumspect treatment of proposals for rapid tapping of

Saving what we have   333

these fields, the grants for which were made illegally in the first place. We need a new set of procedures and priorities that changes the whole atmosphere in which decisions about questions like the pipeline are made. The pipeline would pass over and radically affect areas that legally and morally belong not to the oil companies or a few politicians in Juneau but to the people of the country as a whole (and to some native Alaskans in particular).

WILD PLACES AND OPEN SPACES

Naturally, the first interest of most of us who love wilderness is the preservation of the mountains, rivers, desert, marsh, or shore that we love. The importance of these areas is self-evident to those who lives are entwined with them, but it is equally necessary for those people to concern themselves with more civilized regions—with parks, cities fit to live in, outdoor recreation areas, and the proper use of many open spaces that could not be classified as wilderness by the most generous and citified observer. One reason we need to interest ourselves in such problems is the obvious one that they are vital public problems that concern us all just as do the larger problems of pollution, overpopulation, and perverse waste of resources.

Wilderness lovers must also concern themselves with open spaces close to home for a more self-serving and parochial reason. The members of the population as a whole, or at least those segments of it who have acquired the basic privileges of the society, are turning to the outdoors as a relief from the pressures of their normal lives. They want the relief of open country, unpolluted water, and forested hills. It is important to try to counteract the influence of those who are trying rather successfully to convince these people that they can only enjoy the outdoors with the help of a couple of thousand dollars worth of mechanical garbage. Even if they are convinced that little equipment is needed to enjoy the outdoors, however, there are fortunately a lot of people who have no interest in enjoying the wilderness on its own terms. They want to get out in the country, admire the scenery, go swimming and perhaps camping. Many would be perfectly happy with rather tame woods and beaches and campgrounds close to home, but unless these are provided, and unless they offer at least a taste of challenge and adventure, the national parks and other places that *ought* to be reserved for headier and more Spartan joys will be converted to paved pabulum for recent and temporary refugees from the city.

Those who wish to retain a little of the spice of independence and wildness in areas like the national parks will have to help provide tamer pleasures closer to home, pleasures that are not to be shunned, anyhow, as the suggestions of ski touring on golf courses and power-line cuts in this book should suggest. Clearly, even in these more civilized areas, there are great problems of overcrowding, some of which could be reduced by eliminating excessive mechanization. The imagination needed to design many kinds of areas for outdoor recreation is obvious and should provide a challenge that is urgent. One of the major difficulties involved is in teaching people (or unteaching them) that the best way to escape the pressures of the machine is to get away from it, not to bring it with them.

There has also been a class bias quite evident in most of the conservation groups of the past, which has got to be eliminated if we are to have much hope for the future. This has been the case from national parks to city parks, and it is evident to anyone inspecting the park system in almost any city in the country. Where are all the nice parks? In the "nice" part of town, of course. Small wonder that with urban decay and the spread of slums of displaced and alienated people, the parks that are in the path of the expanding slums become jungles in which it is not safe to walk at night. The park to a ghetto resident is often less a treasured piece of greenery than a remnant of a hated group that now flees the city at night. All this is close to home. It strains one's sense of reality to imagine why someone concerned with starving children should give a tinker's damn what happens to Yosemite Valley or some arches in the desert.

An interest in recreational open spaces in and around the cities on the part of wilderness conservationists is necessary then for several reasons. Places must be available for people to pursue a host of interests and tastes without "developing" genuine wilderness areas. These same areas can also serve as an introduction to the appreciation of the outdoors for many people who are just becoming interested in the pleasures and skills that are needed to travel comfortably in the back country. People who are stuck in

Wild places and open spaces

the cities have even more need for parks to walk in, rivers and lakes to swim in, and open space to look at than do those fortunate enough to live where all these luxuries are more readily available. Finally, if the residents of the rotting cores of our cities, black and white, have no chance to enjoy any of the pleasures of decent open spaces, they can hardly be expected to be tolerant later on when they or their representatives are asked to join in efforts to preserve a distant mountain range. The preservation is more likely to seem to them a frivolous request redolent of privilege. As poverty in this country becomes increasingly an urban problem, conservationists will make a grave error if they allow wilderness preservation to become an issue of interest only to the wealthier classes.

Creation of decent recreation areas should not be at the expense of existing wild areas, both because of the distance from population centers and because of the need to save all the wild spots we have. With intelligent land use and reclamation, it is perfectly possible to create such areas where they are most needed. Millions of people make exhausting drives to distant beaches because the bodies of water within walking distance of their homes are polluted or access to them is prevented by buildings. Cleaning up the river near home is a far better answer to the Sunday traffic than building a new freeway to a beach ninety miles away. A bit of thought and minor expense and effort could create hundreds of miles of ski-touring trails near any of our urban areas with adequate snowfall in the winter, and the same tracks could easily double as bicycle paths in milder seasons. The possibilities for humane use of the environment are innumerable, and attention to them is vital for wilderness preservation. Such possibilities also present one of the strongest means of creating pressures for further improvement of conservation methods. Who can get very interested in an oil spill on a polluted river fronted by a row of factories and warehouses? If the local residents spend their summers on a beach along the shore of the same river, they will not view the same oil spill very tolerantly.

While open spaces around the city call for better use and administration, the wild places that remain are often *over*administered. Policies tend either to total neglect, including a neglect of enforcement of legitimate restrictions on use, or towards a self-serving promotion of what Edward Abbey calls "industrial tourism." For advocates of this latter type of development, the national parks and other wilderness areas become mere tourist attractions, and the success of their administration is measured in the number of people that can be shoved through the gates. Many national parks are turning into syndromes of more roads, more facilities, more rules, and finally citizen campaigns to protect the hurrying tourists against the few remaining pieces of scenery they might accidentally bump against or fall off.

Conservationists are going to have to lend strength to those beleaguered members of the government bureaucracies who are trying to preserve some of the lands entrusted to them. There are many working rangers and administrators in the various federal and state services responsible for parks, forests, and other public wild lands, who know and appreciate and love the wilds, but they are often at the mercy of stupid administrators or of members of the public who want nothing more from them than a scenic rest stop on the highway, amply supplied with bars and immaculate toilets. These men desperately need the support of conservationists and wilderness lovers to reverse the trend of overdevelopment of parks and wilderness areas.

There is a desperate need to reverse the programs of road building in the national parks and in wilderness areas in the national forests and in other publicly owned wilderness. In most national parks, problems of overcrowding would be readily solved by elimination of motor vehicles from the parks. For winter travelers, a particularly urgent battle is now being waged in many parks over the issue of whether snowmobiles are to be permitted. My own position is pretty obvious, as is the importance of this particular issue to those who love the quiet spaces in winter. This is the only one part of the more general problem of motor vehicles in the parks, however. Conservationists spend tremendous amounts of money and effort in the battle for the creation of a national park or the designation of a wilderness area, but the value thus derived is almost as easily frittered away after designation as before. Each of the agencies responsible for administering public lands is subject to many pressures for development, not the least of which is the bureaucrat's desire to increase the size of his department. Conservationists need to understand these pressures and to either create counter-pressures or work to change the administrative structures that enable the pressures to exist.

We haven't much more time to be satisfied with bills that look good on paper and turn out to be frauds. Point Reyes National

Seashore was created, but since funds were never appropriated to purchase the private land making up most of the park area, we may end up with a national park consisting mainly of a housing development. Other national parks are becoming highway projects more than wilderness areas. Recently, one of our best and most militant conservation organizations took the position that the forests of northern Maine would better preserve their wilderness character under lumber company ownership than under the questionable protection of the park service.

We will have to start holding public servants responsible for some of the appalling practices in areas for which they are supposed to be responsible. A lot of hard work is required, however, not just indignation. The existing conservation organizations have much of the political knowledge necessary to put pressure in the right places, and they desperately need and deserve support. A check is not enough. Anyone seriously interested in preserving our remaining wilderness is going to have to exert some pressure of his own—both on existing conservation groups and on appropriate administrators. Pressure points and organizational characteristics have to be learned. The U.S. Forest Service, for example, is structured in such a way that it is particularly prone to local pressures. In many agencies, the administrator of a particular park or preserve has a great deal of personal authority. In any case, the good guys are usually happy for a little pressure in the right direction. The bad guys deserve no sympathy until they are either reformed or out looking for jobs.

We need to stop making our national parks into amusement parks instead of wilderness preserves, and we need to stop making the rangers into traffic cops and office time servers. Quite a few parks, forests, and wilderness areas are going in the right direction because of really creative administration. These should be recognized and held up as sterling examples. Don't take them for granted: there's some guy who's been fighting tooth and nail to keep your favorite mountain in decent shape, and you'd better give him some help. Picking one random example from many that could be chosen, I would like to congratulate the administrators and rangers of Baxter State Park in Maine, site of Mount Katahdin. Despite the greatly increased population pressures, they have done a beautiful job of maintaining the character of the park. Many things could be improved, especially the regulations on winter travel, but they have maintained the park, and that in itself ranks as a fine accomplishment. Rules can be changed at any time, but the wilderness character of much of the park would take years to retrieve if it were once given up.

A FINAL NOTE

As noted earlier in this chapter, I have not been too fastidious in my use of the term *wilderness* while discussing the need for preservation. Many areas to which I have referred have already been greatly influenced by modern man, even when they have never been trodden by him. The great forests of white pine that once stood in the eastern part of the continent are gone. Areas that have experienced less direct contact are still affected. The elimination of many predators has affected ecosystems in places that hunters have never reached. Still, we have to start where we are standing now; we have no control over yesterday's loggers, sheepherders, or campers. If we take "wilderness" as meaning a place where man still has only very slight influence on the current life of the land, aside from past interventions, there is still a good deal of country with a stable life of its own, worth saving and deserving to be left alone.

The value of such land for recreation is obvious, but it has intrinsic value of its own, which should govern recreational use. Man's influence should remain peripheral, and administrative involvement with the environment itself should be concerned mainly with controlling the effects of human beings—fire control, for example. "Game management" is a more difficult problem, and conservationists have occasionally allowed themselves to be oversentimental, leaving themselves open to the sneers of the hunting lobby. By and large, however, the sneerers have shown themselves either ignorant or disingenuous.

The fact that many game animals would experience excessive population growth without hunting pressures is not due to sentimental bird watchers, but rather to the elimination of useful predators by stupid men, with guns and poisons and traps. Nor need the conservationist pay much attention to pious claims that hunters never do anything but good to non-predatory game species. Numerous harmless species in this country have been exterminated by hunters, and many others were saved only by "sentimentalists." Shorebird populations, for example, have still to recover from hunting pressures, quite aside from the reduction in habitat. Many game species are no longer controlled by predators, and hunting may frequently be a useful way to control populations. Similarly, hunting licenses may produce needed revenues for preservation of woods, and the hunters may then help lobby to preserve those woods, but conservationists need to take long hard looks at all the desires of such lobbies. Maximum production of game species is not always the sign of a healthy ecological balance.

Conservationists do not need to take any back seat to howling gun lobbyists. Everyone makes mistakes, but preservationists (that's the current dirty word for conservationists among loggers and some hunters) have made fewer ecological mistakes than those whose only outdoor interest is "harvesting" game. Hunting is often legitimate, whether it suits your taste or not, but it is also an activity that *requires* strict regulation by its very nature, unlike hiking, mountain climbing, and similar activities. Man cannot be a free predator any more. When he took up agriculture and animal husbandry, he increased his population to an extent that cannot be supported by predation.

In any case, the most urgent need in the administration of most wilderness areas is for a style of treatment that respects the balances that already exist and that maintains a healthy conservatism concerning schemes of major intervention. The ancient Greeks used the word *hubris* to describe the overbearing pride and presumption against the laws of nature and the gods that preceded an inevitable and disastrous fall. *Hubris* is perhaps the most applicable term for technological man's attitude towards the natural system of which he is a part. There seems always to be an arrogant presumption that any well-intentioned intervention by people in fantastically complex natural processes will be for the good. The irresponsible exploiter who cares not a whit for what he destroys is bad enough, but sometimes the well-meaning interventionist can do even more damage. If you doubt this, go back and take a look at some of the statements and reviews that followed Rachel Carson's *Silent Spring,* a book that now seems a model of understatement.

We need to save what we have left of the wild spaces of this country and continent not only because they are nice places to ski tour, but because we have already fouled up more than enough of our land. We should feel extremely lucky to have some left to preserve and very jealous of those in a hurry to either exploit or "improve" what we have left. Uses of the wilderness that remains should be of a character that has only minimal effect on the environment, a character that is very much compatible with the cleansing of men's souls. Preserve the wilderness, and you'll have somewhere to go to renew yourself. More important, you'll have saved a little bit of the larger world of life that surrounds us and from which we came. Good touring!

Appendix A

HOW TO MAKE YOUR OWN EQUIPMENT

A few years ago, suppliers of equipment for lightweight winter travel were few and their offerings necessarily rather limited. With the great interest shown recently in the outdoors, this is no longer true. Shops specializing in lightweight equipment are opening everywhere, many making some equipment themselves. There are several major manufacturers of high quality equipment for lightweight wilderness travel. It is rarely necessary these days to go to the expense of having equipment custom made, since satisfactory gear for most purposes can be found in any one of a half-dozen catalogues.

Though one of the major incentives for making one's own equipment—the unavailability of a ready-made substitute—is gone, there are still several reasons for going to the trouble of doing it yourself. The most common one is money—or the lack thereof. Many of the operations in the manufacture of quality outdoor equipment require tedious hand work, but if you're willing to spend your own time doing it, you won't have to pay someone else to do it for you. If you're trying to get through the initial expensive phase of acquiring good equipment on a limited budget, making some of your own gear can allow you to get much more satisfactory items. There are several other reasons for making your own outfit. There's an inherent satisfaction in using something you've made yourself. Very often it is possible to make a piece of equipment that is better suited to your needs than anything available from a supplier: you can incorporate special features ranging from pockets for particular items to special multiple-use arrangements. You may also be able to improve on currently available designs. Most good outdoor gear is still developed from the personal experience and ideas of the people who make the equipment, their friends, and their customers. You can do the same thing with your own equipment. Finally, making a few pieces of your own is one of the best ways to become an expert in evaluating the quality of equipment made by others.

FROM KITS OR FROM SCRATCH

Once you decide to make some of your own gear there remains the question of how to manage the project. There are several possible choices. If you're a rank beginner at sewing and you're not interested in designing your own gear, just in saving some money, your best bet for a first project may be a kit, especially if what you want to make is a difficult piece of down gear, like a sleeping bag or a down jacket. With the kits the planning has been done for you. You receive detailed instructions, precut materials, and sometimes down prepacked in the right quantities for each compartment. You do only the hand labor. Some of the advantages of this method are obvious, particularly the fact that you avoid all the pitfalls of designing and cutting. Less obviously, you may save money on materials. Cutting out is the cheapest part of the operation in making a good piece of gear, and since an outfitter is making many items, he not only can buy materials in quantity, but he can also cut with much less waste than someone making only one or two items—an extra scrap of cloth can always be used for an odd piece on another garment. Kits are to be highly recommended for a beginner who wants to slip into making his own equipment gradually, but no more need be said about how to make them, since all instructions are included.

However, many of the advantages of making your own equipment are lost if you rely exclusively on kits. Selection is much more limited than even the regular manufactured lines, and you may not be able to find a kit that suits your needs. The wise and patient cold weather slogger can also save a good deal of money over the cost of even the kits if he buys his material in the right way. You can't save much by buying just new material in small amounts, but several methods are suggested below which can cut your costs way down. Finally, of course, using kits robs you of both the interest and advantages of designing your own equipment.

Aside from kits, you are still left with several choices in making a particular piece of gear. You may find a pattern in this or some other book and follow it; you may design your own piece of gear from scratch; or you may mix these two methods, modifying an existing pattern to suit your own needs or whims. One other technique which is useful for some items is to modify or copy another piece of gear. Many items in surplus stores are suitable for wilderness use with a few modifications, for example. Or you may have a favorite old parka with a design that seems nearly perfect, but which has finally worn out—just rip out the seams and cut out exactly the same pattern from new material and sew it together, perhaps using the old hardware if it's still in good condition.

GETTING STARTED

Making your own gear successfully mainly requires that you plan things well. You don't have to be any kind of master with a needle to make fine equipment; outdoor equipment is generally rather baggy as a matter of choice and a few irregularities in the seams will not detract from either the usefulness or attractiveness of a finished garment. Proper care and strong work are necessary in outdoor gear, though, and good design is very important. A ripped-out parka seam in a bad storm is no joke.

For large pieces of equipment—sleeping bags, tents, and the like—a sewing machine is almost mandatory, but hand sewing is feasible on smaller items. A normal home sewing machine handles most outdoor equipment with little difficulty, though certain heavy or awkward spots may have to be sewn by hand, especially on packs. Not much other special equipment is needed, and that is usually inexpensive. If snap fasterners or grommets are needed on a particular item, a set of dies is normally required to set them, but these are quite cheap and last indefinitely. A selection of needles with various curves will cost a quarter or so and will enable you to sew in hard-to-reach spots. For sewing very heavy fabric or leather, especially in packs, a sewing awl is hard to do without. This is essentially a hand sewing machine. It costs about $2.50 equipped with extra needles and plenty of thread.

You should plan the whole garment before going out and buying any material or equipment especially for it. The information provided in this chapter should be adequate for a start, but I believe that every lightweight winter traveler ought to get a copy of *Light Weight Camping Equipment and How to Make It* by Gerry Cunningham and Margaret Hansson (see Bibliography), even if he is not interested in making his own gear. This book has invaluable information on materials and design, including some excellent design ideas which are, unfortunately, not included in any commercially available gear.

If you are using a pattern, it will usually be presented as the ones in this book are: either the shape is shown with dimensions or in more complicated designs the shapes are drawn out on a square grid, which each small square on the pattern representing a larger square of a particular size. You simply draw out a grid with the right size squares on big sheets of lightweight paper and transfer the pattern. This is easy to do freehand with the help of the squares, even if you have no drawing talent.

A few tips on using patterns:

1. Check the size of the person the pattern is to fit. If you are much larger or smaller, just enlarge or reduce the size of your squares to adjust the garment size. Remember though, that outdoor clothing should fit loosely, especially if it is to go over down garments.

2. Before your make up your paper pattern, decide on the fabric you will use, if possible, and cut the paper to the same width. If you do this, you can experiment with the most efficient way of fitting the pieces together to use the smallest amount of fabric.

3. When you cut out the paper pattern leave extra margins on the sides. Pinning paper takes more room than sewing cloth. Pin the paper pattern together and try it on. Make *sure* everything is all right before you even buy your material, or at least before you cut it. You'll regret it if you get six inches too little, which you may, if the guy who made up the pattern didn't have your spectacular chest muscles or long, skinny legs.

4. If you are working with coated fabric, as in rainwear, there

is an outside and an inside. Pay attention when you are laying out the pieces that everything is right. Mark each piece on one side of the paper or color it. Then, when you pin things together, all the outside surfaces should have the mark or the color. If they don't, you'll end up with a garment that is half shiny side out and half shiny side in.

  5. If you're not sure about the fit, transfer the paper pattern to an old sheet or some other soft, dispensable piece of material, and sew it together (fast and sloppy—just enough to hold it). This gives you a mock garment to try on.

  6. Once you've decided that the paper or cloth pattern is satisfactory, you can get your material and either pin or trace out the pieces for cutting. (Don't pin on coated fabric.) Pin together the cutout parts before sewing (use paperclips for coated fabrics) and check the fit. Decide what the best order will be for sewing the seams without getting in your own way. Write it down. Then put it together.

An even more satisfactory method than paper patterns is to use an existing garment. Old outdoor clothing is ideal, of course, but normal clothes will often serve, especially pants. The trick is to find something with a proper fit, which will usually be larger than your normal size. One good trick is to go down to your local thrift shop. The starving student and climber types will know where I mean; more affluent readers can look in the yellow pages for the Salvation Army or Goodwill store. Look around and find a good fit, ignoring the cuffs. Don't worry about worn seats or chartruse checks—you're not going to wear this thing. Rip out the seams and, presto, you have a permanent pattern for some part of your anatomy, and if you have chosen wisely, it will have cost less than a dollar.

DESIGN CONSIDERATIONS

Many general considerations for equipment design have been discussed in the earlier sections of this book. Cunningham and Hansson also have excelent material that is worth many rereadings by anyone designing his own equipment. A few points will be made here, however, both concerning general design and specific pieces of equipment.

Fabrics. Many demands are made on any piece of equipment for lightweight winter use, and an actual design is inevitably a compromise. This fact is nowhere more evident than in the choice of fabrics. It is usually desirable that these be warm, light, strong, abrasion-resistant, tear-resistant, ravel-free, free breathing, waterproof, nonabsorbant, condensation-free, impervious to rot and mildew, fireproof, and possessed of several other incompatible qualities. The fabrics available today are pretty miraculous compared with what was available a few years ago, but they cannot now, and never will, fill all the requirements that a difficult environment imposes. The advantage to making your own gear is that you can choose the compromise that most precisely suits your own needs.

The materials useful for our purposes are fairly limited, both by design considerations and availability. The advantages of *wool* have been extensively discussed already. It is not a particularly strong fabric, is weaker when wet, is very heavy when tight woven for water and abrasion resistance, is itchy, is vulnerable to moths, and in most weaves is not easy to waterproof. It is still a very important fabric because of its unique characteristic of wicking moisture and drying first on the inside. It is indispensable for some basic clothing wherever a survival situation may occur in both wet and cold conditions, and many recent accidents can be attributed to excessive dependence on down clothing to the neglect of wool. Because it is heavy when woven for even limited abrasion-resistance and ability to turn wind and water, wool is usually best confined to underwear and to basic garments: socks, mitts, shirts, pants, and sweaters, which under winter conditions are worn under shell clothing. Providing it will not have to serve double purpose as outer wear, it is best in light, fluffy weaves. Pants that may be worn without wind pants should have a hard woven outer surface, however, both to prevent snagging and to keep snow from sticking to the outside. For outside garments and socks, a little nylon is often combined with the wool to improve wearing qualities, but light shell clothing of a different material is as good a solution. Virgin wool is warmer than reprocessed wool.

Cotton is generally an undesirable material for inner clothing. It is clammy when wet, and it dries slowly. However, it is still sometimes useful for shell clothing and tents, since it is cheaper than nylon and is easily made water-resistant. A good quality, tightly woven cotton fabric is still the best water-resistant cloth made which also breathes adequately for use as a general shell garment. Since cotton is not nearly as strong as some of the synthetics, a more expensive nylon-cotton mixture is often used which is nearly as water-resistant as cotton but which is stronger. The best cottons are made from Pima or Egyptian cotton, both of which have very long fibers. I have had good luck with an Oxford weave cotton fabric, but there are others that are good.

Nylon has become the standard material for most fabrics used in outdoor clothing and equipment for the excellent reason that nylon cloth is stronger than any other fabric of the same weight. It can be made fairly wind-resistant while still breathing well. It is nearly always used in covering down garments and sleeping bags, since nylon fabric strong enough for a satisfactory garment is still light enough to allow the down to loft well. The primary disadvantages of nylon for tents and clothing are that it is very difficult to waterproof without using an impermeable coating and that the smooth surface of the fibers tends to condense moisture more readily than cotton or wool. *Dacron* and *Orlon* are somewhat less strong than nylon, and they are satisfactory but not widely available for the uses being discussed here. An exception is fluffed Orlon, which is a slightly inferior substitute for wool, very useful for people who are allergic to wool.

Coated fabrics for quality lightweight equipment should always use nylon or Dacron for a base. The disadvantages of the synthetics are of no consequence in coated fabrics, since they are impermeable and waterproof as a result of the coating. The extra strength of the synthetics is important in coated fabrics, because the coating isolates any tearing force to a small area by gluing the fibers of the cloth together, and this action makes any coated fabric weaker than a corresponding uncoated one. Many types of coating have been developed, but no particular recommendations will be made here, since this is one of the most rapidly changing materials and since the home manufacturer will be limited to those coated fabrics he can find. Most of the ones listed in the catalogues of mountaineering suppliers are quite good, with the weight per square yard giving a good indication of strength. Urethane has been one of the more successful coatings, but other good ones are likely to be found. Keep an eye on what the best manufacturers are using. One development that is not likely is a coated fabric that also breathes enough to avoid condensation problems—none that have been tried so far have been successful.

Other materials are mostly pretty obvious, except perhaps for closures. Zippers, the handiest means to close and open long pairs of edges in garments and sleeping bags, used to cause some problems, especially in cold weather. They are, however, quite dependable if good quality large nylon zippers are used. Good metal zippers are also adequate if rubbed with paraffin occasionally, but nylon is definitely preferred. Smooth operation is the main criterion: don't use surplus zippers. To avoid snagging edges construction details around zippers must be examined closely. Buttons and snaps are occasionally used as main means of closure and often as backup closures which also hold storm flaps in place. Velcro, consisting of paired hook and mat strips, makes an excellent draftproof, snag free, easily opened, and easily installed method of closure, but it has certain disadvantages. The main one is that it is not self-aligning as are snaps, buttons, or zippers. For this reason Velcro is usually used either for backup closures or for quite short openings like pockets and cuffs. When using Velcro in spots where it might rub against the skin, install the hook side to face away from the skin—it's irritating.

NOTES ON CONSTRUCTION

It is important that the seams in equipment designed for lightweight outdoor use be strong and well made. Synthetic thread should be used throughout because of its extra strength. Nylon thread is excellent, but its stretchiness creates difficulties in some sewing machines by causing dropped stitches. This problem can usually be solved by reducing machine tension and perhaps using a larger needle. Textured nylon, nonstretch Dacron, and cotton-wrapped synthetic threads are all satisfactory substitutes for regular nylon thread if the latter causes trouble with your sewing machine.

Nearly all seams in outdoor equipment should be finished seams, that is, the cut edges should be turned under so that they cannot ravel. Alternatively, they may be stitched in two lines to

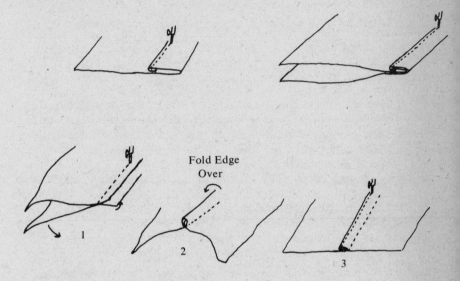

Fold Edge
Over

1

2

3

Good seams for outdoor equipment. At the top are a simple finished hem
and a finished hem seam; in both the cut edge is folded under to prevent
raveling. The bottom row shows the steps in making a finished flat-felled seam,
the main seam for tents and garments.

1. Lay the edges together, with the outsides facing out, and sew them together leaving edges wide enough to fold back on themselves in the next two
steps.

2. Fold one edge over the other and back on itself, so that the whole seam
will form a shingle, *pointing downward in the final garment.*

3. Sew the shingled edge down.

prevent raveling, but with the edge left rough. The only type of fabric that can normally be left safely with a single line of stitching is coated fabric, since the coating prevents raveling. All uncoated synthetic fabrics and webbing ravel very badly, and melting the edges will help prevent this, but melting does not substitute for finished seams.

Details of the more commonly used seams are shown in the illustration. Additional ones can be found in any sewing book, and many special suggestions are shown in detail in Cunningham and Hansson's book. Most clothing can be sewn with nothing more elaborate than flat felled and hem seams, however.

Shirts and pants can be made pretty easily if you get a pattern out of an old piece of clothing, making necessary modifications such as cuffs, hoods, wear patches, and so on. However, because of the bounty of the surplus market for good wool clothing, I confine my activities to making a few modifications on surplus clothes. If you find the right suppliers you can get excellent ready-made cold-weather gear at a fraction of the cost you paid for them as a taxpayer. My favorite winter pants are Air Force flier's pants. They have knit cuffs, snap waist, padded seat and knees, a warm weave that doesn't pick up snow, and they cost me $3.95 a pair, much less than what I would have paid for the materials.

Shell clothing suitable for lightweight travel is not generally available in the surplus market, except for wind pants, so parkas are a common item for home manufacture. Parkas for winter use should be cut *baggy,* so that you can wear your insulation under them. This is especially true if you use down clothing, since a tight shell over the down will compress it and nullify its value as insulation. It is desirable to use shell clothing over the down, so that wind will not penetrate the down layer. The light nylon used in these garments is not sufficiently windproof. Shell clothing for winter requires particular care in cutting sufficiently roomy arms and shoulders. Pullover types of parka with a short zipper at the neck will give adequate ventilation if they are made roomy enough with the bottom left wide, to be closed with a drawstring. Jacket styles are easier to ventilate, but they are more difficult to make and zipper failure is a slight worry in bad weather. Suit yourself.

Another question for the winter traveler to decide is how heavy to make a parka. Good all-purpose mountain parkas for summer and winter wear should be made of strong, fairly weatherproof cloth, perhaps cotton-nylon cloth weighing about 4 oz. per square yard. They should also be made double throughout. The winter traveler who is not planning on struggling up rock chimneys or summer bushwacking may elect to carry a light single layer garment to break the wind and shed the snow. In cold weather when rain is likely, waterproof rain gear is desirable, so double layering the parka for rain protection is unnecessary. The pattern given for a cagoule can be shortened a bit and used for a very simple parka pattern, with a pocket sewn into the front closed by a Velcro taped flap. A good design for a more sophisticated parka is given in Cunningham and Hansson, but I recommend a hood that extends farther out than theirs for storm protection. Try sewing on a hemmed rim around the edge of the hood, containing a drawstring. Incidentally, drawstrings are better made of some material other than nylon, since nylon won't hold knots well. Try a round cotton boot lace.

Rainwear can be made very light, usually with a single layer of coated nylon. For heavier duty and longer wear, the garment can be made double throughout, with the coated sides facing in toward one another to prevent their rubbing off and to reduce the clammy feel of the coating. If a single layer is used, the coating should face in to prevent its being rubbed off. Rainwear should preferably be designed with as few seams on the shoulders as possible, and if the garment is made double, the seams on the inside and outside layers should not be sewn through or overlap, since the seams are the main leaking points of rainwear.

Take care in sewing rainwear to avoid mistakes—in most garments a bad seam can be ripped out with no harm done, but coated fabric is permanently punctured every time the needle goes through. After sewing, the seams of rain garments should be sealed with spray sealant or seam cement. Renew the sealer once a year. All rainwear should fit very loosely to allow ventilation. The bottoms should open as wide as wind permits, and some sort of zipper or drawstring openings around the neck and cuffs are mandatory. With a long garment like the cagoule shown here, the legs can be protected by rain chaps. Shorter tops require rain pants.

Tents are larger projects than most clothing, and more care is required in designing and sewing them. For forest use open front tents may be used with fires in front, and it is possible to design models that are convertible to closed cell models. For use at high altitudes, in open spaces subject to severe storms, and for general use without fires, small closed tents are the most practical solution. The usual design for one or two people is a mountain tent, which may be designed with one high end or two. For more people the Logan design is more practical. The mountain tent is a refined pup tent, and the Logan a modified pyramid tent. Many good suggestions will be found in Cunningham and Hansson, which is required reading for beginning tent makers, but probably the best preparation for anyone designing tents like these is to visit a good supplier and study the construction of his tents. Material for tents that may have to withstand high winds should be strong—either nylon or a cotton-nylon weave—but forest tents can be made of a good cotton. Waterproof material should be used for floors, but never for the upper parts of closed tents designed for winter use. Waterproof tents require very good ventilation, and in blizzard conditions such ventilation will insure a snow-filled tent. All nylon tents will require flies if they are to be used when rain is a possibility.

The large areas of cloth supported by the seams and suspension points of tents require considerable attention to their strength. Make a number of drawings of your tent and think about the lines of strain. Well-made seams are strong, and they will reinforce lines of strain; nylon tape will serve the same function. All pull-out tabs, stake loops, pole tubes, and suspension points must be reinforced to prevent their pulling out, especially in storms. Walls of tents will tend to bow in, especially under a load of snow, and they should be held out with pull-outs or wands. Pull-outs are easy to sew in, but they require additional staking points. Wands are a more difficult solution to construct, but they make pitching simpler. Light fiberglass rods are inserted in sleeves arranged so that they force the rods to bow out and hold the tent wall up. Wands must be carried with the tent. If you take ski poles, make sure to design any pole sleeves wide enough to allow the handle ends of the poles to go through; this eliminates the need to remove pole baskets in order to use ski poles to hold up the tent. (If this is done, pockets ought to be substituted for the standard grommets at the tent corners, to accommodate the handle ends of the ski poles.)

A frost liner is a worthwhile addition to any tent designed for use in very cold weather. It is generally made of very light nylon material which forms an inner tent wall suspended a couple of inches inside the outer one. Its purpose is to keep the tent warmer by channeling cold air blowing through the walls around the living space of the tent and to catch frost falling from the outside wall before it falls on your face. Liners require numerous suspension points to keep from sagging more than a few inches from the tent walls. Ties are commonly used, but I do not recommend them, since they can only be tied in the proper order. Snaps are better, since they can be fastened even when the whole liner is in, as can single ties on the tent wall which are knotted through small grommets in the liner.

A good first tent project is the mountain tent described in Cunningham and Hansson. Study it carefully and make any design modifications you think appropriate.

Sleeping bags and down clothing involve much more complicated problems of construction than other equipment, though they also present a good place for the poverty-stricken outdoorsman to save some money. Since materials are expensive, however, so are mistakes. The beginner would be well advised to use a kit if he wants to make a down garment or sleeping bag as his first project. The best kits have the special advantage of prepacking the down in bags separated for each tube or pocket in the piece of equipment. If you start from scratch you will have to experiment to get just the right amount of down to fill each compartment; do it outdoors —you would not believe how elusive those bits of down can be when they get loose in the room, which they will surely do if you work indoors.

Proper design of down equipment requires that the down layer be held in compartments which are small enough to keep it from shifting and which exert as little compressive force on the down as possible. The best designs have the largest number of compartments and thus require less down fill, since extra down does not need to be added to compensate for shifting. The baffling that forms the inside walls of the compartments is best made from very lightweight nylon material—its only purpose is to prevent the down from moving about. The best designs will result in many compartments shaped to allow the down to expand them easily, but requiring as little fabric as possible. Such combinations require a great deal of thought.

One of the first principles of designing down equipment is to use a differential cut. All garments and most sleeping bags for lightweight camping must fit the body fairly closely. If the inside

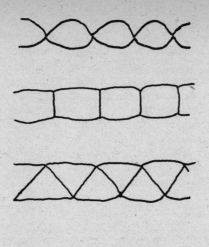

Basic methods of construction of down equipment. Top to bottom: sewn-through tubes, box baffling, triangular baffling, overlapping tubes.

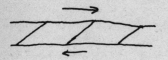

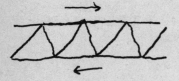

One of the advantages of triangular baffling over box type. When force is exerted to turn the inside layer with respect to the outside one (when you turn in your sleeping bag, for example), the box construction tends to pull together much more than the triangular.

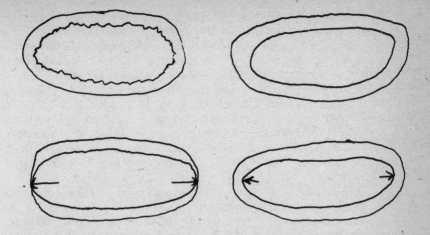

The advantages of a differential cut. The sketch on the left shows a cross section of a sleeping bag with the outside and inside sheaths cut to the same diameter. When your elbows push against the sides of the bag, the down is compressed and the cold seeps in. In the differential cut shown at the right, the inner layer can't be stretched against the outer one, and you stay warm.

and the outside are cut to the same dimensions, then when you stretch around inside, you will stretch them both out to their maximum circumference, which will also push the inside and outside walls together and compress the down. By cutting the inside layers smaller, it is impossible for the body to push the inside wall against the outside one: you may still be cramped in your sleeping bag, but you won't be cold as well.

A differential cut is mandatory for down-filled parkas. It is desirable for sleeping bags. Quiet sleepers won't care much. Restless sleepers will. Don't let anyone tell you a differential cut doesn't make a warmer bag. Because it is harder to sew the differential cut bags, the kit-makers don't use them, but I still maintain that a good differential cut improves a bag, and more down is needed to make up for its omission.

Several methods of down construction are shown in the illustrations. They are not the whole story, though, since various advantages can be gained by installing cross-baffles to prevent down from shifting along the tube, by slanting the tubes in particular directions, and so on. Major methods are fairly simply discussed.

Appendix A 357

The easiest method of construction uses *sewn-through* seams to block shifting of the down. The outer and inner shells are simply sewn together in a quilted or tubed pattern. This is a very satisfactory and simple method to use with supplementary down equipment like down vests and the light jackets often called down sweaters. These are among the most useful pieces of down equipment you can have. They are very light and take up little space, but provide lots of extra warmth when it is needed. They are worn under shell parkas, so the sewn-through seams and light outside material do not detract from their value. Sewn-through seams provide a major heat leak, however, and can only be used in light garments. They must never be used in big down parkas or winter sleeping bags.

Sleeping bags and big down parkas use one of the methods of packing down without sewn-through seams. The simplest is to construct two sets of sewn-through tubes and then overlap them to eliminate cold seams. This is reasonably effective, but it is heavier and less efficient than other methods. Probably the most common method is box-type construction, in which baffles are sewn straight across between the two walls of the sleeping bag or garment. Even better is a triangular pattern as shown in the illustration. This is more efficient than the box-type because it controls down shifting more effectively and because the walls cannot be pulled together by having the inside shell turned with respect to the outer one.

A useful down garment which is not available commercially is shown in the patterns. It is a pair of down shorts, about the length of Bermuda shorts, using sewn-through seams and a very simple construction with a wide waist at the top held by elastic. These shorts are worn over regular pants and under wind pants, if any. They are much less complex and bulky than full down pants, but they cover the major source of heat loss in the legs—the femoral arteries in the inner thighs. Make sure to compare your own measurements (with clothes) before making the shorts, but there is a good deal of leeway in a garment like this.

The biggest complication in making down equipment comes from the closures. These require interruption of the pattern of the insulation, and they generally create cold seams. The most common solution is to install a zipper closure and to sew in a down tube behind it to stop drafts and heat leaks. Velcro can be used to advantage as an alternative means of closure, since it can be sewn to the clothing shells and used without collapsing the down tubes.

APPENDIX A   358

Again, much attention is due to *Light Weight Camping Equipment* for anyone seriously interested in making his own gear. A few other suggestions for making down gear: include insulated, down-filled pockets for warming your hands; make your sleeping bag long enough to accommodate your boots at the-bottom beyond your feet, and then put them in a plastic bag at the bottom of your sleeping bag; make some down booties as a cheap, light, welcome luxury; don't forget head protection in designing down equipment —that's the most important source of heat loss; plan your equipment so that your down gear is enclosed in a windproof shell.

Packs are easy to make for day use, since they require less sewing than many other pieces of equipment, the main trick being to make the pack large enough to prevent its becoming a hard little ball on your back. At the risk of being repetitious, I again refer the interested reader to Cunningham and Hansson, since there is little point in repeating their many useful points. The main difficulty in making bigger packs lies in fabricating the frames. For contour frames, the solution is simply to buy the frame and make your own packbag to fit it. Rucksack frames cannot be so readily purchased, but several of my friends have been reusing the same rucksack frame for years. When the old bag wears out, they rip out the seams, cut a new set of pieces from coated nylon pack fabric, and sew it together, using the same hardware and always having a ready made pattern. I know a couple of people who like the design of the old army ski mountaineering packs (still available), and who have each put three or four new nylon sacks on the old frames.

Many of the best rucksacks made in the last few years use the principle of semi-rigid frames, a principle that is readily adapted to the home craftsman's use. The most common method is to rivet together flat strips of aluminum or magnesium into a triangle. (For home construction replace rivets with machine screws.) The corners are flexible enough to have some give, but the shape gives it strength all the same. The strips can be sewn into the pack and can be bent to fit the back. This principle can be combined with some tubular pieces, fiberglass mat, mesh or lacing, all of which can serve to hold the pack away from the back and to transfer some of the load to the hips. Such a pack, if it is well designed, can be used to carry reasonable loads very well, though the capacity is never as good as the contoured frame. Semi-rigid frames hug the body better than rigid frames, and are thus less confining, but they will carry greater loads than frameless rucksacks.

Bivouac equipment is simply an extension of regular gear, but anyone who expects to bivouac very often should give special consideration to his equipment. He can choose a cagoule for rain gear, sew a pocket in it for an Ensolite pad, carry down booties to go inside his overboots at night, and so on. Some practice in bivouacing in milder seasons will give the winter beginner a proper respect for conditions. If you plan to sleep regularly in snow caves, the sleeping bag cover shown will be a help, and it can double as a general emergency sack or as a summer shelter when it is not raining. One side is waterproof, usually the ground side, while the other side is permeable. The snaps permit folding it into a waterproof footsack.

GETTING YOUR MATERIALS

Many outdoor suppliers carry materials, but they are naturally quite expensive. If you are in a hurry to make a piece of equipment, this is the source you will probably use, but there are a number of methods you can use to cut your costs if you make your own equipment regularly.

If you live anywhere near any outfitters that make their own equipment, you can do very well buying both ready-made equipment and materials at the annual clearance sale that most of them have. Most of these suppliers do much of their business by mail order, and since they are likely to modify their equipment each year, they have to clear out their back stock of discontinued models, at which time they often get rid of odd bolts of cloth, discolored items and material, rental equipment, parkas with off-colored pockets, and so on. Find out when the places near you have their sales, and plan to be there early—you may find ready-made stuff on sale cheaper than you can make it, but you will probably also find some good material for future use.

The surplus stores are not the source they once were, except for some special items: ski mountaineering packs, pants, sweaters, parachute cord, and a few other such items. You may make occasional finds, though, especially if you make friends with the owner. A less frequently tapped source is a possible local manufacturer of clothing and such items for the military. Quality control is pretty good, and there are all kinds of items with a few skipped stitches, etc., which you can readily repair and modify for your own use, or which is good for material. If you can find a source, you can get this stuff for a song (you pay with your taxes, brother). You may get tired of that khaki, but the money you save will console you. Two more possible methods of saving costs on materials are a bit more involved, and they will not be worth the trouble for everyone. The first is to band together with some friends to buy materials directly from the manufacturers, and the second is to take the trouble to become authorized to bid on government surplus sales directly (the red tape involved deserves a special adjective all of its own).

Making your own equipment, at least a good deal of it, is not really too difficult, once you have gained some familiarity with the advantages and disadvantages of various commercially manufactured items. You will find soon after you head for the woods that each design has its advantages and disadvantages. By making your own you can pick the compromise that suits you best. A worthwhile technique is to match your equipment; pieces can be made to fit together in a way that cannot be managed with commercial equipment. Compartments in a pack sack can be designed to fit a camera, jacket, or sleeping bag perfectly. Snaps or ties can be used to rig rain gear, and packs can be designed to bolt to skis for emergency stretchers. Possibilities are endless, and the ingenious outdoorsman can use his poverty-stricken condition to get him the best possible set of equipment—with a little work.

CAGOULE

You will need ten feet of coated nylon fabric 44 to 46 inches wide, nylon thread, something to sew with, four grommets and a setting tool, a few snaps, and a setting tool, about three yards of drawstring, and a zipper, open at one end, 12 or 14 inches long.

Directions: First lay the pattern out on paper or scrap material, cut it out, put it together, and try it on. After making necessary

Layout on Material (45″ Fabric)

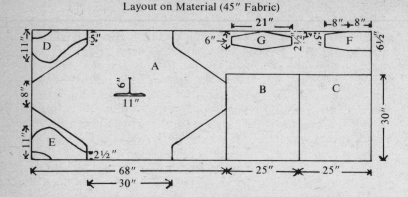

modifications, lay it out on the fabric and cut it out. Sew the skirts B and C onto the bottoms of A, using finished fell seams lapped downward. Then sew the edges together from the bottom to the sleeve ends, again using finished fell seams, and leaving the bottom and the ends of the sleeves open.

Next, sew the three main pieces of the hood together. F goes between D and E, with the narrow end facing forward. Sew the hood into the opening in A, fitting it carefully first with paper clips. Piece G now fits around the front edge of the face opening, forming a visor and holding the drawstring. It is folded double with the wide part in the center above the forehead. Before sewing it on, punch holes on one side at each end and install grommets for the drawstring. Sew it on. Sew in the zipper. Velcro may be substituted for both the zipper and wrist snaps.

Put in grommets at the bottom front of the parka, just high enough for the hem to fold over them. Sew in a finished hem at the bottom and at each wrist. Install the drawstrings. A small safety pin is good for threading them through. Install snaps to close the wrists.

The size shown is a fairly versatile medium. To lengthen or shorten it, simply change the 30 inch dimension of the skirts— room is left for this on the layout. An alternative wrist closure which I prefer is the friction tab shown in Cunningham and Hansson. An illustration of this cagoule will be found in the clothing chapter.

APPENDIX A   362

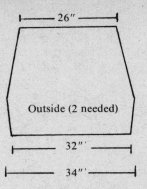

26"

Outside (2 needed)

32"

34"

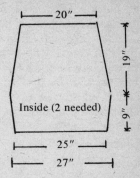

20"

19"

9"

Inside (2 needed)

25"

27"

Quilting Pattern

DOWN SHORTS

These shorts are basically very simple, but they require some care in construction. They should be made of a light, downproof nylon. After trying the pattern with paper or scrap cloth, get enough fabric of whatever width is cheapest to cut out the four pieces. Then sew together the outside edges of the inside pieces of the shorts and the crotch. Do the same with the outside pieces. You should now have two rough pairs of shorts, one larger than the other. Put the inside pair in the outer one, with the rough parts of the seams

Appendix A

in the space between. Turn it all inside out and sew the legs of the two pairs of shorts together. Sew twice to prevent raveling. Make two loops of elastic (sold in any sewing store) the right length to just tighten around all the clothes you wear in winter. Insert one of these at the bottom of each leg, and sew them in. Now you have a pair of shorts with two layers, and open between the layers at the top. Sew the vertical lines of the quilting pattern. Now start filling with down (probably a total of about eight ounces). As you get the lower part of each down compartment filled, sew it off. When all the lower ones are full, do the top ones the same way. Then fold the top over a waist band of elastic, do a finished hem, and you're done.

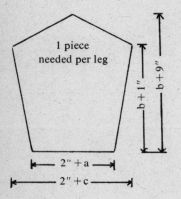

RAIN CHAPS

1 piece needed per leg

$b + 1''$

$b + 9''$

$2'' + a$

$2'' + c$

RAIN CHAPS

These are very simple to make from coated nylon. All you need is the material, a little elastic or some snaps and a little nylon tape for the tops. "A" is the length of the shortest loop of string or cloth that will fit easily over your boots, "B" is your inseam length to the floor, and "C" is the diameter around the top of your thigh with all your clothes on—measure loosely. Sew the two sides of each chap together with a finished fell seam, and hem the bottoms, either inserting elastics or installing snaps. Then hem the top edges and install belt loops with ties or snaps at the top corners.

APPENDIX A   364

BIVOUAC SACK AND SLEEPING BAG COVER

Take two rectangular pieces of cloth, one of coated nylon and the other of light cotton element cloth. Sew them together to form a bag open at one end, with the coated side of the nylon facing in and the seams finished. In the top install a hem with a drawstring. I prefer not to taper the bag, since the bottom provides space for my pack and gear. Grommets or snaps along the sides will allow you to make it into a half-size, double-layered footsack for use with the cagoule. The half sack is waterproof; used as a whole bag cover the bottom is waterproof and the top water-resistant.

Appendix B

SELECTED READING

Hopefully, this list will help the interested reader looking for additional information or different viewpoints on particular aspects of lightweight winter travel. It is also, in part, an expression of some of the debts incurred by the author, since many of my own ideas were derived from or modified by some of the books mentioned here. Some portions of this list are rather complete, since the literature on modern camping techniques is limited. Other parts of the list merely suggest a starting point, not necessarily the best one, for further reading.

GENERAL

This book has assumed a basic knowledge on the part of the reader of fundamental summer camping and backpacking methods, so a few books on those subjects ought to be mentioned. The best general survey of modern camping methods from hiking and kayaking to camping machines is Paul Cardwell's *America's Camping Book,* published by Scribners. For backpacking, Colin Fletcher's *The Complete Walker* (Knopf) is excellent and charming. Robert Colwell's *Introduction to Backpacking* (Stackpole) is brief, but the beginner will find it trustworthy. My own *Complete Backpacker's Guide* is to be published by Scribners.

For winter techniques, even the snowshoer will find much useful information in the old Sierra Club *Manual of Ski Mountaineering,* edited by David Brower. The new paperback edition issued by Ballantine is largely unchanged, except for the excellent chapter on avalanches by LaChapelle. This book has become the standard guide for the subject, though the sections on technical climbing are now quite outdated. Because mountaineers generally backpack and often climb and camp on snow, mountaineering literature generally is of use to the winter tourist, even if he lives in Iowa. The best general mountaineering book is published by the Mountaineers, *Mountaineering: The Freedom of the Hills,* edited by Harvey Manning. A recent British handbook, published by Penguin, is Alan Blackshaw's *Mountaineering.* An older but still useful guide is Kenneth A. Henderson's *Handbook of American Mountaineering* (Houghton Mifflin).

A very different point of view will be found among those whose experience derives mainly from the old north woods type of camping for long periods in the great northern forests. Most such books are really not of too much use to the modern backpacker in heavily used wilderness areas. The major exception is Calvin Rutstrum, whose *New Way of the Wilderness* is a classic and a mine of useful information. His book on winter camping, *Paradise Below Zero,* is also good, but it is more anecdotal in style and does not add a great deal to the winter chapter of the earlier book. Both are published by Macmillan.

Also in this tradition are the many books written by those who have lived for months or years in the great northern wilderness. These are often entertaining and sometimes instructive. One of the best is John Rowlands's *Cache Lake Country* (Norton). From a different part of the country and in a different spirit, there is John Muir's *Mountains of California,* reissued in a paperback edition by Doubleday.

All the books just mentioned will give some advice on problems of clothing, camping, sleeping, and cooking.

FOOD AND COOKING

The beginner will probably be able to develop his own recipes according to his preferences with only a minimum of practice, but if further advice is wanted Ruth Mendenhall's booklet on *Backpack Cookery,* usually available at mountaineering and backpacking stores, is very good. All moderns will delight in Bradford Angier's *Wilderness Cookery* (Stackpole) which includes many traditional woodsmen's recipes that have been foolishly forgotten by many modern wilderness travelers.

Those going on reasonably short trips hardly need worry about nutritional problems, and can usually judge caloric values well enough by guesswork. Longer trips or stringent weight requirements demand a more precise approach. A very good discussion of nutritional needs and food characteristics can be found in the 1959 Yearbook of the U.S. Department of Agriculture, *Food,* available from the U.S. Superintendant of Documents in Washington, as is the very comprehensive list of food values, *Composition of Foods* by Bernice Watt and Annabel Merrill.

SNOWSHOEING

The books by Rutstrum mentioned earlier contain much useful information on snowshoeing. On mountain snowshoeing the best summary of techniques and equipment modifications is the introduction to Gene Prater's *Snowshoe Hikes in the Cascades and Olympics,* published by the Seattle Mountaineers. Prater advocates a different type of shoe for steep terrain than this book, perhaps because of experience with different types of snow, but his wide experience is compelling.

SKIING

The Sierra Club *Manual of Ski Mountaineering* has already been mentioned. A very useful little booklet, *Ski Touring in the Northeastern United States,* is published by the Adirondack Mountain Club, Gabriels, New York. *Ski Touring: An Introductory Guide* by William Osgood and Leslie Hurley (Tuttle) is satisfactory.

Complete Cross-Country and Ski-Touring by William Ledener and Joe Pete Wilson (Norton) is good.

Touring technique with lightweight Nordic equipment is discussed in two excellent books: Johnny Caldwell's *Cross Country Ski Book* (Stephen Greene) and Michael Brady's *Nordic Skiing* (Dreyers Forlag).

Books on downhill technique are innumerable, and quite a few of them are good. One comprehensive treatment is the *Official American Ski Technique* put out by the Professional Ski Instructors of America.

FINDING YOUR WAY

I think the best book on this subject is Calvin Rutstrum's *Wilderness Route Finder,* which includes some discussion of the sophisticated techniques needed for extended trips in extremely remote and featureless terrain. It is published by Macmillan. Robert Owendoff's *Better Ways of Pathfinding* (Stackpole) is good, and the makers of Silva compasses put out a book by Bjorn Kjellstrom called *Be an Expert with Map and Compass.*

STORMS, AVALANCHES, AND SNOW

Any textbook on meteorology will reward the outdoorsman with some insight, whether it helps his forecasting ability or not. A good layman's introduction is provided by the little Golden guide, *Weather* by Paul Lehr, R. Will Burnett, and Herbert Zim. A very useful book on predicting the course of the weather is Alan Watts's *Instant Weathercasting* (Dodd, Mead) which, despite its rather misleading title, requires and deserves considerable study. With some practice, his crossed-winds rule is a great help in prediction.

Avalanches deserve all the study that can be afforded them by anyone going into the mountains in winter. The standard guide is the U.S. Department of Agriculture Handbook #194, *Snow Avalanches.* Like most avalanche work done in this country, it is the product of the dedicated snow rangers of the U.S. Forest Service, centered at Alta, Utah. The best brief guide is Edward LaChapelle's booklet *ABC of Avalanche Safety,* published by Colorado Outdoor Sports. This booklet is reprinted with few changes as the avalanche chapter of the paperback edition of the *Manual of Ski Mountaineering.* LaChapelle's *Field Guide to Snow Crystals* and his chapter on "The Cycle of Snow" in *Mountaineering: the Freedom of the Hills* are also very worthwhile. The former is available in paperback from the University of Washington Press.

Two narrative books contain a great deal of practical wisdom on avalanches: Colin Fraser's *The Avalanche Enigma* (Rand McNally) and Montgomery Atwater's *The Avalanche Hunters.*

Malcolm Mellor's *Avalanches* is recommended to the technically minded and to those looking for a comprehensive bibliography. It is published by the U.S. Army Matériel Command, Cold Regions Research & Engineering Laboratory, Hanover, New Hampshire. *The Snowy Torrents: Avalanche Accidents in the United States, 1910–1966,* edited by Dave Gallagher, is instructive. The latest in avalanche rescue technique is *Modern Avalanche Rescue* by Ronald Perla. Both are published by the Alta Avalanche Study Center. The pictures of avalanche terrain in *Snow Avalanches Along Colorado Mountain Highways* are educational. It is U.S. Forest Service Research Paper RM-7, from the Rocky Mountain Forest & Range Experiment Station, Fort Collins, Colorado.

STEEP SNOW

Aside from avalanches, the techniques for climbing on steep snow are discussed in the books on mountaineering already listed. For pictures of a master showing how it's done on *really* steep snow, see Gaston Rebuffat's *On Snow and Rock* from Oxford University Press.

EMERGENCIES

The standard book on first aid is, of course the American Red

Cross *First Aid Textbook* (Doubleday), and this should be everyone's starting point. The *Ski Patrol Manual* published by the National Ski Association is good. Two books for ambulance personnel by Carl Young are worth studying: *Transportation of the Injured* and *First Aid and Resucitation* (both C. C. Thomas). For summaries of first aid that can be carried in a pocket, check your local mountaineering store. Several good ones are available.

For advanced techniques going beyond first aid, the standard book is *Medicine for Mountaineering,* edited by James Wilkerson and published by the Mountaineers. The standard book on wilderness rescue methods, including many drawings of improvised splints, sleds, and stretchers in Wastl Mariner's *Mountain Rescue Techniques,* distributed in this country by the Mountaineers. Also excellent is the booklet *Mountain Search and Rescue Operations* put out by the Grand Teton National Park rescue group. Good discussions of many problems of wilderness first aid and medicine are contained in *Mountain Medicine Symposium,* available for a dollar from the Appalachian Mountain Club in Boston. The best volume on frostbite is Bradford Washburn's booklet *Frostbite: What It Is and How to Prevent It* published by the Museum of Science in Boston. Theodore Lathrop's booklet on *Hypothermia: Killer of the Unprepared,* put out by the Mazamas, is excellent.

NATURE AND WILDERNESS

Even a brief bibliography on this subject would take a book of its own, so only a few suggestions will be made here. Many general books of appreciation have been written by the great naturalists, and all of them contain a wealth of information. A few, selected at random, are: John Terres's *From Laurel Hill to Siler's Bog: The Walking Adventures of a Naturalist* (Knopf), Sigurd Olson's *Listening Point* (Knopf), Aldo Leopold's *A Sand County Almanac* (Oxford University Press), and Sally Carrighar's *Wild Heritage* (Houghton Mifflin).

Ann Morgan's *Field Book of Animals in Winter* (Putnam) is a good handbook for winter travelers. A brief guide is Margaret Buck's *Where They Go in Winter* (Abington). A wise and useful guide to the winter tourist's main animal signs is Olaus Murie's

Field Guide to Animal Tracks (Houghton Mifflin). Another book on tracks is Ellsworth Jaeger's *Tracks and Trailcraft* (Macmillan). For four-footed animals, there is *A Field Guide to the Mammals* by William Burt and Richard Grossenheider (Houghton Mifflin).

For birds, a good introduction is Roger Tory Peterson's paperback *How to Know the Birds* (New American Library). I think the best field book is *Birds of North America* by Chandler Robbins, Bertel Bruun, and Herbert Zim (Golden), but the older standard Peterson guides are preferred by some. *A Field Guide to the Birds* (read Eastern) and *A Field Guide to the Western Birds* are both published by Houghton Mifflin.

For trees, a good field book is C. Frank Brockman's *Trees of North America* (Golden). G. A. Petrides's *Field Guide to Trees and Shrubs* is excellent for winter use, but it only covers eastern trees. A fine set with much more information on trees than the field books is Donald Peattie's two volume (eastern and western) set, *A Natural History of the Trees.*

In addition to the many general books on photography, two that may be of special interest to the wilderness traveler are David Linton's *Photographing Nature* (American Museum of Science paperback) and Russ Kinne's *The Complete Book of Nature Photography* (Chilton).

MAKING YOUR OWN GEAR

Lightweight Camping Equipment and How to Make It by Gerry Cunningham and Margaret Hansson is published by the Colorado Outdoor Sports Corporation of Denver.

Appendix C

WHERE TO BUY IT

This is a selected list of companies that deal in equipment particularly useful for lightweight winter camping. In many cases local stores have begun to carry the products of some of the better manufacturers, which were difficult to obtain a few years ago. Even so, catalogues from some of the mail-order houses specializing in quality lightweight equipment are useful for comparisons; they are also the only source of information concerning many recent developments in equipment.

Some of the sources listed carry a general selection of equipment, while a few others are worthy of special notice because of one product. Unfortunate omissions have probably been made, especially in the case of some of the new firms that are popping up like spring flowers. An asterisk (*) indicates a supplier with a particularly complete line and a standard mail-order catalogue.

ALPINE DESIGNS, Box 1018, Boulder, Colo. 80302
  Makers of high quality sleeping bags, tents, packs, and clothing.

ALPINE HUT, 4725 30th Ave., N.E., Seattle, Wash. 98105
  General Equipment.

ALPINE RECREATION, Warehouse, 4-B Henshaw S.E., Woburn, Mass. 01801

BACK COUNTRY CAMP AND TRAIL EQUIPMENT, 8272 Orangethorpe Ave., Buena Park, Calif.

EDDIE BAUER, Seattle, Wash. 98124
Expensive sleeping bags, clothing, and luxury items.

L. L. BEAN, Freeport, Me. 04032
Some excellent equipment including the original rubber-bottom boot, together with various gentleman—outdoorsman accessories.

BECK OUTDOOR PRODUCTS, Box 3061, South Berkeley, California
The best neoprene-nylon crampon and snowshoe bindings.

BERNARD FOOD INDUSTRIES, Box 487, San Jose, Calif., 95103
Dehydrated food.

BISHOP'S ULTIMATE OUTDOOR EQUIPMENT, 6804 Millwood Rd., Bethesda, Md. 20034
Tents.

BLACK'S, Ogdensburg, N.Y. 13669
Outlet for English and Continental sleeping bags, tents, clothing and other items.

CAMP AND TRAIL OUTFITTERS, 21 Park Place, New York, N.Y. 10007
A good general selection of equipment.

CARIKIT, P.O. Box 1153, Boulder, Colo. 80302
A new supplier of well-designed kits.

CHOUINARD, P.O. Box 150, Ventura, California 93001
Outstanding technical climbing equipment.

CHUCK WAGON, 176 Oak St., Newton, Mass. 02164
Dehydrated food.

CMI, 5800 East Jewell Ave., Denver, Colo. 80222
Superbly made technical climbing equipment.

NEIL CREAMER, 10643 Lindamere Dr., Los Angeles, California 90024
Children's snowshoes, made by Huron Indians.

DRI-LITE, 11333 Atlantic, Lynwood, California. 93001
Dehydrated food.

* EASTERN MTN. SPORTS, 1041 Commonwealth Ave., Boston, Mass. 02215
One of the most complete outfitters, with a good mail order service.

APPENDIX C   374

FROSTLINE, Box 2190 Boulder, Colo. 80302
Pre-cut, well-planned kits that you sew yourself. Tents, down clothing, etc. A good way to cut expenses, but selection is necessarily quite limited.

GERRY, 5450 North Valley Highway, Denver, Colo. 80216
Quality lightweight equipment.

HIGHLAND OUTFITTERS, P.O. Box 121 Riverside, Calif., 92502
A good general selection of gear.

HIRSCH-WEIS/WHITE STAG, 5203 St. Johnson Cr. Blvd. Portland, Ore. 97206
Sleeping bags, tents, etc.

HOLUBAR, Box 7, Boulder, Colo. 80302
Makers of high quality clothing, tents, and down equipment, fairly reasonably priced, especially sleeping bags. Some other items.

KELTY, 1801 Victory Blvd., Glendale, Calif. 91201
Makers of the original contour pack frame. They now handle other equipment also.

PETER LIMMER AND SONS, Intervale, N.H. 03845
Custom and ready made boots, some other equipment.

MOOR & MOUNTAIN, Concord, Mass. 01742
Good selection of non-mountaineering lightweight equipment. Some useful items not usually carried by mountaineering shops.

MOUNTAIN PRODUCTS, 123 South Wenatchee Ave., Wenatchee, Wash. 98801

MOUNTAIN RESEARCH, 631 South 96th St., Seattle, Wash. 98108
Excellent newsletter—catalogue dealing with mountaineering equipment. The ice axes should be considered by anyone planning on going on to serious mountaineering.

MOUNTAIN SPORTS, 821 Pearl, Boulder, Colo. 80302
Handles Gerry, Camp 7, and others.

NORTH FACE, 1234 5th St., Berkeley, Calif. 94710
Very high quality equipment.

PERMA-PAK, 40 East 2430 South Salt Lake City, Utah 84115
Dehydrated food.

* RECREATIONAL EQUIPMENT, 1525–11th Ave., Seattle Wash. 98122
Very complete and reasonably priced selection. Recreational Equip-

ment is a cooperative (membership fee $1) which refunds some of your money at the end of the year. Generally the cheapest place to get good equipment, but mail service is slow and quality on some items needs watching.

RICH-MOOR, P.O. Box 2728, Van Nuys, Calif. 91404
Dehydrated food.

SIERRA DESIGNS, 4th & Addison, Berkeley, Calif. 94710
Makers of some of the best shell clothing, tents, and down gear on the market.

* SKI HUT, 1615 University Avenue, Berkeley, Calif. 94703
One of the best and most complete stores in the country. Sells and manufactures very high quality equipment, often at very reasonable prices.

SKIMEISTER, North Woodstock, N.H. 03262
General equipment.

SMILIE COMPANY, 575 Howard St., San Francisco, Calif. 94105
Backpacking gear and items for large groups: portable wood stoves, aluminum Dutch ovens, etc.

TRAIL CHEF, 1109 S. Wall St., P.O. Box 15598, Los Angeles, Calif. 90015
Dehydrated food.

STEPHENSON'S, 23206 Hatteras St., Woodland Hills, Calif. 91364
Well made and thought out sleeping bags and tents using interesting design principles different from those advocated in this book.

UNITED STATES GEOLOGICAL SURVEY, Washington 25, D.C. or Federal Center, Denver, Colo.
The standard source for maps. Index maps for each state are free.

WEST RIDGE, 11930 W. Olympic Blvd., West Los Angeles, Calif.
A good selection of equipment.

Appendix D

CHECKLISTS OF WHAT TO TAKE

The following checklists hopefully include everything that would
be needed for tours lasting from a few hours to a couple of weeks.
Not all the items are necessary on all trips. Rainwear is quite unnecessary in some areas at some times of year, for example. Quantities also clearly vary. More spare food and socks are required on
a two-week mountain trip than on a weekend jaunt near home.
Quantities are thus left for the reader to calculate, but the lists can
serve as a memory aid if they are used systematically as the pack
for the trip is made up.

Items generally needed even on day trips:

> Underwear
> Shirt
> Pants
> Sweater
> Shell parka
> Mittens or gloves with extra set of liners
> Hat or balaclava
> Socks with extra set
> Boots or equivalent
> Goggles or glasses
> Watch
> Food, including some extra
> Emergency kit
> Pack

Water bottle
Matches in waterproof container
Map in case or plastic bag, onionskin paper, pencil
Compass
Pocket knife
Flashlight or headlamp with alkaline batteries and extra bulb
Toilet paper
Chapstick
Sunburn goo
Gaiters or anklets

*To which you may need to add, depending on conditions, means
of transportation, and individual needs:*

Rain gear
Extra wool clothes
Wind pants
Face mask
Down clothing
Overboots
Bivouac sack
Foam pad for bivouacs
Avalanche cord
Avalanche probe
Saw
Shovel
Skis
Pole(s)
Snowshoes
Ice ax
Touring waxes with scraper or putty knife, waxing block, hand
    cleaner
Climbers (for skis)
Touring attachments for ski bindings
Arlberg straps for skis
Crampons
Ski or snowshoe crampons
Wands
Route markers (plastic strips)
Water purification tablets
Extra eyeglasses
Eyeglasses strap
Antifog compound for glasses
Camera
Film

Nature and area guides
Thermometer
Barometer or altimeter
Alarm watch or clock
Innersoles
Boot liners
Protractor
Firestarters
Can opener
Handkerchief(s) or facial tissue
Toothbrush and powder
Hand cleaner in tube
Soap
Comb or brush
Sanitary napkins or tampons

For overnight camps and longer trips, you'll need:

Tent with the necessary pitching equipment or tools for building
    an appropriate shelter
Sleeping bag
Sleeping pad
Eating utensils
Pans
Cup
Salt, lots of it to replace losses
Pepper and other desired seasonings
Stove or firebuilding necessities appropriate to the area (saws,
    etc.)
Stove accessories: funnel, pricker, windscreen, etc.
Fuel in can
More matches (in waterproof container)
Plastic bags for trash, etc.
Changes of some clothing like socks, undershorts, etc.
Addicts' needs: cigarettes, etc.

To which you may want to add:

Bowl or plate
Sleeping bag cover
Large plastic bags
Extra batteries
Extra fuel containers
Pocket sharpening stone

Appendix D   379

EMERGENCY KIT

The contents of the emergency kit will vary depending on your prudence, equipment, plans, experience, and access to helpful doctors. Whether you carry them in one container or separately, it is essential to be able to give certain basic first aid and to repair some types of equipment failures whenever you are traveling far from the beaten track in winter. You will have to figure out some items for yourself—what tools you need for repairing and adjusting your ski bindings, for example. Locking pliers or a plier-wrench-screwdriver combination may be needed by skiers but not by snowshoers. An emergency ski tip should be carried by skiers unless they are using metal skis. In general, one emergency kit is sufficient for a group that doesn't intend to break up, but some care must be taken that spare parts, ski tip sizes, and similar items are given consideration.

General repairs of equipment are facilitated by:

>hank of parachute cord for laces, packs, tent ties, etc.
>length of strong malleable wire for ski, binding, snowshoe, pole, pack repairs
>needles and nylon thread for repairing rips
>ripstop fabric tape for tent and clothing repairs
>adhesive tape from first aid supplies makes repairs if warmed to body temperature so that it sticks
>pocket knife already carried
>spare parts that may be needed for bindings, stove, pack, etc.
>tools needed for installing the above

In all cases, more elaborate repair kits are clearly advisable on more extended trips. A snowshoe repair adequate for getting you over a few miles will not do for a week of rough mountain travel. More spare parts are prudent for longer trips.

First aid and medical supplies range from very small kits to the elaborate field hospitals of expeditions. For long trips in remote areas especially, I would advise consulting specialized books and a physician. Since this is a necessary step to get prescription drugs, none will be discussed here.

A basic first aid kit is suggested.

waterproof container

summary of first aid and emergency medicine (several are listed in the reading list)

large roll of 2″ wide cloth adhesive tape—not waterproof—on cardboard roll which can be collapsed (can be ripped into narrower strips—warm near skin before using)

4″ x 4″ sterile gauze pads—at least 10

ace bandage

moleskin

bandaids

triangular bandage

2 single-edged razor blades in sterile packages

1 pair tweezers

1 pair scissors

thermometer

aspirin

pHisophex—small plastic bottle

aqueous zepharin—clear antiseptic

antacid tablets

milk of magnesia tablets

tube of vaseline

SAVING MONEY ON YOUR OUTFIT

The lists just given are likely to seem insurmountable obstacles for the impoverished beginning tourer, but winter camping really is a cheap recreation. Some of the principles of getting equipment have already been mentioned, the most important of which is to buy equipment in the order you will need it, especially if you are paying standard prices. Outdoorsmen on a budget should get most of their wool clothing from attic trunks or the surplus market. Some other good surplus buys are mittens, bearpaw snowshoes, and army ski mountaineering rucksacks, which are not quite as good as some modern designs but will serve well at a quarter the price.

Another good source is the secondhand market. The bulletin boards of mountaineering shops are often productive. Haggle!

Mountaineering shops themselves generally have annual or semi-annual sales of rental equipment, discontinued models, irregulars, etc. Find out when the sales are, check the advance lists, if any, and go early, armed with a list of what you *really* need and how much you can get it for in the cheapest catalogue. This is often the best way to get down gear, tents, parkas, and skis.

Finally, if you *have* to pay catalogue prices, write for all the catalogues and compare—prices for identical items often vary considerably. Despite shipping costs, local sales taxes often make it cheaper to shop by mail. Some suppliers give quantity discounts —get together with friends. Prices and offerings change annually, but a few suppliers should always be checked by the outdoorsman on a budget. Recreational Equipment in Seattle is consistently lower in *most* prices and gives members partial refunds at the end of the year as well, though a few items are not up to standards they should meet. Ski Hut and Eastern Mountaineering give good competition on some items and Holubar has always been one of the best priced suppliers of top quality sleeping bags.

Index

INDEX

INDEX

INDEX

Index